W9-AVT-416

IMPOSTERS AT THE GATE

A Novel About Private Equity

Aseem K. Giri

Tusk Publishing Inc.

Copyright 2007 Tusk Publishing Inc.
ISBN 978-1-60502-001-3

Library of Congress Cataologing-in-Publication Data available upon request.

First Edition.

Tusk Publishing books may be purchased for educational, business or sales promotional use. For information, please write to main@tuskpublishing.com.

www.tuskpublishing.com

Publisher's Note

Thank you for purchasing this book. Our publishing company was launched recently and we are proud to present this work as the inaugural novel of our imprint, Tusk Publishing, Inc. Tusk will focus on a multi-cultural genre; works that have racial, religious or ethnically diverse themes, particularly where two or more races, religions or ethnicities are interacting. We also would like to provide our readers with experiences, not just books. You will notice on the front inside flap of the cover a BIN™ number. This is the work's *Book Identification Number*. Please use it to register on our website www.tuskpublishing.com to receive additional benefits and services. We hope you enjoy this work.

Author's Note

Thank you for purchasing this work. As with most, this was written with you, the reader, in mind. My aim has been to relay a story to you and have you be engaged by it. I hope you find it as entertaining, moving and thought-provoking as I set out to make it. If I have fallen short in any regard, I encourage your comments and feedback. In our era of technological possibilities, writer and reader are able to forge a new relationship hinged on interactivity. I am thrilled to be affiliated with Tusk Publishing Inc., a company which embraces and nurtures these possibilities and is developing innovative ways to foster them. I look forward to a long working relationship with them. I encourage you to register your book on their website. I intend on contributing additional content and material that will only be available to registered readers.

Lastly, while it may be tempting to associate the names, people, places, companies and events depicted in the book with actual names, people, places, companies and events, I assure you that any resemblance or similarity is strictly coincidental. This is a work of pure fiction.

To my wife Kavita,
for saying yes
&
To my daughter Naina,
whose innocence as an infant
was the wisdom her father needed
to bring him home

IMPOSTERS AT THE GATE

A Novel About Private Equity

CHAPTER 1

Ash caught the motion out of the corner of his eye. He stood at the top of his driveway. His car door was open and his arm rested on the roof of the vehicle. The spot where his attention was directed had simply been, on every other day, the back edge of his neighbor's house. He never would have had a natural desire to look there, but he was forced to, every day, as that fringe invaded his line of sight and obstructed his view of the Los Angeles skyline. He would strive to look around that corner on a daily basis, his neck and eyes attempting to defy geometry, before he backed out his car and headed to work. Today, he looked right at it.

There, dangling from the light ochre-colored stucco, was what at first sight looked like a piece of excrement. Fitting for my mood thought Ash. Had his neighbor chosen a darker color he never would have seen it. The object quivered again, as if trembling from self-consciousness, keenly aware it was being observed by Ash.

Ash's engrossed trance was disrupted by the sound of his cell phone ringing. He remembered when a ring was just a ring. Back then he'd snap the phone open in seconds. Lately, it had become an alarm clock shocking him back into the reality of his life. When this sensation first started, he would react to it as if it were a just a gentle nudge waking him. He would answer after two rings. As his desire to stay in his dream state increased, it was like the sound of cymbals crashing; nonetheless, he would succumb at four rings. Today, as he began to feel more at home in his blissful reverie it was like an intense shock of voltage to his heart attempting to resuscitate him. He swore he had heard the moving object in front of him shouting "*CLEAR!*" even before the phone rang. He saw the call was from his office. He was about to capitulate at six rings.

He held the phone in his hand, yet his gaze remained transfixed on the gyrating form before him. Slowly, clumsily, in a manner that disturbingly reminded him of his own life, Ash watched as a majestic butterfly broke free and flew gracefully away. Although he couldn't see the animal anymore, Ash kept looking in the direction he thought he saw the symphony of blue, yellow and lavender fly.

Ten rings. I'll reward them for their tenacity thought Ash.

"Yeah."

He remembered when he used to say hello.

"Ash, is that you?"

It was James from the treasury department at his firm.

"Yeah, I'm here."

"The wires are all set to go. The banks are on standby awaiting your approval."

"What's the total amount?"

"Three hundred twenty-nine million four hundred sixty-two thousand eight hundred thirteen," James offered.

Sounds close enough thought Ash. I'm sure someone really wants those thirteen dollars he continued to think. Sometimes the feigned precision would make him laugh. He remembered taking the time to immerse himself in the detail when he first started his career, memorizing all of the key statistics of a transaction, readily available on the tip of his tongue. He couldn't bring himself to do it anymore. It wasn't that he had become sloppy or careless; he had simply grown callous. Numbers numbed him. They didn't speak to him, captivate him or engage him. He never had the patience for numbers or a taste for the analytics requisite for his chosen profession. It was a necessary skill set to have, so he mastered it, even though he could not find the inspiration in it.

James had just quoted the dollar amount for the largest private equity deal Ash had ever funded. The code name for the transaction, to ensure confidentiality, was Project Emancipate. The amount was the equivalent of the combined average earnings of over seven thousand five hundred Americans. By approving this, Ash would move more money than most small towns in America had control of.

Ash was part of a fifteen billion dollar private equity fund. The amount they managed was bigger than the GDP of several African countries.

"Send it," Ash confirmed.

With those words Ash ended an intense two-week mad dash to the finish line. The process had been made even more complex because of the ineffective people he had at his firm. It was a zoo. In most of the personnel's actions, they were following commands even though they were defying logic. It would have been a great show, if it were a circus. He was tired of having to think for them. He had heard rumors of orderly transaction closings; he had just never been a part of one. Maybe that was the elite reserve of the more prestigious firms. Or, maybe it was him. There was even drama when he closed on his mortgage. The lender made errors on the documents, the escrow agent didn't process the title change properly, and the title insurance policy never showed up. Buying a company or buying a house thought Ash – it's the same thing.

Ash climbed into his car. He took another glance of his impeded view. It was another morning in Los Angeles when the buildings downtown and the mountains north and east of them were not visible. Ash knew they were there. After a day or two of rain, the smog would clear and the ensconced view would emerge from its treasure chest, where it had been preserved, revealing picturesque splendor for the eyes.

What irony if the smog was there to keep the view fresh thought Ash. Ash wished he could have the benefit of a storm to clear the dour thoughts clouding his own mood. Rain, even a swift downpour, could lather away his despondency. Hope might bloom again. The roots were there; they had just been forced down to greater depths – a preoccupied mind only had so much waterfront property. He had listlessly shoved some papers and his laptop into his bag, and he now threw them on the front passenger seat. He noticed his bag was a little closer to the edge of the seat than would be safe; he knew that if he had to unexpectedly slam on his brakes, the bag would topple over. He didn't bother to move it back.

Ash had been waiting patiently for the last two months to see if he made Partner in the firm or not. Truthfully, he had been waiting the last five years. He knew he would be under consideration this time around. The Partners had stalled the announcement, however. All Ash could think about was the countless hours on airplanes, the sleepless nights and the killed weekends he had devoted to his job. And now they took their time to let him now where he stood.

"I always respect their timelines," Ash whispered to himself. The Partners had wanted Project Emancipate closed today and Ash had made it happen. The Partners were desperate to hit their quarterly numbers. Ash felt like he was always coming through for them. When would it be their turn to reciprocate?

He suddenly smiled to himself as he thought he could stop for coffee on the way in to the office. Quickly, Ash frowned and shook his head over how something so trivial could inspire him. He just closed the biggest deal in his career. Shouldn't this feel better?

Waking up that morning to do the nationwide conference call at seven am took some doing. He remembered opening his eyes and hatching a scheme to fall back asleep. I can say I had to be on a conference call with someone else, I had a breakfast meeting or I had to go see a doctor. However, Ash realized these options were all either not convincing enough, had been used too often or were just plain silly – he couldn't think of a single doctor's office or clinic open that early. By then, his brain was sufficiently active enough where he could quell the alluring voice proselytizing sweet slumber and the moral arguments campaigning for duty and obligation grew louder and louder. He tossed the covers to the bottom of the bed and went to the phone.

Ash remembered how even on those days when he let temptation win the argument, the joy was short-lived. The inevitable doldrums of his current existence were always there, and try as he might, he couldn't avoid it.

● ● ●

As Ash drove, he noticed a sign announcing a new store opening. "Good Times Wines" the sign read. What a miserable name for a store Ash thought. Yet, he couldn't help himself; he drove into the lot. They weren't open until ten am. He had thirty minutes to wait. Ash shrugged his shoulders. He went to get coffee and sat back down in front of the wine shop.

When he walked in once the doors were unlocked, Ash recognized the owner.

"George, is that you?"

Only some of the wire wine racks demarcating the aisles had been set-up, and only a few of the placards labeling each row had been suspended from the ceiling. There were shelves along the walls – most of them were in place, but they had not all been stocked. Boxes and crates of wine were everywhere.

"Ash? Ash, my guhd vriend, you vound me!"

George Abramovich's voice cracked as he spoke. It must have been the strain of his weight or the tension of life's decisions. George was a Russian immigrant in his late fifties. He had lost his farm back home and had migrated to Los Angeles ten years ago to live with his mortgage broker brother and his family. George worked in the business with his brother for a while, but only just long enough for him to earn the cash to do what he loved.

Ash always found the story of George's life inspiring. He smiled to himself.

"Of course, George, you know I'd never let you go!"

George's portly shape was overflowing from the edges of the apron he would often wear. He would rest his arms on his stomach and smile broadly when he was happy. He was missing two side teeth, only noticeable when he did smile, and his remaining teeth, stained from years of use and lackadaisical maintenance, looked like they had their days numbered. He had square eyeglasses that were twenty years out-of-date – and although the style didn't reflect the times, it complemented George's attire. His hair was cut very close to his scalp, similar to the stubble on his cheeks, giving his head a continuum – where did his face begin? – making it seem like a one-tone white soccer ball. When he was really happy, he would tilt his head to the side when he smiled. This morning, he was at full tilt.

"So what will you do with the shop on Pico Boulevard?"

"I run dhem both."

"That's great," said Ash, "You are growing!"

"Vee shtart like little vine, and now, vee grow!"

He added a nodding motion to his head tilt.

Ash was curiously touched by that thought. He couldn't help but feel that his own growth had been stunted.

"What do you have that is new?"

"I just geht dhis tomorrow, er, yesterday, 1961 Chateau Lafite Rothschild."

Ash's eyes widened, and he couldn't help but smirk.

"Dhee odhers, I sharge six dhousand for dhee case. For you, I say five."

George put his hand forward depicting five fingers.

"George, you always tempt me with such exquisite wines, but I can't do it."

"Maybe vhen you is pardner?"

"Touché!"

"Vhat?"

"You got me."

George was still grinning. Ash was reflective. He had used that excuse many times with George to demurely decline from making an extravagant purchase. He enjoyed knowing what exotic wines were available, but he had a hard time taking the plunge.

Seeing that George was still in his jovial mood, Ash decided to purchase something.

"How about a '99 for a hundred fifty dollars?"

"Vhery guhd. I get for you."

He gave Ash an emphatic thumbs up before he walked away to get the bottle.

"I zhee you zoon," said George as Ash left the store.

Ash walked back to his car. He placed the wine in a net he had in his trunk to secure it to the side of his seven-year old BMW 5-Series sedan. It would be cool and protected in there. As Ash drove away, he looked over to his bag on the front seat. He pushed it back.

● ● ●

They were all called into the conference room of the office later that afternoon. Ash hated being disturbed, but these meetings were mandatory. It was also irritating the haphazard nature with which they were scheduled. He felt like a whistle was being blown to announce a sporadic shift change, a pan was being struck by a ladle to announce an arbitrarily chosen mealtime or a security guard was ordering everyone out of their cell for a random search. Eddie had called the meeting. He was lucky that half of the people in the office sauntered into the conference room after his announcement. The other half would show up when they saw, through the glass panel, Ash seated at the conference room table. Ash was second-in-command in the office; holding the title Senior Vice President. All he needed was the Partner title to be on more of an equal footing with Eddie. Ash knew deep down that this standing was somewhat illusory. Eddie would always be the head of the office. Yes-men were virtually impossible to dislodge.

Into the conference room entered the rank and file. It always amazed Ash that after four years the improvements around the office had not been finalized. It had reached a point now where new problems were arising although the original renovations had yet to be completed. There was a musty smell to that conference room now. Electrical outlets were missing their cover plates, there remained unsealed a hole in the drywall where a disgruntled employee had projectiled a chair two years ago and there was a projector screen that could not be closed.

It was also a room where time stood still. Literally. The clocks on the wall ceased to function. There had been some ambition in purchasing this clock. There were three clock faces on the panel. Below each was a city name: 'Los Angeles', 'London', 'Hong Kong'. Now it was a promise unfulfilled, the suspended animation of ambition, aspiration held in abeyance. Twice a day these clocks were right. Apparently, that was good enough. Somewhere, in some stack of papers, there was a three-year old purchase order for its replacement. Eddie had convinced Ash of that. It's a shame he has to control the finances thought Ash.

Ash pondered how much time he had spent in that room. Rooms like these were where you had to build your career as a private equity professional he mused. Ash thought about his emotional highs and lows in that space. It was a football field where touchdowns were scored, a movie set where you attempted your Oscar-winning performance, a concert hall where you dazzled as a pianist. The conference room had usurped other more illustrious, romantic and enthralling settings. Warriors had their lush battlefields, pirates their high seas and brokerage houses the chaotic floor of the stock exchange. Forget storming a castle, firing cannonballs at unsuspecting ships or fighting to be heard above the fray for your trades. Modern takeovers, pillaging and speculation had opted for four walls, fibre-optics and wireless e-mail. There was a muted approach now. And it all happened from a conference room. It allowed a new breed of conqueror to emerge. One where strength of character, presence or resolve were not really necessary. You could camouflage all of that with distance, a phone line and the Internet.

"Where's David?" asked Eddie.

Oh it's good to see you too Eddie, thought Ash. *Let's just ignore the fact that I congratulated you on the last two deals you closed and all I have gotten from you for the last five I closed in the same period of time is this clueless expression on your face.*

Ash looked around, but he didn't see David. It was the third time in the last week David had taken an extended lunch. Eddie had threatened disciplinary action. Ash worried Eddie might use it as an excuse to fire David. Eddie didn't like David all that much, most likely because he was an Associate in the office who preferred working with Ash.

"He's looking into something for me," Ash explained.

"Oh really? And what would that be?" challenged Eddie.

"It's for one of my deals," offered Ash. "Project Emancipate."

"I thought it closed today."

Oh so you do know about it? thought Ash. Still, no congratulations.

"David is tying up some loose ends," Ash assured.

He looked Eddie straight in the eye. Eddie was the first to back down.

Everything about Eddie was short. Short in stature. Short in his responses. Short purse strings. When he didn't have an agenda he was pushing, people would barely acknowledge his presence. The quiet mouse in the corner. When he did have an agenda, there would be an irritating hum emanating from him as if he were an old household appliance with insufficient electricity. His one distinguishing physical characteristic was that he had once broken his right arm, and although it had long healed, he had yet to break the habit of holding it in front of him, parallel to the ground, hand clenched in a fist. Onlookers wondered if there was an imaginary sling holding it up. For Ash it was like a weathervane, a dog's tail or its ears. Ash would take mental note of the times Eddie would move his arm – when he was over-emphasizing what he was saying, generally trying to convince you of a lie. He kept it at his side only when he was nervous, when one of his prospective deals had gotten shot down or on those rare occasions when he got angry. Otherwise, his imaginary sling held it in place. When he was triumphant, Ash could see that he clenched his fist more tightly. Ash wondered if Napolean's adversaries had benefited from this type of intelligence by the time they defeated the French ruler at the battle of Waterloo.

Eddie commenced the meeting. It was forty-five minutes of him grandstanding, talking about his deals. Incidentally, he did very little of the actual talking. He called out the names of his deals on his punch list and he would prompt others in the room, namely Jason and Bob, to do the talking. They grandstanded on his behalf. Or maybe he just got a kick out of having his potential transactions highlighted back to him. Jason and Bob were Eddie's favorite insubordinates. Jason was an Associate and Bob was a Vice President, one step above Jason and two steps below Eddie. They worked on all of his deals. Ash actually hated working with either of them. He sensed the feeling was mutual. Behind their backs, Ash would refer to them as the ELVES (*E*ddie's *L*ackeys *V*igilantly *E*ngrossed in *S*ucking-up). Eddie and the ELVES. Sounds like they could be a rock group. Or a circus sideshow.

Eddie's cell phone rang. He observed it, scrunched his forehead, stood up and answered it as he walked out the door. The door creaked as he walked out of the conference room. Ash overhead Eddie apologize for the sound. Ash knew who it was. Eddie's behavior indicated that the caller was Lasi, the President and Founder of the firm.

Lasi favored that hands-on approach, all of his Lieutenants at his beck and call, a mere speed dial button away. Ash had received a few such calls. Ash had made the bold maneuver lately of not answering. He allowed the message to go to voicemail and between one (initially) to four hours (lately), he would respond. It was fabulously effective at encouraging Lasi to curtail the frequency of his phone calls to Ash.

Lasi's centralized controls had a clear origin. He was an atypical head of a multi-billion dollar firm claiming to do private equity. Most heads had built their careers in the deal business, plying their trade and perfecting their craft over decades of experience. They had a following of people, respect from the industry and admiration from their peers. Instead of building his way up the finance ranks, Lasi had spent the early part of his career as a communist insurgent. He would move from country to country, scouring the world to be a mercenary for populist causes. It was hard to get him to divulge details, but his former comrades had placed him in Cuba, Romania and Hungary. While the heads of competing firms were managing deals when they were in their twenties and thirties, Lasi was buying weapons and orchestrating demonstrations. Somewhere along the way, he shed his birth name of Richard Chester, and then he abandoned the nickname Pepito to settle on Lasi Nescu. One former soldier suggested that Che Guevara had given Lasi the nickname Pepito, but it seemed sensationalized – the dates didn't quite work.

People questioned him often about his transition from communist to capitalist, but it was nearly impossible to pin him down. One could only imagine, he must have hit some crisis with a need to actually earn a living. Perhaps he decided one day that conviction was great, but he wanted the cash. Maybe he saw the Michael Douglas movie and decided to agree that "*greed was good*". Maybe he read *Barbarians at the Gate* and thought he would give it a try. Or maybe he just realized what Eastern Europe finally acquiesced to in the late eighties and early nineties – communism was a flawed system.

When Lasi did make the change, he managed to convince an industry veteran to join forces with him to launch Popular Capital. The model had been familiar enough, get a seasoned guy where you can trade on his name and reputation and the young people around him would do all the work. The veteran participant loved it because he made money simply by being him and the junior guys loved it because it allowed them to play the game. Without this they wouldn't have made it past the proverbial 'gate'. It was their backstage pass. The bouncer would have cut them off otherwise.

Lasi looked like a man of the people. He blended into a crowd. He had no discerning physical characteristics.

He wore characterless glasses, had salt and pepper hair, was 5' 6" tall, neither thin nor fat, and looked perfectly non-descript. His one unique physical feature, in no doubt another throwback to his earlier years, was his beard. He was one of a very small number of finance professionals that sported facial hair.

Lasi certainly did aim for lofty goals. You couldn't help but give him credit; he did build a multi-billion dollar entity from scratch, figuring out clever ways to get people to part with their money. And he was the one hiring when Ash needed a job.

David stumbled into the room. Unfortunately, Eddie finished his phone conversation simultaneously and took note of David's entry. David Weltz was about medium height and would always walk as if he was in a hurry to get somewhere. His glasses were round and wire-rimmed. Ash found it curious how he would spike his hair. He also recently got braces to better align his jutting canine teeth. He looked like he would fit in more in an Internet start-up than in a private equity fund.

"Did you get what you needed for Ash?" asked Eddie, using a pointed, accusatory tone.

David looked at Ash.

"You know, David, for Project Emancipate?" Ash hinted. His tone was matter-of-fact.

"Yes," said David, trying to suppress his panting, "Yes, I got the info."

"Perhaps you can show it to me first, before we present it to everyone," suggested Ash.

"Great idea," said David.

"Take a seat," Ash advised.

Once he sat down and a few seconds had passed, he looked up at Ash, who happened to be glancing in his direction. David mouthed a silent "thank you" to Ash.

Ash smiled and nodded.

Ash knew David's girlfriend's parents were in town and were only there for a few days. Unfortunately, David had been stuck in the office until midnight every night working on various tasks for Eddie. Eddie didn't cut him any slack. Ash also suspected that Eddie called this impromptu meeting knowing that David was not around.

This was the time of the meeting when Ash's thoughts would begin to wander. Eddie's soporific voice made him think about how soft his bed had been that morning. He would certainly heed that call back to bed now. I need to get my car serviced, Ash recalled. Did I pay my credit card bill? Should I call that girl back?

Ash was short for Ashwin. Ashwin Gyan. Ash was a useful Westernization that was easy to pronounce and rolled off the tongue as if he, or those talking to him, were saying Joe, Tom or Sam. He felt blessed he didn't have a polysyllabic last name that people would eye with dread. It was a wonder to him though, "*gyan*" would still be butchered to "*guy-an*."

His ancestors came from India. His father had migrated to the US before Ash was born. Nonetheless, Ash's frame of reference and everything he knew was American. India was as exotic to him as it was for those whose grandparents or great grandparents had settled in the US from Europe or Africa. There were some threads of having been born Indian, and Ash was cognizant of this, that would always be a part of him. These were some of the ideals his parents espoused while he was growing up. Ash always liked the concept of guests being treated with a holiness that juxtaposed them next to God. He found that a useful aphorism of how to deal with people. He also always intuitively understood the concept of karma. The concept was explained to him when he was a teenager, and it felt like he was being told the sky was blue. It was a basic truth of the universe – how could anyone deny it? Later in life he would come to realize that it is specifically taught because it is broadly ignored, with equal disregard, by those of Indian and non-Indian origin.

Ash was rubbing his chin as he rode the merry-go-round of thoughts in his mind. It was a round chin, the sides of his face coming to a blunt point. It served as a suitable demarcation line for his oval face. At 5' 10", Ash was medium-height for most Americans and on the tall side compared to his ethnic Indians. He was about medium-build and at times he would develop a round belly, particularly when he attempted to find inspiration for life in fine food. He had soft eyes, a rounded nose and he loved to laugh, even though he knew those laugh lines would haunt him as wrinkles later in life. He had olive-toned skin. In Mexico they would speak Spanish to him, in France they thought he was from Algeria and in South Africa they asked if he was Arab.

There was a scar at the base of Ash's neck. It was a source of great embarrassment for him. As a five-year old he had allowed curiosity to get the better of him and his kindergarten classmate who happened to be his neighbor. While behind closed doors and without any clothes on in a game most aptly described as *"I'll show you mine, if you'll show me yours"*, little Ash had decided to impress young Julie by doing karate moves, that he didn't even really know, while simultaneously admiring himself performing such stunts in front of a mirror. Unfortunately for him, he noticed a knife on his mother's dresser, and had the flash of inspiration that a karate kick with a knife would surely impress Julie even more. His excitement overwhelmed him – little Julie was clapping her enthusiasm – and he accidentally lodged the knife in his neck. It must have been a loud scream, because his mother bolted into the room within seconds. Ash recalled how her eyes looked like they were going to pop out of her head. Her scream topped his on a pure decibel basis, causing Julie's mother to drop her cup of tea and come bounding into the room as well. Ash resented his mother for quite a while after that. When older, he realized that she probably thought he had cut off something that would become very important later in life in extending the family line. Ash had a hard-time facing Julie's parents after that. It always seemed like Julie's father was sneering at him. He avoided that house at Halloween. He was really relieved when the Applebaums moved away several years later.

Ash wasn't sure he had heard it clearly after it was said. He was being called out from his stupor to the present once more. Were those paddles coming towards his chest? Was he going to be violently jerked back from his daze? He recalled a movie – what was its name – something to do with running in the 1924 Olympics – where everything fell to a frame-by-frame crawl in a race and the winner crossed the finish line, cutting the tape, the reaction played out slowly on the screen, almost painfully slow. *Chariots of Fire.*

He had to think over the words just spoken. They were delivered with the same robotic, lifeless, monotone voice as the deliverer of the news had used throughout the beginning of the meeting and indeed through most of his communicating life. The fact that it was Eddie who delivered it gave Ash a sense of repugnant whiplash.

CHAPTER 2

"Ash has been named Partner."

The applause yanked Ash from his thoughts to the present goings-on. His mind had wandered to another movie – a nuclear bomb exploding in slow motion, an ominous mushroom cloud over the horizon – what was the moral of that – oh yes - do we really want this monster we have created? That was macabre though; this was supposed to be joyous.

Ash forced a smile. It was the right thing to do. He was happy – he had to be happy. Who wouldn't want this? It was all he had been working towards. It was his articulated goal. He had to admit, he had spent the better part of the recent past tormenting himself about when and if it would happen. Now he knew. It was happening, and the time was now. There was suddenly a lot of pressure lifted … maybe.

Eddie rose from his end of the table. He and Ash always sat as far away from each other as possible. As he moved from his side of the long conference room table, made to hold twenty, towards Ash, one could see the alliances within the office shift. Beginning with his closest allies seated next to him, the ELVES, down to his enemies, who were, coincidentally – or perhaps it was by design – Ash's allies.

Ash thought he ought to get up and meet Eddie halfway. It would have been the gentlemanly thing to do. However,

Ash merely sat there. He focused his gaze on the smiles and the high-fives being exchanged at his end of the table. Good people, Ash thought to himself, at least those sitting next to me. David kept clapping his hands every few seconds. Ash found this behavior really strange, yet endearing.

Eddie approached Ash. He had his right hand out, but he also had his left hand and arm opened out wide. It seemed like an invitation for a hug. Ash had to think quickly. Perhaps it is better not to spurn him here, Ash thought, in front of all these people. There may be repercussions as a result. It would also tarnish the image Ash was eager to project – he wanted to be known as the good guy.

Ash went in for the hug. Eddie was stunned. Their bodies met in this awkward side-by-side embrace. Eddie quickly jumped back and Ash responded in kind. It was like cotton candy touching the tongue, a soap bubble making contact with the ground, a man deprived of sexual intimacy for too long - *it ended in a flash.*

Both wanted to resume their normal activities as quickly as possible. That situation was just too weird.

Ash folded his arms across his chest and with his right thumb and index finger he stroked his neck up and down while holding his chin up. He only stopped once when he shook the hand of an insubordinate, Steven Reynolds, who was congratulating him. Steven was extremely tall, over 6' 5", very thin and had short brown hair.

Ash thought back to Eddie's announcement. The presenter of the news that Ash had waited so long for had to be none other than Eddie Cache. Ash hadn't envisioned it that way. He thought it might be more like his graduation, or a Presidential swearing in to an official post with his hand on a Bible or those ceremonies he had seen on television of someone being knighted. Not that he would have trusted

Eddie with a sword.

Ash had to fight the urge to call him Johnny. It was the irony of the impulse which amused Ash. Eddie was the diametric opposite of "The Man in Black." Ash could never imagine Eddie *"walking the line."* He looked Chinese, but when prompted about his name, he had spent the forty-plus years of his life saying that it had French-Canadian origins. It was odd, thought Ash, he would presume nobody knew the French had occupied Vietnam. Eddie had been born and raised in Southern California.

Ash remembered the trip he and Eddie took to China together to meet with suppliers of a company they were contemplating buying, named Project Flow. Ash was delighted when Lasi and the others had asked them to make the trip. He had been to China several times and had learned some key phrases in the language. Eddie attempted to conjure a litany of excuses why he couldn't go. His guises resonated a similar desperation to Ash's recent reluctance to wake up in the morning for the nationwide conference call. Ash watched as Eddie boarded the airplane with brooding shoulders and his right arm firmly at his side.

During their stay, one of the hosts asked Eddie where he was from through a translator.

"Orange County," had been Eddie's response.

The translator gave a multi-second response. Ash paid attention. He caught *"America"* and *"Chinese cannot."* "Orange County" was never repeated. At least someone in the group had the good sense to protect Eddie from himself. Later that night, the translator caught a few minutes alone with Ash.

"You are more Chinese than Eddie," said the translator.

"Try hard very I," said Ash with a sheepish grin.

He knew he had butchered it. The two laughed together.

Ash also recalled the time that one of the portfolio companies that Eddie had invested in had sent him a box of mandarin oranges for Chinese New Year, a key tradition. Ash watched in disbelief as he threw them in the trash, violently. *I'm not sure what those oranges did to you* thought Ash.

Ash also recalled the time that they were looking for a new Associate in the office. Ash felt that Eddie tended to favor the white, Anglo-Saxon, Protestant candidates that they were interviewing, although half of the candidates would be Asian-American or Indian-American. Ash quickly dismissed this thought, thinking it improbable. When they had screened each applicant, Ash had settled on a Chinese-American candidate and Eddie had favored Jason, who was ultimately victorious.

Ash soon learned what had gone wrong. The candidate that Ash favored made the mistake of trying to talk to Eddie in Chinese. Needless to say, Eddie was emphatic about not hiring him. Ash thought it was a shame. The candidate was a Harvard Business School graduate who had several years of private equity experience and genuinely had an interest in joining the firm because his father, who was very ill, resided in Los Angeles. He was actually desperate.

Jason had a mediocre background in comparison. His previous experience had solely been running a mobile phone equipment retail outlet. At least that's what he put on his resume. Ash envisioned Jason along the boardwalk of a beach, perhaps even Venice Beach, hawking knock-off cell phone ear pieces and carrying cases displayed on a blanket. Jason had other options. He specifically told Ash he was contemplating continuing to surf and live off the rental income being generated from his grandfather's real estate investments that he had inherited. He might even re-locate to the Caribbean, he pointed out, if he didn't get this job. He didn't strike Ash as particularly desperate.

Desperate candidates were the best suited for Popular Capital. Ash knew. He had been one of those desperate candidates years ago. Desperate candidates were easier – they complained less, but most importantly, they didn't leave. No matter how much they hated it. Non-desperate candidates did such things as throw chairs at you, creating holes in your conference room walls, when you failed to deliver on promises of bonuses and promotions. Desperate candidates didn't insist on such things as the firm delivering on what it promised or paying a market rate of compensation. Or for that matter, they never demanded intelligence or consistency of thought from their superiors. They tended to think less and fall into line more. It was exactly what Popular needed.

• • •

Ash returned to his office. There were a few of his junior people loitering around his door. He liked them. They had been intensely loyal to him, and he had gone to bat for them as well. It was a positive relationship. It was how he had always envisioned working in such a setting would be.

"Congratulations, Ash!"

"Way to go!"

"It took them long enough to acknowledge your talent," said Steven.

Ash placed his right index finger and thumb on his chin and started to rub it. He was pondering this last comment. He had recently turned thirty-two. He was the youngest Partner of all around the country. Some of the Associates and Vice Presidents working for him were older than him. Steven was giving him a *Blow Smoke Up The Ass* comment. This wasn't a term found in any finance book, but everyone in private equity knew the term and was guilty of using it. Ash could never figure out the origins of the comment. Perhaps it was a reference to what beekeepers do to hoodwink bees into not stinging them. Although why the reference to that anatomical part of the body? It wasn't as if directing it through there was an obvious means to impair someone's ability to see or think clearly. It must be for dramatic, although misguided, effect. Ash got such supplications from time to time. And, Ash had to admit, he had played the role of sycophant himself. He decided not to harass Steven, however disingenuous his comment was.

It was more interesting to reflect on how the recipient of the news reacted. While the person making the statement would be a toady, Ash decided that if the recipient enjoyed the comment, that person was a FROG – one who *F*ailed to *R*ecognize the *O*bsequious *G*rip. Ash loved the term. He had shared it with David.

"You have the added benefit of hinting at control," indicated Ash.

"Like the tail wagging the dog," highlighted David.

The best FROG that Ash and David had known was the former head of the office, Martha Landis. She had a tendency to attempt to exert her control often. Ash could easily manipulate her by faking adulation. Others seemed to know that as well. When a local industry group wanted to sequester a donation from her, they sent her an award entitled "Top Twenty-Five Banker in the Los Angeles Suburbs". Everyone in the office thought it was a hoax. Even if it were real, Martha should have refused it since she *wasn't a banker*. Instead, living up to her FROG distinction, she accepted the award, donated $500 and proudly displayed the plaque in her office.

One visitor to her office quipped, "Martha must have come in last place and I bet numbers seventeen through twenty-four were ATMs." Ash laughed uproariously at the comment. There was such joy in taking delight at a FROG's expense.

While it was easy to control her, Martha on the other hand, had complete control of Eddie. Eddie failed to see that she was a FROG and also lacked the ability to leverage that phenomenon in his favor. Martha had initially hidden the office in a suburb of Los Angeles, over an hour away from all other participants in the private equity industry. This required Eddie to drive two hours to the office and two hours home everyday because of where he lived. Rather than raise an objection, being a Partner and having near equal status, Eddie complied. Ash was sure this was a key reason he was one of Lasi's favorites.

"Why don't we go out this evening to celebrate?" Ash suggested to David, Steven and the others standing outside his office.

"Really?" asked David, his eyes growing wide.

Ash knew why he reacted with such surprise. Eddie would never sponsor such an event.

"Don't worry," said Ash, "It's on me."

● ● ●

The late afternoon sunlight bounced off the beige walls illuminating the wood furniture while Ash sat in his office. It made the room golden yellow. He looked out the window and rubbed his chin.

He thought about many things while he sat there. There was a knock at the door. Damn glass doors, Ash cursed under his breath. He turned around. It was David. He motioned for David to come back. Ash picked up the phone, dialed his home number and kept the phone to his ear. There was no one home. Two thousand five hundred square feet laid out over two floors, with high ceilings, dark amber hardwood floors and minimalist furniture all to himself. The exterior was in the fashionable Mediterranean style. The exterior color was lighter than his neighbor's choice, some hue in between beige and khaki the builder had told him, and the house was covered with characteristic rust colored roof tiles. It was located on an incline, to call it a hill would overstate its altitude, and its back faced the city of its address.

The announcement for his answering machine finished, and Ash had silence. He had deliberately placed a ninety minute tape in there for times like these. This way the receptionist and others in the office could see from their desks that Ash's line was engaged and those passing by his door would see the phone in his hand if he was facing forward. Of course, if he was in his preferred position of looking out the window, passers-by would see the phone cord disappearing behind the chair.

He continued to rub his chin.

Why aren't I happy? he thought to himself.

He had dreamed about this moment since he was in high school. It was the pinnacle of his career. He had reached the top. All of those purchases he postponed – the latest model BMW 7-Series, the Rolex, the larger house in Hollywood Hills, the vacation home, he could now do. He *should* now do he thought to himself. Ash wanted to achieve something before he acquired these luxury goods, as if it were a rite of passage. But the last thing he wanted to do was go to the car dealership, the jewelry store or the realtor.

Now I guess I am one of them. Why doesn't that make me comfortable? As he considered the Partners he had worked for in the last ten years of his career, there were several he had admired.

Maybe Ash was disturbed that it had been Eddie who relayed the news. He decided that he should call Lasi.

"Hello?"

"Hi Lasi, it's Ash."

"Yes Ash."

There was a few seconds of silence. *Okay, I'll start* thought Ash.

"Well, I wanted to say thank you for promoting me to Partner."

"Yes, right."

Back to a few seconds of silence. *Okay, I'll carry the conversation* thought Ash.

"It's a great honor," added Ash.

Silence again. This was wonderfully uninspiring thought Ash.

"How is the sale of your portfolio company GeldXpress going?"

Gee, glad to see that you took the plunge and uttered more than two syllables. You usually aren't at a loss for words - but are you kidding me? This is supposed to be the biggest day in my career and you are asking me the status of one of my deals? Instead of the fireworks he had longed for, Ash got a candle. A very short candle. One that went out in five seconds.

"It's fine. I'll report more next Monday," replied Ash.

"Okay."

"I'll see you then, Lasi."

"Bye."

That was anticlimactic Ash lamented. It was like delivering a masterful performance and the string of the violin snapping, leading in the 100 meter dash and tripping before the finish line or preparing to go on your dream vacation and a work crisis holding you back.

After so many years, there are still so many things that I don't understand regarding people's behavior in this industry thought Ash.

But as he thought about the Partners in that first firm he worked for or the two companies he was subsequently with, he realized it would have been an honor had the people of similar rank to Lasi and Eddie asked him to join them as an equal. Why did he not feel that now?

Ash called his mentor. "Samuel, how are you?"

"I'm well, Ash. How are things with you?"

"Well, I just made Partner."

"Congratulations! Hey, now you're a member of the club, a walking representation of the firm, an icon of its ideals. You get to set the tone. I remember how excited I was when I made Partner."

The words made Ash's head spin. He suddenly felt like Atlas, shouldering a huge burden.

"Did you get your carried interest package?" continued Sam.

"Uh, not exactly."

"How about access to the private firm chef?"

"Not really."

"A time-share for the corporate jet?"

"No."

"So what *did* you get?"

Ash began stroking his neck.

"Samuel, can I call you back?"

"Certainly."

Ash hung up the phone. Ash felt puerile in abruptly leaving the conversation with Samuel. Samuel had asked about his carried interest package. This was the ownership that Ash should be receiving as a Partner in a private equity fund. And it was nonexistent. Ash knew why he still spoke to his mentor. Samuel would ask Ash all of the questions Ash was himself afraid to hear the answers to.

Ash knew that he couldn't avoid his mentor forever; he would be in touch with him again soon. He simply couldn't cope, at least not at that moment, with the sense of disappointment he felt that he was responsible for creating within his mentor. I can only handle that disappointment in small doses, he thought to himself. It almost felt like he was letting Samuel down, and that seemed to trouble Ash even more.

Ash found himself thinking about the Marx brothers. He remembered how fond his good friend Max was of them. There was a particular quote:

"I'd never want to join a club that would accept me as a member."

● ● ●

Ash let several days pass. Something continued to be missing. Why couldn't Ash figure it out? Wasn't there supposed to be more to this? Everyone else seemed to think so. Ash had gotten that confirmation from Samuel. Ash thought he would feel more excited. He had to keep reminding himself that it had actually happened, a variant of the pinch-me conundrum.

He certainly didn't feel any differently, and he surely thought he would. Ash thought of a friend whom he was confident would cheer him up, Max Chu.

Max had a great set-up. He worked in a small private equity firm, just Max and two other Partners. The three of them had all joined around the same time and had taken the reins from seasoned private equity veterans who wanted to retire. Ash had always been jealous of the mentoring Max received. Max's firm had ten loyal investors who gave them significant leeway. He never had excessive pressure to get deals done or requirements in terms of how he managed his portfolio company investments. As a result, his fund had been extremely successful. He was able to take the time to make smart bets, spend considerable time at each portfolio company and create value through the consistent application of hard work and perseverance. When problems arose, Max was able to devote the proper time and resources to resolve them, and not be forced to spend countless hours preparing for bureaucratic meetings and then lose another several hours in the course of the meetings themselves.

Ash picked up the phone.

"So how's life, Max?"

"Not too bad. I'm planning another vacation to Tahiti."

Max Chu was a Chinese-American immigrant success story. His father had escaped with the family during the Chinese Cultural Revolution. Mr. Chu had been an entrepreneur, founding several electronics companies in the US. He had long since retired.

Max looked like an athlete. He was six-feet tall and well built. He had an exceptionally friendly demeanor. He exuded an aura of peace, instantly making those around him comfortable and at ease. When anyone spoke to him, he would lean his head forward towards that person. People responded well to that gesture and to him.

"It must be nice to be able to get away," indicated Ash jealously.

"Yeah, I try to do it once every few months. It is one of the pearls of wisdom from my father. He makes sure he takes multiple trips throughout the year. In fact, all three of us who run the place do. The other guys here are great; we always cover for each other."

Ash decided to end the conversation. He became lost in thought. He wondered what it was like to be able to leave and have your back covered. He was always afraid to be away too long from his job.

Ash decided to give his abysmal sentiments time to clear up. He thought he would live with the new situation for awhile – wear the new suit about town, break in the fresh pair of shoes or test-drive the car for a few days. He hoped it would help him come to terms with what was troubling him and he could finally enjoy his promotion.

He waited until Max came back. Unfortunately, the status quo prevailed.

"How was your trip?" Ash asked Max.

"Oh, it was great, very relaxing."

"You should try to get out there sometime," Max

suggested.

Ash chuckled to himself but agreed overtly so as not to stifle the conversation with negative comments about his job. And then Ash stalled.

"So, watch any good Marx brothers lately?" asked Ash.

"Ash, it's 9:15 am. Did you really call me to ask that?"

"Well, I made Partner," offered Ash, finally.

"Hey, that's great!" said Max.

Max enquired about how long it had been and what the new perks were going to be. Ash then described to Max the salary and the ownership package.

"You are joking, right?"

"No, unfortunately not."

"Do you know that we pay our Vice Presidents more than that?"

"Yeah, I figured as much."

"And at Benson's firm, they pay their Associates that much. You know, people with ten percent of the experience that you have."

"I know," Ash conceded.

Ash stood up from behind his desk. He began stroking his neck, again.

Benson Wong was a good friend of theirs. He landed at the most prestigious firm in the industry, the one credited with founding private equity, TTW. The initials were for the founding Partners. The first "T," Thornburg, had been a seasoned Wall Street veteran, and the two younger ones, Tate and Wolseley, had been the aggressive drivers of the business. There was even a rumor the two were related. Since its founding, Thornburg had actually left the fund to start another one, on his own.

TTW had a stellar reputation in the industry. While their performance hadn't been the best compared to others, they had been one of the originals. They never had difficulty in raising money for their funds. People invested in them simply because they were TTW. For years, TTW had the distinction of completing the largest buyout in history. The investment ended disastrously, but there was tremendous notoriety the firm had gained as a result of acquiring the large tobacco and consumer products conglomerate. Books had been written about them and on that deal in particular. Tate and Wolseley were heroes in the industry. Everyone who was in private equity or aspired to join the industry, the list of the latter being a multiple of the list of the former, had heard of their names.

Benson had the best pedigree of either Max or Ash. Princeton undergrad, Harvard MBA, and two years at the most prestigious investment banking firm on Wall Street, Gunner Salk & Co. Benson had been one of 250 people who wanted, and had been qualified enough, to have that job. Benson was the lucky one. Ash and Max would later admit that he was also the one who seemed to want it the most. Benson expended a great number of hours studying every transaction TTW had done. He knew intimate details that some of the deal members who had done the transaction originally had long since forgotten. Such was his nature. Benson had amassed an encyclopedic knowledge of private equity and its workings. Ash was sure TTW benefited immensely from his overzealous approach. Benson was making millions of dollars a year.

He had rimless glasses. All of those hours that Benson spent sitting – at his desk, in conference rooms, on airplanes – had given him a portly figure. He would slick back his hair to present to the world a sense of control. His gaze was intense, even intimidating. Ash could visualize how Benson would be effective in meetings. When he walked into a room, he evoked a reaction of *"be afraid, be very afraid"*. While Benson was determined, he had no malice. He wasn't attempting to take advantage of anyone; he just wanted to achieve the best he could given the circumstances. All of his time spent preparing and his knowledge of arcane facts were just his attempt to make the odds more in his favor.

"When was the last time you spoke to Benson?" Ash probed.

"Well, you know how it is with him, you leave five messages across three months and then he calls you when he is sitting on a plane right before take off..."

"...And he has to hang up within two minutes," Ash completed Max's comment.

● ● ●

Ash would later come to learn Eddie had told the receptionist that whenever Lasi called, even if he had asked for Ash, the phone call should be given to Eddie first. When Ash finally did speak to Lasi, he could literally count to between fifteen and twenty seconds and Eddie would be standing outside his door.

"So what did Lasi say?"

Ash would enjoy having fun with him sometimes. He would note Eddie's arm was at his side.

"He was asking me to take over the company. He wants to retire soon."

Ash had been able to deliver the comment with just the right touch of nonchalance. He enjoyed watching Eddie's reaction with glee. Eddie would lower his head and tighten the focus of his eyes, before he would finally lean back.

"Oh, that's a good one," he would say. It was presented with a bit of laughter, but Ash could always detect the slightest tinge of nervousness in his delivery.

Ash watched as Eddie lifted his arm to his imaginary sling.

"Lasi actually has some major changes he is looking

to implement," said Eddie.

That's funny thought Ash *he didn't say that to me and I'm a Partner now, I would hear about such things. You're not going to frighten me, Eddie.*

"He set-up a committee and asked me to be on it," said Eddie.

Okay Eddie, you win, I'm a little frightened. Ash could see Eddie clenching his fist.

Lasi was able to take himself out of a communist construct, but it was never very clear if the communist mentality ever really left him. Sure, he enjoyed the money. His current one hundred million dollar net worth certainly provided a comfortable existence for him. But he never shook his autocratic tendencies. He had a legion of committees that reported to him. The most powerful such committee was the Capital Commitment Committee of Popular Capital, CCCP or "The Commies", as it became referred to by employees. The Commies made all investment decisions. Any potential transaction had to be approved by them. Lasi exerted his full control over The Commies. Even though there were several senior Partners on the CCCP, and votes were held, they were largely symbolic. Of all the members, Henry Exeter, Jake Roberts and Ted Fulsom, nobody voted against Lasi and no investment was approved without Lasi agreeing to it. He never invited or welcomed diverse viewpoints. His decision was always the final one, his power absolute.

Being asked to join one of Lasi's committees meant you were an insider.

"There are going to be some pretty radical changes around here," continued Eddie in a smug tone.

Okay, I give.

"Such as?" enquired Ash.

"Oh, well, in due time, you will come to learn of them. When the others know," Eddie trumpeted.

He attempted to look Ash straight in the eyes, but it was clumsy, he looked away repeatedly. He was also flailing his right arm a little. Eddie's attempts at being intimidating were sloppy. But, Ash should not have taken as much comfort in that as he did that day or in subsequent such encounters. There should have been enough clues from these and other comments Eddie would make for Ash to realize he should have been increasingly more guarded with him.

CHAPTER 3

Rather than merely calling Samuel back, Ash decided it was time for a visit. When he reached Samuel's home, more properly his multi-acre estate, he found Samuel in the garden seated in a lawn chair, a stack of books piled on the table in front of him. Ash had brought with him a bottle of wine.

Samuel was slightly shorter than Ash. He was a thin man. He had an oval face with a prominent forehead. It was even more pronounced due to his receding hairline. Samuel's ears seemed a bit bigger than would have been proportionate for the rest of his head. They protruded outwards slightly. Upon them and his pointed nose rested round rimmed glasses when he was reading.

After enjoying a bit of the wine, Samuel offered Ash some advice.

"There are two types of people in this world not to trust."

"Tell me," encouraged Ash, a smile creeping up on his face.

"Those who don't drink or drink very little and those who drink too much."

"Why is that?" asked Ash now fully smiling.

"Those who don't drink or drink little haven't experienced enough pain in their lives and those who drink too much don't know how to cope with it."

Samuel was always good about savoring the moment. He waited until the bottle was nearly empty before he dug in again.

"So let me get this straight. If your expenses are over your budget, it comes out of your hide, but if you bring in revenues more than your budget, you don't have any upside?"

"Yeah. That's how it works," Ash corroborated.

Samuel was grilling Ash on how his compensation was structured. Ash felt like a sideshow freak. Ash was the man with three eyes, the elephant trunk as a nose or the one who could insert himself into an unusually small barrel. Ash was stroking his neck again. He recalled how in the past he would derive so much joy from impressing his mentor. Now he felt like he just made himself out to be a donkey. He could only imagine what was going through his mentor's mind – why am I talking to you?

"That's not how it is supposed to be, Ash," Samuel assured and added, "You are supposed to get a fair share of the profits you bring in."

"Sounds like a dream," Ash surmised.

Ash had fantasized about private equity for so long. Private equity was the top of the totem pole for the financial services industry. A group of Partners would raise money from investors. They would use that money to buy businesses, grow them, try to increase their value, and then sell the companies after three to five years, churning a profit. This excited Ash immeasurably. Ever since he came to know about the industry, he would think about different companies he would hear about and he'd determine whether it would be something he'd like to own or not.

The real roots could probably be traced to high school. Ash loved flipping through *BusinessWeek*, *Fortune* and the other popular business rags. Private equity didn't have center-stage status then as it does currently. He had to dig up the information by searching through the available resources for it.

He, like his classmates, had an image of an omnipotent, super hero, Wall Street finance jock. Men wanted to be him and women wanted to be with him. Everyone respected him for his money and his ability to make more of it. Who really knew what he did? It was glamorous, it was seductive and every one of Ash's peers wanted it.

The media helped feed the frenzy. There were exciting transactions Ash read about in the late 1980s. The biggest was the large tobacco and consumer products conglomerate bought by the firm Benson eventually worked for, TTW. And then of course there was the movie that epitomized the era. *Wall Street.* Who didn't want to heed the call that *"greed was good"*? It became every teenager's dream to become a stockbroker or an investment banker so that they too could become a *"Player."* Everybody wanted to be *Bud Fox.* And then the stakes were raised by Richard Gere. "How great would it be to live Richard Gere's character from *Pretty Woman?"* Those were the Gods; private equity was the goal.

When Ash graduated high school, he ended up at the University of Pennsylvania, a breeding ground for the Wall Street set. That is where he met Samuel. Samuel was a professor when Ash started college, but prior to Ash graduating, he left to start a series of consulting and advising businesses. Samuel was a man whose practical side found it too stifling to remain in academia for the rest of his career.

Ash's time in college was a euphoric experience. He found himself in a sea of aspiration that seemed to know no bounds. However, his individualism got lost in the mix. Suddenly he wasn't *THE* stellar Indian student, he was *A* stellar Indian student. Furthermore, there was no direct access to private equity at the time. There were two options for those coming out of school to get into private equity: it was either investment banking or consulting. Ash attempted both avenues. The best consulting groups didn't want him.

They preferred candidates with a better pedigree. Furthermore, those who talked "shop" well had an upper hand. Ash hadn't learned enough about how to play the job-seeking game at that point. With the help of friends like Charles Adams and Pedro Fritz, masters at the interviewing song and dance, Ash figured out the catch phrases, sound bytes and other parts of the script that would land him a job in investment banking. By then however, most jobs had been taken. Ash went to the alumni database and began sending letters to everyone and anyone in investment banking. It was probably two thousand in total he sent. He managed to get some interviews. The mergers and acquisitions and raising capital activities that he discussed in his interview were crammed into his head. At the time Ash was saying it, he still didn't fully appreciate what investment banks did. His performances were enough; he landed on his feet, ending up at one of the top six investment banks in the world.

"The fees, Ash, the fees are the reason to be in private equity," Samuel had told him many, many years ago.

"Investors pay the private equity fund two percent to manage their money," began Samuel, "There would be a few million in fees that the private equity fund would earn when it completed a deal, there would be a few million in annual management fees that they would pay themselves from the companies they owned, and when an investment was sold, the gains were split twenty percent for the Partners of the private equity fund, called General Partners, and eighty percent for the investors, called Limited Partners. The twenty percent for the General Partners is called carried interest."

Ash recollected reacting to this by growing excited. He was having a virtually Pavlovian response to the figures Samuel was throwing around. *I feel like that shark in the series of movies* Jaws *or like the dinosaurs from* Jurassic Park, *– hey, wasn't it the same director who did both?* Ash remembered understanding at that instance why they named the book *The Predator's Ball*.

"Now, the General Partners do have some monetary responsibility, it's not just a one-way street."

Darn, thought Ash.

"The General Partners are required to put their own capital in, usually two percent of the fund. Nonetheless, their split coming out of a deal remained so favorable to them. Some funds could even charge a three percent management fee and take a thirty percent carried interest. It is like the housing market, sometimes the market would favor buyers, sometimes sellers. Hence, sometimes General Partners have the upper hand, and sometimes Limited Partners have the upper hand."

That made sense to Ash.

"I guess you'd better get while the getting is good," said Ash.

"Well, it's already been modified a little bit. What I described is how it has been. Over time, the terms have become less favorable for General Partners. Limits were placed on the number of years that a two percent management fee could be earned and sometimes the carried interest payout would be calculated only after the Limited Partners were reimbursed the fees they had given the General Partners."

Even with the revision in terms, thought Ash, this is a great business to be in. When he was ready to leave investment banking, and would interview for those private equity jobs, his peers again advised him of what the moves were, the playbook of buzz words and phrases one had to use in order to get hired. Some of them Ash felt were bogus. But some of the reasons for desiring the job that he articulated, unlike investment banking, actually resonated with him. In investment banking, you had a deal you had accomplished, but it ended there. It was merely a transaction and you moved on to the next one. Ash always found that a bit maudlin. He learned so much about a company, in many ways he had grown close to it, and now he had to abandon it. Wouldn't it be nice to be involved with these companies for more than just a few months?

Ash continued to try to gain entry into the prestigious private equity firms, but he wasn't able to make it. The top firms just weren't calling him back. He tried joining some start-up private equity funds. It proved to be a disastrous career choice. He started with one, which eventually folded and then went to another one where history repeated itself.

Coming through those experiences, Ash's proverbial star had fallen considerably. What a precipitous decline it had been. He had gone from solid pedigree to mediocrity. There was only one place available for him. Popular Capital.

After thinking about those days when Ash's appetite developed, his thoughts came back to the present day, over ten years since graduating college and five years since landing at Popular. In the past year, Ash had brought in eight million dollars in fees to the firm. Seven-and-a-half million of it had been pure profit. He shared these details with Samuel.

"You should be making over a million a year," said Samuel, shifting his weight in the garden chair.

Ash thought about his paltry salary in comparison to this. It was less than twenty percent. It occurred to Ash that had he been in Benson's or Max's position he'd be making the millions that he had envisioned.

"Why don't you go elsewhere?" suggested Samuel.

● ● ●

Ash had been trying for a long time to join another firm. In fact, since he had joined Popular Capital five years earlier, he had never pulled his resume out of consideration for any other position. There just weren't any suitable positions available for a period of time. And when options did open up, Ash had been at Popular for over a year - long enough that he had become tainted. He couldn't say "them" anymore, he had to use "we". And that killed the likelihood of any transition. As Ash's desperation grew, he was even prepared to take a step back to a lower position or a cut in pay, but prospective employers didn't even want him for that.

Ash called several of the headhunters once again. He thought he was making some headway with one group. The headhunter was enthusiastic about a job for which he had recently been engaged. And then Ash mentioned with whom he had been working.

"Are they a real private equity firm?" asked the recruiter.

"Ouch," said Ash aloud.

He did what he had grown accustomed to doing. He began to defend Popular Capital with the recruiter. When he met the recruiter, he tried driving the point home again.

"Look, I have been doing traditional private equity deals. My experience is on point. Just because the firm does debt deals as well doesn't mean that I have solely been doing them," Ash insisted. He noticed he had begun to breath heavily.

"Okay, okay, okay," said the recruiter.

Ash heard the sound of a file cabinet closing, a door slamming shut, a computer being switched off.

As the headhunter was typing something, Ash remembered something more to relay to him. The recruiter saw Ash was about to say something, and he quickly interrupted. "So how are Jason and Bob doing?"

Ash was stunned.

"Steven is with you too, right?" he also asked.

So everyone is trying to leave thought Ash.

"How do you know those guys?" Ash enquired.

The recruiter grew quiet and tried to provide a plausible explanation of how they had come to see him long ago and that he simply knew they were with Popular Capital at this point.

"Oh," said Ash, "So it's not like they are also all looking for jobs or anything?"

The recruiter looked at Ash. He attempted to say something and then stopped. He changed the subject. It was enough of an indication for Ash. He got his answer.

• • •

In preparing to call some additional headhunters, Ash thought through his experience at Popular Capital and thought about some of the transactions that had particular meaning for him or the people with whom he had formed a nice bond over the years. He thought back fondly to when he first learned of Project Emancipate, the deal he funded the day he became Partner. It was a company called High Performance Systems Inc. They were involved in testing equipment sold to medical and biotechnology laboratories and were a division of a multi-billion dollar medical instruments company. However, the parent was looking to do a spin-off. All other operations of the business sold their products to hospitals, clinics, doctor's offices or other centers where there was delivery of healthcare. It was a certain segment of the market that played by its own distinct rules. Selling into the laboratory segment, where High Performance Systems sold its products, was often not a priority for the large sales team. Hence the division became a bit of an orphaned child.

The head of the division was Boas Cole. Boas was considered youthful to be head of an entire division, only in his late thirties. He had risen through the ranks of the parent company at a young age. He became particularly skilled at fixing problem divisions. He was appreciated because he could conceptualize the best strategy for a business and had the tenacity and the resolve to be a master at execution.

Ash recalled his first meeting with Boas as the most memorable he had experienced with the head of a company Ash was looking at buying.

"*Namaste*," said Boas to Ash.

They were meeting in an airport restaurant. Ash was speechless to hear a greeting in his ethnic Hindi. He didn't have time to react.

"You seem surprised," offered Boas.

"I am," responded Ash.

"You are from India, correct?"

"Yes. You know, I usually don't interact with many people who know about or appreciate my background. At least not in this industry. Or in this country for that matter. Most Americans in finance want to discuss business right away," replied Ash.

"*Mera naam* Boas *he*."

"I can't believe you just told me your name in Hindi," exclaimed Ash.

Boas was a tall man of average build. He didn't wear glasses. He had brown hair that was neatly groomed and a sharp nose. Boas confidently looked Ash in the eye, without wavering. When he talked with you, he was 'in the conversation', he leaned forward and spoke in earnest. When he was thinking, contemplating what to say next if he didn't already have a game plan, he would sit back and cross his arms. This wasn't done in a defensive way. It was his way of carving out some space to 'step out of the conversation' momentarily, to collect his thoughts. When he came back to the conversation, he would lean forward again, arms unfolded.

"I can't believe we just went through half of our meeting and we have yet to discuss business," marveled Ash.

They had both spoken at length about India and their respective families.

"My father was an anthropologist," explained Boas.

"Hence your name," pointed out Ash, "and your knowledge of India."

"Exactly."

Ash really didn't want to, but he knew he needed to begin discussing some business matters.

Boas seemed to sense the same.

"Well, I know you finance types like to dive into the numbers, slice and dice them a number of ways, so we can get into that. If you ask me, they are the punchline, and what's really happening, what should really be of interest to you, is the story behind those numbers, not the various ratios you guys like to calculate," Boas stipulated.

Ash was elated with what he was hearing. The ideas were Ash's but the voice was Boas's. Ash didn't want to make Boas feel like he was treating him like a FROG, so rather than adamantly agree with him, he opted for a more restrained approach.

"Sounds like a good idea. Let's get into the story," replied Ash.

Boas smiled broadly. He had been flipping pages in a presentation to get to the section he desired. He immediately stopped, leaned back and folded his arms for a few seconds. He then leaned forward.

"So you aren't a victim of paralysis through analysis?" Boas asked.

Ash smiled. He had heard the term often.

"No. I am capable of making a decision quickly and I don't have to rely on the excuse of 'we need to run some numbers and get back to you'."

Boas smiled broadly. Ash knew that many of his colleagues wielded that excuse freely to avoid making a decision.

"I wish others in your industry felt the same way," commented Boas.

Ash responded with a smile.

"Why don't you tell me the history of the company and I'll be straightforward about my concerns?" suggested Ash.

Ash's primary concern at the time was that Boas may not come with the business. Ash was worried the parent had placed Boas at High Performance Systems just for the sale process, and they would wrench him back to another division as soon as the deal closed.

"I don't want to do this deal without you," Ash explained after Boas had talked about the history of the company and its future growth plans.

He watched Boas's reaction. It concerned Ash that he took his time to respond. That convinced Ash he was considering other possibilities. With his talent, there were a number of places he could go.

"If we happened to work together, I would enjoy our interaction very much," responded Boas.

"What would it take to convince you to stay with the Company?" Ash asked directly.

"You're not afraid to get to the point," Boas noted, smiling at Ash, "How very American of you."

"You deserve for me to be straightforward with you," Ash avowed, laughing as he spoke.

Ash knew Boas wouldn't be so crass as to tell him. It was a bit like the honor of a gentleman, one never kisses and tells. Ash decided that if Boas had told him, it would have indicated something very different about the character picture Ash had begun to formulate of him. It was a rather useful litmus test. Boas passed it well.

• • •

Another quarter had ended and Popular Capital, being a publicly traded company, was required to announce its earnings. This was a unique phenomenon for Popular Capital. Ninety-nine percent of other private equity firms had *private* investors as their backers. Most private equity firms reported to their relatively small group of investors on a discrete, non-public basis. They didn't have to divulge financial performance to the public as Popular Capital was required to do. This structure allowed them to be more long-term in their thinking. Short term hiccups could be easily absorbed. Not at Popular Capital. Every quarter, the financial performance, good or bad, had to be revealed.

Lasi had a tendency to issue the results as if he were delivering a proclamation. He had little patience for the questions asked by shareholders, as they tended to exploit inconsistencies in Popular's performance to see if it was a sign of impending demise. It was a marvel to Ash that the shareholders had allowed Lasi to go on for so long, tolerating his dictatorial behavior and his irreverence towards them. To Lasi's credit, he would mask his indignation effectively. He knew he had to placate the shareholders and assure they were happy. He never took out his anger on them. He was a great actor in that regard. However, with a little provocation, he would lash out at them for what he perceived was impudent behavior.

Lasi's attempt at restraint was exclusive to shareholders. He preferred to do a full release of his pent up frustration with his yes-men. With non-shareholders Lasi Nescu was very swift to become combative. Anytime any non-shareholder attacked the sanctity of his business model, he would get belligerent.

Performance had been average for the quarter. The number of new transactions and the fee income was up significantly, but the profitability remained the same and the net income was actually less.

Ash knew the reasons why – he was living it. However, he enjoyed listening to the shareholder calls to see if the portfolio managers could figure out the reason, deciphering the numbers to see what was really going on.

That's their biggest problem, Ash would joke out loud, they rely so much on numbers, getting upset over percentage point shifts in performance without thinking through the reasons for why it was happening.

The operator came on the phone, "We have a question from William Crest of Balmoral Investments."

"What happened to all of your fee income?" demanded William.

"Well, it was used to cover our expanding operations," explained Lasi, with a slightly irascible tone.

"You mean you frittered it away on hiring too many people you don't actually need," challenged William.

"It's all a part of our expansion plan," Lasi offered, trying to appease him.

Lasi sounded like he was trying to conquer Europe, Ash thought.

"You know," said William, "I am your third largest shareholder, and I've been in your stock for nearly ten years. Not once have you shown me an expansion plan and not once have you stopped expanding your operations."

"Well, that's just a function of…" attempted Lasi with a sense of dismissal.

"Maybe you ought to increase your profitability and reward the guys who have stuck it out with you all these years," William suggested, interrupting Lasi.

"Well, I guess we'll have to keep that in mind," Lasi agreed, the acerbic tone of his voice seemed like it would melt the phone line.

Lasi struggled through a few more questions.

"I'd like to wrap up the call by announcing our recent promotion to Partner," Lasi declared.

Uh-oh, thought Ash. I didn't know he was going to do this.

They had all been seated in the conference room. Eddie, who had been leaning on his chair with his feet up, suddenly fell backwards. His action caused the phone cord to be ripped out of the wall. Ash had his doubts in his mind regarding Eddie's motive, and he had a brief vision in his mind of shoving Eddie into the unsealed hole in the wall, but rather than dwell on either of those, Ash grabbed his cell phone and dialed into the call.

"Eddie, are you on, is Ash there?" he could hear Lasi calling.

"Yes, hello, sorry, Lasi, Ash here," Ash advised.

Great, he had to ask for Eddie.

"Why don't you say a few words?"

Thanks for the offer, but I'd rather not, thought Ash.

"I would like to thank Lasi and the other Partners for deeming me worthy of this recognition," Ash proclaimed.

That came out well, he thought to himself. It's best to make it seem like I really wanted this and I'm really happy to have it. Which I am. Really.

CHAPTER 4

Each one of Ash's deals was like his own child. While it is hard for any parent to say they are partial to one child over another, deep down, in places few people like to talk about, everyone knew that favoritism existed. For Ash, his favorite deal was GeldXpress.

He discovered the Company at a conference on the marriage of manufacturing and technology. He was exhausted from travel prior to arriving at the conference, and he had to admit, he probably had consumed more wine than he should have the night before. He walked into the booth and had been fortunate enough to meet the founder and President straight away, Lothar Landsmann.

Ash often wondered whether if he had heard about the company's products from a regular employee or if he had to browse through product catalogs on his own if he would have been as enthralled. Lothar's love of the company, his passion for his products and his steely resolve to accomplish his stated goals enraptured Ash. It was the human element that hooked Ash from the onset.

Lothar had been a senior product development expert with Stieger, an enormous industrial conglomerate, the General Electric of Europe. He had a comfortable position, a great pension, a company car and all the other perks that a well kept executive in Europe would have. He had discovered an enhanced way for machines to accept cash – vending machines, slot machines, parking meters, etc. His concept allowed people to avoid the treacherous rejection of that crumpled, folded, end-is-cut-off bill. Who could stand waiting there, rejection after rejection? Suddenly that soda, candy bar or bag of chips wasn't worth the frustration.

He couldn't get any advocates in his company to pursue it. So he left. Lothar struggled for three years with no salary, trying to convince customers to try it. He had to sell his car, his house and had even gotten to where he had to eat only half a can of soup a day. He never relented. He got his lucky break with a small vending machine company, and the business slowly grew.

And then, in a classic example of being at the right place at the right time, and in resounding support that it is better to be lucky than smart, the conversion to the single banknote, the Euro was announced in Europe. *Everyone* needed to replace their bill acceptors. Sure, competitors could scramble to adjust their systems, but they didn't have the efficiency that Lothar's devices did. Nor did they have a chance to devise a better system *and* change the currency simultaneously. The big incumbents never saw him coming. Suddenly, Lothar was everywhere. And he was faster, cheaper and more sophisticated than the others. Business fell upon him like an avalanche.

Who else other than the person at the epicenter of the storm could have explained that with the same zeal and fervor? Ash felt all of the emotional oscillations of the experience through Lothar's intonations, the flailing of his hands and the symbolic pulling out of his hair. There was poetry there. And Ash developed an instant admiration.

Lothar agreed to have dinner with Ash and David that same night. He was already waiting for them at the bar when Ash and David arrived. Lothar was watching the television.

"Oh, I am begging your pardon," said Lothar in his learned, unpolished English, "I watch Bayern Munich will host Eintracht Frankfurt this weekend. It is our fussball.

You call it soccer, yes?"

"Eintracht Frankfurt doesn't have a chance," Ash predicted.

"Ah, just so," said Lothar, getting very excited.

"They barely qualified for the Bundesliga this season," added Ash.

"Wunderbar! You are knowing very much about it," said Lothar. His face had lit up with child-like exuberance.

"I enjoy watching," admitted Ash.

"You are a minority of Americans," Lothar pointed out.

In more ways than one, thought Ash.

They spent a good portion of the rest of the evening talking about soccer.

Ash was tingling with excitement on his way back to the US from Munich. It was the first deal that he had sourced on his own. He was still a Vice President, so he knew he needed to convince a Partner to champion his cause at Popular Capital. The only option he had was Martha, Eddie's predecessor.

When Ash made the pitch to Martha, her eyes glazed over. She was not looking Ash in the eye, she would occasionally shuffle some papers and had gotten into the steady rhythm of "uh-huh" every few seconds.

"This guy really understands technology trends. He is a visionary."

"Uh-huh"

Ash was getting frustrated.

"He murdered his mother and wears his underwear outside of his pants."

"Uh-huh."

Ash stopped talking and just sat there in Martha's office. After a few seconds passed, she looked up at him.

"Anything else?"

"Martha, this company has thirty-five percent profit margins, twenty percent year-over-year revenue growth and sixty percent market share."

She looked up at him.

Ah yes, finance people always react to numbers. He should have known better. Ditch the words, give them the figures.

"Oh. Why didn't you say so earlier?"

"I did. I just peppered in some trivial details about what the company does, how it came to exist and how great the management team is."

Martha frowned.

"Sorry to confuse the pitch with relevant facts."

"Well if you want to pursue it, we can present it to the CCCP."

"That's what I was hoping for," said Ash.

●　●　●

Every Monday began the same way ... with that dreaded national call. In the beginning, Ash remembered waking up early and taking it from the office. Back then, the update meetings in the office would be held immediately after the nationwide conference call. That structure soon fell apart when Martha failed to show up to take the nationwide call in person after making demands that others do so. Having destroyed her credibility with a blasé response to her own policies, how could she enforce a schedule with others? Where leaders go, others will follow. Even if they were pseudo-leaders. Everyone began taking those nationwide calls from home, so there was no consistency of when people would show up to the office. Grooming habits were vastly variable, even among finance people.

On this particular Monday, everyone around the country heard the sound of a toilet flushing. People knew it had to be coming from the West Coast. Rumors that Martha and the others were doing the call from home had spread to the other cities. It was general courtesy to keep the phones on mute while listening.   With over one hundred people, there could be a lot of background noise.   It was also a clever way to give yourself a few extra moments of thinking time when presented with a question – "Oh sorry, I had my phone on mute" when a few seconds of dead silence passed and they began insisting you respond to the question.   This morning, Lasi tried to play down the instinctual biological emergency as "someone forgot to put their phone on mute."   Most people snickered at the comment.   They laughed even harder, however, when the toilet flush was heard for a second time.   And then a third time.

Ash amused himself by thinking it was actually a commentary about what was being said.   There was a rather large web of excuses Lasi was attempting to weave about why there wouldn't be a bonus this quarter.   Ash could just imagine someone saying "that's just ridiculous" and flushing the toilet for emphasis.

Ash pondered to himself that it was a good thing everyone took the national call so seriously.   They were meant to review their deals.   There was a vagary to it though. There was never any set agenda. It would mostly be talking about what the powers that be wanted to talk about.   And that meant Lasi.   You could discuss deals about to close and their status, which was more frequently done when the end of the quarter approached, or you would talk about new deals that came onto Lasi's list.

Over time, Ash realized that it functioned as a confessional.   Lasi was really doing it to assert his control. He wanted people to have to justify where they had spent their time in the past week and what they had to show for it. That is also why Lasi's deal list and the silly associated statistics that Eddie was so concerned about received so much scrutiny.

It was always amusing how the directive would be simple at first, "why don't you talk about so-and-so deal?"

The speaker would start and inevitably be cut off by Lasi who asked a very specific question. The answer to which, of course, would be the topic that Lasi had in mind when he first asked the person to speak about the deal. The fact that it would have been more efficient for Lasi to ask the specific question at the outset must have been lost on him. Or, there was an expectation of clairvoyance on the part of Lasi. Unfortunately, he was disappointed more often than he was gratified.

You were someone important if you talked on the call, or so Lasi wanted people to believe. Partners with their initials next to a deal were the ones asked to speak by him. If a more junior member of the team spoke, that just meant that he or she would soon be taking the helm and becoming a Partner in their own right. Many of those waiting for the promotion to Partner would become envious as their peers in a similar predicament would get airtime. In some cases, they would scan the deal list to make sure that any other Partner-hopeful hadn't put a deal on with only their initials and not with an actual Partner's initials.

Ash remembered doing that himself on occasion. He did it with GeldXpress. He put only his initials and not Martha's. It was meant to spook his competition in the other offices and make it seem as if he was in charge of running the show. For the most part, Lasi didn't seem to mind. But Martha, she threw a fit. Ash changed it for the following week.

More importantly than the stage time, there was a fear of looking stupid. There were several people on the phone ready to point out how inane your ideas were. You didn't want to look foolish in front of them. Your intelligence and capability were judged on nothing tangible like deal savvy or experience. It was more important with what assurance you made your claims. There was always the guy who was nervous avowing the sky was blue that everyone laughed at and discredited and the guy with the wildly esoteric references that nobody understood, but at whose comments everyone would pretend to laugh. You didn't want to seem like you didn't 'get it'.

Partners didn't give the call quite the importance that Lasi did. They would strive to miss the call from time to time and have their junior people respond. It was a symbol that you were too busy – out there doing deals and making money – to be troubled with an administrative matter like actually talking about the deals you were pursuing. Ash would laugh, however, with the infamous post-call scramble – a series of e-mails where the Partner who missed the call would frantically attempt to undo some damage done by a person of insufficient rank.

The most amusing situation was when an entire office seemed to be out and eight transactions had to be discussed by the most insignificant person on the deal team – an analyst. His rote response was "I don't know" for every question. He was never heard from again on the call.

At all costs, one avoided having to admit the dreaded, "I don't know." If you didn't know, you invented something to fill the void. And then you backtracked the following week.

It was dangerous to miss these calls when you didn't have comments for your deals scripted with your junior people, particularly if you were not on the best terms with the other Partner or Partners in your office. Ash learned this lesson the hard way. Ash had planned a vacation for himself. He had achieved a major milestone in a transaction by convincing the seller of a business to stay with the company for five years. Previously, the seller was eager to take his money and retire. Ash told Eddie about it. With this particular deal, called Project Condor, there was keen interest on the part of Lasi. Ash couldn't be on the call that particular morning, and he had forgotten to give the update to

David. Lasi enquired about it.

"Yeah, I don't think Ash got anywhere on that deal. He hasn't been all that on the ball with it actually. He skipped off on vacation for a few days."

The following Monday, when Ash was back, Lasi commented, "It's a shame that Project Condor has been lost."

"It hasn't been lost," insisted Ash.

"You should check with Eddie, he seems to have been on top of things while you were away," Lasi's voice was laced with a reprimand.

"He doesn't know what he is talking about," asserted Ash.

Maybe I shouldn't have been so forceful thought Ash. I'm just reacting to being chided publicly.

There was silence on the line.

"Well, huh…now come on, Ash…that's just not true…" Eddie was feigning a chuckle.

"This deal is still on," said Ash affirmatively.

Ash was now angry. Eddie didn't even know the seller's name. It was Ash who had spent the last nine months courting the seller, flying out to Tampa, Florida six times in order to develop a relationship.

The President, Lasi, finally said, "You two sort out whatever the hell is going on. If it should stay on the list, keep it on."

Ash figured out what was going on. He looked at the numbers tallied at the bottom of Lasi's deal list. There were fifteen Partners around the country with an average number of eight deals each. Eddie had the average eight tentative deals on the list, and Ash would have had nine with Project Condor. Eddie hated being outrun by Ash.

I'm not sure what I did to invite this Eddie. I certainly wouldn't have cared if you had nine and I had eight. Just don't push yourself on my deal Ash was burning to say.

It didn't surprise Ash that Eddie never showed up to his office to discuss the matter. Ash certainly had no intentions of soliciting Eddie's further comments. Ash had Project Condor re-added to *his* list.

The following Monday, Ash noticed Eddie had added two more deals to his list. Ash was hoping Lasi would ask him about it. Ash was willing to wager that Eddie didn't have a clue about them.

"What are these two new ones about, Eddie?" asked Lasi.

Ash was thrilled.

"Uh…yeah…we got two new deals in…these look like great opportunities…I feel really good about these," stammered Eddie.

"Yeah, but what do the companies do?"

"Uh…is Jason on?"

There was silence.

"How about Bob?"

Further silence. Neither of the ELVES was on the phone.

"Uh…I guess…uh…we'll have to get back to you," surmised Eddie.

"Don't clutter my list with garbage," Lasi hissed.

Ash was so excited over what he was hearing. He wished he could take a victory lap and talk about one of his deals that was going well. "Oh how great it would be to kick the guy while he is down."

Ash's mirth gave way to introspection. Ash surprised himself with that last thought. He didn't like feeling that way.

"I've changed," he whispered to himself.

He didn't like it. He rubbed his chin. Ash couldn't remember the last time he would have taken such delight in someone else's misery. He should just be feeling sorry for him.

• • •

Ash called his friend Charles. There was a time when Ash considered going into venture and he and Charles worked together briefly. Ash realized he didn't have the optimal skills for it. Charles was successful because he had a dual degree in engineering and finance. The two hottest areas in venture were information technology and biotechnology. Ash found the guys who had technical backgrounds always did much better than those without. They had a distinct competitive advantage. They could quickly determine what part of an entrepreneur's pitch was going to fly and what was a bit too much of a reach. Charles could also command the respect of the technical guys. He wasn't just a suit to them. He was a suit who understood how things worked and could talk shop with the best of them.

Those without technical backgrounds not only didn't garner the respect of the entrepreneurs, but they also lacked the ability to grasp obscure concepts swiftly, in real time, or find the holes in an entrepreneur's arguments. They would have to go back to the office and spin their wheels for countless hours researching various topics to see if the idea was a plausible one or not.

"How's it going, Charles?"

"I'm all right. A bit tired."

"Doing the conference tour?"

"Yes, it's rather exhausting. Other than that, it's fighting with entrepreneurs and beating them down to reasonable levels on value. Everybody thinks they are the next Google and they want us to pay fifty million dollars for a bunch of resumes and a half-baked idea in a PowerPoint presentation."

"Okay, breathe, Charles."

Ash enjoyed teasing Charles. He would always joke he was the fastest speaking man he knew. He once visited Charles at his office and saw him interact with a bunch of engineers immediately after a meeting. He was going back and forth at a frenetic pace. Ash had vertigo by the end of the conversation.

"You get used to it," Charles explained, "Engineers tend to throw ideas around and talk about concepts at a quick pace. I just need to hang on for the ride."

"Hey, by the way, I made Partner."

Sharing this news with Charles was innocuous to Ash. He was in a completely different tree branch of the finance and private equity labyrinth. There were so many nuances within venture itself to remember – seed, early stage, late stage, otherwise known as Series A, Series B or Series C – referring to what stage of the company's growth trajectory you are investing in – that it was hard to keep track of the sub-branches in other disciplines. Each segment within finance also tended to be insular, so you would only really see the other practitioners in your field. It was a lot like medicine or law in that regard.

"Congratulations," offered Charles, "that's really great news."

Charles seemed busy to Ash. Ash recalled the last time he spoke with Charles, securing a large favor from him for Project Emancipate.

"Charles, I'm looking at this deal in the medical instrumentation space. Can you take a look at the technology and give me a sense of whether it is good, falling out of favor or cutting-edge?"

"Yeah, no problem, send it over."

"You know, normally, I'd have to make you sign a confidentiality agreement," Ash advised him.

"Oh, don't even start with that."

"Okay. Just kidding."

Within an hour, Charles called Ash back. That's one of the things he loved about Charles. The guy was always so loyal, helpful and responsive.

"How does it look?"

"The technology is pretty robust. They've introduced some new products lately which will have a relatively long life cycle. You're good to go for a while."

"Great, thanks so much," said Ash.

"You know, from time to time I see some opportunities that might be good targets to add to this platform."

"That would be fantastic! I love buying and building," exclaimed Ash.

● ● ●

Ash also got in touch with another friend from college, Pedro Fritz. After spending a few years in investment banking, Pedro went to work at a hedge fund. At first he was doing merger arbitrage – analyzing trends in various industries to see who might be an acquisition target and subsequently buying a sizable stake in them. He then switched to long/short where he would buy positions in stocks and short them or buy derivative products around them, trying to maximize his gains.

"I could never do what you do," Ash had told Pedro.

"Sure you can, why not?" Pedro asked.

"I'd have a hard time sitting in front of a Bloomberg terminal all day long, staring at stock charts and reading press releases," he replied.

"Oh, but it's exciting," Pedro gushed.

"Of course it is, but I need to get out, see the action that is happening with a business. You know, be able to kick the tires," said Ash.

"That's because you lack imagination, my friend," Pedro teased.

They both laughed together.

"Okay, I'll give it to you. I lack imagination.....That's why I made Partner!" Ash boasted.

"Hey, congratulations!"

Telling Pedro had the same effect as telling Charles. The hedge fund universe had its own various tentacles, depending on what strategy you employed to achieve your returns and what type of security you invested in. There were event-driven funds focusing on distressed investing or arbitrage funds dealing with bonds, convertible bonds, perceived risk or historical statistical relationships. In all aspects though, everything was tied to a market.

● ● ●

In seeing the load that Ash was now putting on David, he decided to get Steven involved in some of the deals.

"Steve, I'd like you to join the Project Emancipate deal team," mentioned Ash.

"Oh great! That's a really neat deal," exclaimed Steven.

"Good. I'm glad you feel that way," responded Ash, encouraged by Steven's enthusiasm, "Let me bring you up to speed on what happened before the deal closed."

"Sure."

"It may take a while," admitted Ash, "but it's important you appreciate the flavor of what transpired so you can get to know Boas. It's critical in having the background when dealing with him. Let me start with the uphill battle I had in convincing him to join and the difficulties The Commies gave us prior to close."

Ash began.

"What are your other possibilities?" asked Ash of Boas, knowing he would never reveal this to him.

Ash and Boas decided to meet again. It was the same restaurant chain in another airport from their first meeting. Ash had spent some time studying the industry based on research that David had done. Ash had also investigated the competitors. He was becoming more and more interested in doing the transaction. His concern remained not having surety that Boas was going to manage it. Ash sensed that he was the key to the Company being successful.

Boas smiled.

"I think you could guess what would motivate me," said Boas.

There was a level of trust Boas was extending to Ash with that comment. There was an acknowledgment that Ash could appreciate and understand the way Boas would think and feel. It genuinely made Ash a bit nervous. He personally could shoulder the responsibility, but he didn't feel very confident about Popular Capital doing the same.

"You know," Ash felt compelled to reveal to Boas, "my Partners and I don't always think alike."

Ash worried whether he should have said that or not. It was troubling. He knew saying it may endanger his prospects of winning the deal, or of winning Boas over to run it, and he knew not saying it would be disingenuous.

"I would be really surprised if you all did," responded Boas.

He looked Ash in the eye.

"I'd really like to work with you," Ash stressed again.

"And I with you," Boas commented. After a few seconds passed he added, "Plus I have the whole karma thing going."

"What?" asked Ash, chuckling lightly.

"You believe in karma. *What goes around comes around.* You won't forsake our relationship senselessly."

"You see, Steven, at the time, I was sure I wouldn't. But I was actually pretty nervous about representing the same about Popular Capital."

Ash's phone rang. He saw who it was. "Steven, let's continue later."

CHAPTER 5

"You aren't going to get this deal approved," stated Martha as they stood outside the conference room prior to a meeting with The Commies.

"Do you know that for a fact? Did The Commies say something to you?" Ash implored her.

Ash had submitted the financial model detailing the transaction, with David's help, and a twenty-five page analysis of the transaction to the CCCP prior to the meeting.

"No, I just have more experience than you do, and I know what The Commies will like and what they won't. You are still naïve and haven't had a chance to develop your deal selection skills," she continued.

Thanks for the pep talk, thought Ash.

"You are going to fail, but it is a good experience for you to do so," she concluded.

When they walked into the room, Martha began the conference call, cutting Ash off as he attempted to speak.

"I'm sorry to waste your time, but Ash had this little deal he wanted to present, and well, he worked so hard on it. But, I just wanted to let you know that it wasn't my idea. I actually suggested we not waste your time," said Martha, feigning a laugh.

"Okay," said Henry with a chuckle.

A few seconds passed. Ash wore a frown on his face. Or maybe it was a scowl.

"Go ahead, Ash, don't waste any more time," Martha invited.

"Hold on a second," said Henry.

Ash thought his chance to make his pitch just got killed.

"I'm reading this thing now. Are you telling me this guy cornered the European market in a few years and has yet to enter the US market?"

"That's right," said Ash.

"And by your estimates, the US market is double the European market?" asked Henry.

"Triple if you include slot machines," said Ash.

"Yeah, I'm really sorry for wasting your time…. Why don't we just excuse ourselves from the call," said Martha, growing concerned.

Ash threw his hand in the air, indicating wait. There was a long tedious silence. Martha was getting increasingly more uncomfortable and more desperate to hang up. Ash was curious about what they were going to say next.

"This opportunity is huge," Henry exclaimed.

"Yeah, this could have enormous potential," agreed Lasi.

Ash began to smile. So did David.

"You know that's exactly how I felt when I saw this deal. This could be a huge hit for Popular Capital," said Martha.

Ash and David stared at her in disbelief. Ash turned his head so fast he strained the back, right hand side of his neck.

Martha looked up at Ash and David. Ash deliberately held his stare.

"What?" she asked, placing the conference call on mute.

How do I tell you exactly how I feel about you and do it concisely, pondered Ash. I'd barely get my diatribe started and the day would be over he thought.

"This is a full price you are suggesting we pay." Jake

commented.

The three in the room turned back to the call.

"Well, it is fairly valued if we look at similar companies in their and related industries," argued Ash.

"Now wait a minute," said Ted, "You overstated your projections."

"How so?" asked Ash.

"Well, you cite that industry growth has been 14.9 percent over the last five years," said Ted.

"Right," said Ash while looking at David.

"Yet, your model shows fifteen percent projected growth," Ted pointed out.

Ash closed his eyes and shook his head. He was becoming a frequent guest at the house of disbelief. Should he bother to explain to Ted that they had actually done a pretty sophisticated analysis to take out the conversion effect to the Euro in their industry numbers? Or that fifteen percent was conservative given other industry trends. Ash knew he should, but he just couldn't make himself do it. How could they appreciate how thorough Ash and David had been? I bet Rod Serling would love this story, he thought to himself.

"You should change it," Martha encouraged Ash.

"Okay," Ash acquiesced.

"Are you going to re-send the model?" asked Ted.

"Uh, no," said Ash tentatively, "The projected rate of return on this deal went from thirty-five percent to......."

Ash stalled deliberately for added effect, ".....thirty-five percent."

"Oh, so it didn't change anything," Ted declared.

"Shocking, isn't it?" Ash muttered under his breath.

"Okay, you don't have to re-send it then," said Martha to Ash and David.

I'm so glad you stopped me, thought Ash.

"Go after this deal," said Henry.

Ash laughed to himself as he reminisced about the time of the deal. The situation got worse when Lothar had to fly over from Munich to meet with The Commies. He made it to page three of his slide presentation.

"So remind me of what your company does," Ted had asked.

There was a downward spiral of questions from there.

"Don't you think not entering the US market thus far makes you a failure?" asked Lasi, "You have failed."

Ash hated when Lasi would take out on prospective management teams the haranguing that he received from the shareholders.

"Your profitability went up so much in your second year. What took you so long? Why couldn't you do that sooner?" asked Jake.

Luckily, Henry was buried in his laptop. He, like the others, kept their computers open the entire meeting. While the others would periodically type, Henry stared at his computer the entire time.

Ash could see Lothar's face turning red. Ash sympathized with him. He didn't need to be treated that way. Ash wanted nothing more than to end the torture for him, but he was powerless. Stopping it prematurely today just meant that it would happen on another day. The best option was to struggle through it. Ash sat through the meeting, stroking his neck.

When they had dinner together later that night, Lothar had a chance to vent.

"Ash, if not for you, no deal. I almost walk out and get on my flight during that meeting," Lothar said in an accelerated tone that belied his frustration.

Ash suddenly felt the weight of responsibility. He wasn't so sure he could control the CCCP. Actually, he was sure, he *knew* he couldn't control The Commies.

"I am many things, but not a failure," said Lothar,

getting more agitated.

Ash wanted to reassure him. Lothar cut him off before he had a chance.

"I did not fail. That is false! False! FALSE!" Lothar roared, the intensity increasing with each instance he said the word.

"Lothar, I know they were really derogatory and demeaning," said Ash, in an attempt to calm him.

"Ah, just so," said Lothar, the pace of his speech slowing slightly.

Ash had to take a deep breath.

"I can understand if you don't want to do a deal with us," said Ash.

Ash thought to say more, but he decided to leave it at that. A part of Ash felt he should try hard to encourage him. But what faith could Ash have in anything he would need to say in order to convince Lothar? Ash had no evidence or belief that it would get better, that his interaction with them would be minimal or that he could somehow make the CCCP "get it."

Ash was amazed when Lothar called a few days later.

"We move forward, yes?" he inquired.

Ash was elated with the response. He knew that was a large favor that Lothar was doing for him in agreeing to proceed. He also knew in that question of Lothar's that there was a tacit burden Ash had to assume to manage dealings with the CCCP as best as he could going forward.

Luckily, there wasn't that much interaction between GeldXpress and The Commies. When things went well, the CCCP never heard about a portfolio company. Lothar would always exceed budget and would sometimes leapfrog his numbers.

This prompted Ash at one point to question Lothar, "you are understating the performance you are capable of when you budget, aren't you? Just so that you can beat your budget each time."

Lothar smiled, "Ah, just so."

Ash smiled back, "There's no reason to make them so high - you can go even lower next time, if you'd like."

• • •

Another week, another dreaded Monday morning call.

"Looks like you have a few new deals this week, Eddie. Why don't you go through them," Lasi suggested.

There was silence. "Eddie, you there?" repeated Lasi.

"Is there anyone on the phone who can talk about Eddie's deals?"

Ash realized that if ever needed to be off the call, he'd better ask someone to talk about the various deals. Ash was about to say something to break the silence when he heard another voice.

"I'm here, Lasi."

It was Jason's voice. This was curious, thought Ash.

"Can you talk through these deals?" questioned Lasi.

"Sure I can. I've got a handle on this," he said.

"Walk us through these new deals then," encouraged Lasi.

Jason started.

"I got Project Sinister from an investment bank in Chicago. We're reviewing the book. Project Wallet was sent to me from someone I know in Minneapolis. We're also reviewing the information. And lastly, Project Distill is one I am probably going to kill."

"You sourced those first two deals, Jason?"

"Yeah. Sure I did," he insisted.

"It was you and not Eddie or Ash?"

"That's right. All me."

Very interesting, thought Ash. Ash knew those deals had gone directly to Eddie.

• • •

Ash recounted for Steven how David and he had gone to the CCCP to pitch Project Emancipate.

"I thought the meeting was going well. However, there was still plenty of time left for discussion and furthermore, Lasi hadn't joined us at that point yet," Ash indicated to Steven.

And then Ash continued to relay the meeting.

"You know, this deal is pretty rich for this President guy. He is getting a lot here," remarked Jake.

"This is the kind of deal that it's going to take to get him to stay," countered Ash, "Otherwise, he was not interested in coming with the Company."

"Well, this deal can't happen without him," said Ted.

"I know that. That's why we are offering him as many incentives as possible," said Ash.

Lasi had just joined.

"So we are going to give him five percent of the business and maintain his existing base salary," remarked Lasi, "Is that it?"

"No," said Ash, "There is also the ongoing capital commitment he wants from us."

"Yeah, I am trying to read through that part of your memo," said Henry.

"Are there any questions on it?"

"Let me get this straight. This guy wants to have a commitment from us that we will fund ten million dollars in acquisitions every year?" asked Henry.

"That's right," Ash confirmed.

"But we aren't going to give him a blank check," Jake added.

"That's not what he is asking for," explained Ash, "We have the right to review the deals he presents and either approve or reject them."

"So we really don't have to give him anything?" Henry clarified.

"Just the commitment," Ash assured.

"Yeah, we can commit to anything we want right now, we want to get this deal done, but later we can just reject each deal that he proposes," said Lasi.

"I'm not comfortable with doing that," said Ash.

There was a few seconds of silence. Ash strained to listen. Ash put it on mute.

"Are they talking amongst themselves?" Ash asked David.

David shrugged his shoulders.

"Okay, that's fine," came Lasi's voice.

"Fine as in what exactly?" asked Ash.

"We'll give him the commitment," said Lasi.

"Is that a real commitment or a fake one?" Ash posed. Ash was concerned now that they were going to be disingenuous.

There was silence. Ash worried that maybe they didn't like his comment.

"Look, what he is after is to be sure that when he goes and meets with these acquisition targets, that he can represent that he has access to capital. All he is basically asking for is a pre-approval on a mortgage! Nothing more!" pleaded Ash.

"Okay, we get it. He'll get a real commitment."

Somehow, Ash wasn't completely convinced.

"How much do one of their machines cost?" asked Lasi.

"As we indicate on page thirty-six of the report, they range from five hundred thousand to three million dollars," stated Ash.

"What?" demanded Lasi. "Henry, did you know about this?"

There was silence.

"Why didn't you tell us that earlier?" demanded Lasi.

"I did. It was in the initial meeting when we talked about this deal. It's been available for discussion all of these times we have spoken about it. We included it in the report at several points," contended Ash.

"If they lose one of their deals to sell a machine, it could kill their financials," declared Lasi. "A small hiccup and they perform miserably."

"We can't have any more companies performing miserably," Jake advised, "That headache with Project Elba is already too costly."

Ash put the phone on mute and turned to David, "Isn't that one of Eddie's deals?"

David nodded his head yes.

"What's wrong with it?" asked Ash.

"I don't know," said David.

"Yeah, well we aren't discussing that now," reproached Lasi, "anyway, the point is that we can't do a deal like this. It is too different than the others," said Lasi.

Ash thought about the comment for a moment. He didn't understand what Lasi was saying.

"How exactly are the others?" asked Ash.

"Low price point and big volume," Lasi retorted. "I don't know if you appreciate this business model or not," defended Ash, "Sure the machines are expensive, but that is a one-time expense. Once you buy the equipment, you have to buy all of the supplies from the company. Every time a test is done, a whole new set of supplies have to be purchased. These labs are running an average of one hundred tests a day per machine. Half of the Company's revenues come from the sale of these supplies. The average replacement supply is $1.72. Hence the company has elements of that business model."

There was silence from The Commies.

"Why don't you enlighten me, what kind of deals are you looking for?" Ash attempted.

Still silence. *Thanks for ignoring me you guys* thought Ash. He then remembered a shareholder call from many months ago.

"Aren't our shareholders asking for diversity in our portfolio?" asked Ash.

"Yes, we should try to be different...while sticking to the same thing," said Lasi finally. It was as if he was looking for something to latch onto. He desperately sought a concept he could leverage so that he could speak with the authority he preferred utilizing when speaking to the troops. It was clear he didn't have a way of defending his comment. It was hard to imagine Lasi not having a response. He generally always had something to say. That day he seemed like a drowning man in need of a life vest.

"Different while sticking to the same thing," mumbled Ash under his breath. *Sounds like a really confused request - do you guys want to think some more about what you are saying* thought Ash. Ash remembered where he had heard it. Eddie had used the phrase.

Several minutes had passed.

"Look, we'll approve this TENTATIVELY but you HAVE to come back to us before you fund the deal. We'll e-mail you a list of ADDITIONAL questions and FURTHER deal requirements," demanded Lasi.

Ash thought it would be fitting if Lasi were to laugh maniacally. He didn't however; he just hung up the phone.

Ash turned to David, "Looks like we're being punished."

"And we were being punished," Ash said to Steven, "some of their requests were really onerous, particularly the parts about cutting the pension and the healthcare benefits."

David stepped into Ash's office, "I need you to look at something."

"We'll continue later, Steven."

CHAPTER 6

David came into Ash's office and collapsed in a chair. It was late one night and they had both just come back to the office after having dinner together. "Are you all right?" asked Ash.

"I'm exhausted. Ted of The Commies is driving me nuts with all of his nitpicking of the model. He keeps asking me to run all of these scenarios. It's so meaningless, because it doesn't alter the results," complained David.

"Well, you know we've always had that problem with Ted," Ash pointed out.

"I know. I know. He's an INMATE. *I*nsists *N*umbers *M*ust *A*ffirm *T*he *E*vident," declared David.

"No matter how painfully obvious...," began Ash.

"Yes, yes, no matter how painfully obvious the answer, INMATEs insist they rely on their numbers."

David got up and dragged his feet out of the office. Ash recalled the number of conversations where he and David had discussed financial modeling.

David had asked Ash a while back, "Why do we spend so much time on these financial models?"

David had just completed a few nights of working until two in the morning.

"Well, look," started Ash, "to a large degree, people in our industry try too hard to make it an exact science. They live and die by the results of the numerical analyses that these models churn out. People forget that it is just meant to give a ballpark feel for a deal to test some assumptions. For example, if a company grows at ten percent a year, can it handle the amount of debt we want to put on it. If yes, then you can play around with scenarios – what happens if it is only two percent growth, do we run into trouble with the debt? Or, what happens if we have a ten percent increase in our costs because gas prices or interest rates go up? What happens in those situations?"

"Right, that makes a lot of sense," David concurred.

"Too many people get caught up in the specifics. The growth rate has to be precise; the cost structure has to be precise. They argue about what to predict with interest rates and exchange rates. They get caught up in whether a deal yields a 29.4 percent rate of return instead of a 31.2 percent rate of return. At the end of it, it's not going to matter. People forget that an argument is only as strong as its weakest link. If you put garbage assumptions into a model, you are going to get garbage results. In fact, I have never known a company to hit its budget. They are either woefully below or exceptionally above it. There are too many variables to predict. Nobody can be that precise," Ash assured him.

Ash looked at his watch. It was 10:30 pm. Time to stop reminiscing and make his way home.

"As much as I have enjoyed our evening together, I am afraid I must take my leave," said Ash using a haughty tone to be comical as he walked to David's cubicle.

They had been working late together to try to finalize their work for Project Emancipate so that they could get final approval from The Commies.

"Sounds good," said David, "Have a good one."

"Don't work too hard," Ash admonished. He couldn't help but sneer as he said it. Ash felt the guilt for making David work late, but he knew that The Commies were the ones responsible. Their bureaucratic forms, processes and requests were a tremendous burden on deal teams. Ash had tried many times to encourage the CCCP to curtail their operations. As he looked back at David while walking away, he knew why they never bothered. They didn't care enough for people at his level.

• • •

Ash recounted for Steven the time when he had to break the news to Boas regarding the meeting with the CCCP.

"I stressed a lot about how much to divulge to Boas. And ultimately, I didn't tell him about what the specific new demands from the CCCP were," Ash indicated to Steven.

Ash described from there.

Ash arrived late afternoon the day they scheduled to meet for dinner. He wanted to allow enough time for Boas and him to spend some time together prior to the meal.

"Boas, I have to tell you, I got the commitment for acquisitions, but I have a fear the CCCP may string you along on these," Ash lamented.

"Well, there's always that risk. I know nothing is set in stone. I know that each potential transaction has to stand on its own merit and survive the deal approval process."

"So you're okay with it?" asked Ash.

"Yeah, let's move forward," Boas instructed. There was a bit of resignation in Boas's voice that Ash detected.

There was a quiet lull in the conversation.

"I feel like I am entering this as if it were a lop-sided marriage," said Ash, "you're bringing so much and we…"

"Don't worry. If I was really having cold feet, I'd bolt," said Boas.

"And, mind you, I'm not afraid to leave you at the altar," Boas added.

Both laughed. It was strangely relieving for Ash to hear those words. It would be frustrating to disappoint him, thought Ash, particularly when his hands would become tied by The Commies so frequently on matters. Ash had control, but yet, he really didn't.

"By the way, I've got to go back for the final approval on this. There are a bunch of other requests The Commies made which we have to comply with."

"Time's up," said Ash to Steven, abruptly ending his recounting of the history, "I've got to respond to this e-mail."

● ● ●

Eddie received a new deal which he didn't have time to review. Indications of interest were due the next day. Eddie thumbed through it.

"This doesn't look all that intriguing," he said to one of his ELVES.

"What industry is it in?" asked one of the ELVES.

"Plumbing."

"I don't think that is all that interesting. Pass it to Ash," suggested one of the ELVES.

Ash reviewed the information. The transaction had a great deal of merit in his mind. The Company was called ProMax Plumbing Products. Ash called it Project Flow and presented it to the CCCP.

"These guys have had a high gross margin and profitability and have consistently grown their revenues each year," pitched Ash. "They have only twenty-five percent of the market, but they have a relationship with all of the customers," he continued.

"It would be easy, as they have done in the past, to keep adding products to their existing line and watch their revenues grow like clockwork, as it has done historically."

"Well, what if they don't grow revenues each year?" asked Henry.

"As I have indicated, I don't think that is a big concern. I thought you might be more concerned they have been operating in a favorable economy and housing market for the last several years and what could happen if there is a downturn in the housing market," replied Ash.

"Oh, well, yeah, why don't you answer that then," said Ted.

"I got an e-mail here from Eddie," interrupted Lasi.

Ash assumed it was on something else.

"He wants to know how the discussion on Project Flow is going."

Ash was taken aback. What the hell is Eddie up to? he wondered to himself. He *gave* me this deal to work on.

"I'm going to tell him that we will approve it," said Lasi.

Ash and his team were beyond excited. Ash proceeded to answer the question the CCCP had presented as well as a few others.

Lasi piped up when Ash was done, "Oh, Eddie says that he was supposed to be on Project Flow? I guess we'll just add him then."

How convenient, Ash seethed. He waits until the deal has been approved. After my team and I have done all the work.

They presented the deal to the Board of Directors. Because they were publicly traded, all of the transactions of Popular Capital had to be approved by the Board.

David turned to Ash.

"Are you worried?" he asked Ash.

"Not at all," said Ash.

Ash looked up from his computer and could see the anxiety on David's face.

"What are you so worried about?"

"We've put a lot of time into this," David explained, "I don't want it to not get approved."

Ash smiled broadly.

"Don't worry," said Ash, "The Board has never rejected a deal that the CCCP has approved."

"Oh really?" asked David, "So what's the whole point?"

"It's just so Lasi can cover himself and say the Board approved each transaction."

"Who is on the Board?" asked David, "A bunch of who's who from private equity?"

"No. It's a bunch of sycophants who are Lasi's friends. Not a single one of them is in private equity. The best way to get a Board to always approve the CCCP's transactions is to have one that is made up of all of your friends and has no deal experience whatsoever."

"So this Lasi guy is pretty clever?" asked David.

"No. He's wily," retorted Ash.

● ● ●

Ash sat on the plane heading to the East Coast. He looked down from the window. The weather had cleared quite a bit, and their altitude didn't seem that high. It was the middle of the country. Flat land was everywhere. Ash wondered to himself, if I could see my life from 30,000 feet – would it look just like this?

He had gotten the call from Lasi a week ago. As per custom, it had gone to Eddie first, then to Ash.

"I'd like you to come by in person."

"Sure," said Ash.

"You've just made Partner and there are things we should talk about," asserted Lasi.

Oh, thought Ash. A Partner's meeting. He liked the way that sounded.

"No problem, Lasi, I'll be there."

He arrived the night before and stayed at the hotel within walking distance to the office. In the morning, there was a long line to check out, so he decided he would do it at lunchtime.

The receptionist led him to Lasi's office.

Ash was shocked when he walked in the door. Seated there was Eddie. Lasi was on the phone.

"Oh, I didn't know you were going to be here," said

Ash.

Eddie stood up, arm in position with the imaginary sling, and responded with a dismissive tone.

"Yeah, I thought I would make my way out."

"We could've come on the same flight," said Ash.

"Yeah, er, well, it didn't work out that way," responded Eddie.

Lasi hung up the phone.

"Ash, welcome," Lasi beamed.

He stood up and shook Ash's hand.

"Congratulations," Lasi said.

"Why, thank you," said Ash.

Ash tried to be as gracious as possible. He kept his own indecisiveness hidden and acted out the part of an excited, eager employee who was thrilled at having just been hand-plucked for the firm's highest honor.

"Now that you are a Partner…" began Lasi.

Ah yes, thought Ash. Here come the list of revised expectations. He thought that this might be one of the possible topics of discussion. He wasn't all that keen on hearing about it. *Couldn't you have done this over the phone?* Ash wondered.

"It is important you take on some initiatives to help out the firm," said Lasi.

Ash pretended to listen intently. On the inside he was growing concerned with what he might be asked to do.

"We have a few investments we would like you to manage," continued Lasi.

Ash cringed.

"We need you to take over Triangle Cosmetics, VirtuTech and Diversified Metals."

Ash's eyes opened wide. These were some of the worst performing companies in the portfolio. He had to think quickly.

"Lasi, I feel like that is a lot. Look, I appreciate your trust in my capabilities," started Ash, "but I am already Chairman of three companies, on the Board of four others and I have Projects Flow and Triumph expected to close in the next three months or so."

Lasi was playing with his computer mouse and looking at his monitor while glancing occasionally back at Ash.

Ash turned to Eddie who was fiddling with his laptop.

Eddie looked at Lasi, "Two of Ash's companies are in a sales process and will likely be sold in the next three months."

Ash turned to Eddie. "And those are getting replaced by the new deals."

Eddie avoided eye contact with Ash.

"Yeah, but I am assisting on Project Flow."

If by assisting you mean adding needless time to the process because I have to explain everything I am doing to you, then yes, you are assisting.

Lasi sighed and turned his attention to Ash.

"Having the title comes with some responsibility," Lasi reminded him.

Damn you, Ash wanted to say to him. He had displayed enough responsibility flying 350,000 miles a year – a trip a week – and by working eighty hours a week. He knew no other Partner who pulled all-nighters. Except for maybe Benson. But Ash didn't have the cash to look to as a motivator. He tightly pursed his lips and listened.

"I worry I won't be able to do a good job for you, Lasi," Ash confessed convincingly.

Ash was pleased with the comment. It had just the right touch of corporate servitude and obsequiousness to it without seeming like he had shoved his nose up Lasi's ass.

"You'll find a way to make it happen," said Lasi.

Oh sure, thought Ash, *I'll just increase the number of hours in the day, or clone myself, or hire more people* – wait a minute, that last thought actually had some legitimacy.

"Lasi, I may be able to manage better if I could hire some additional people," Ash proposed.

Lasi turned to Eddie. Eddie shook his head emphatically and then looked down.

Lasi turned back to Ash, "You'll have to manage with the resources you have."

Ash felt like a bee had just stung him. Multiple times. Perhaps there were a hundred bees stinging him. He felt like his head was swelling up. He continued to sit in the office. Lasi continued to say a few more things, likely what the companies he would have to assume responsibility for were about, and perhaps what Lasi would like to have done with them, but Ash couldn't hear it. He started rubbing his chin.

"Lasi, I wanted to ask you about compensation," Ash raised.

Eddie looked up from his laptop and then proceeded to close it.

Lasi stared straight at Ash. Ash was beginning to feel laser beams.

"What's your problem?"

"I don't have a problem," said Ash, "Just a question."

Lasi continued to look at him. The stare felt like it was boring a hole in Ash's head.

"I feel like my compensation is below what my peers with similar positions in other firms make," Ash opined.

Lasi kept looking. I think the laser is through all of the bone now and is heading for the brain.

"What is the firm's policy with respect to market-based compensation?" Ash asked.

That's good, he thought to himself. They always teach you that when interviewing or asking tough questions – ask the question *without really asking it*.

"We don't have a policy."

And sometimes it backfires.

"Is there any desire on the firm's part to make compensation on par with the market?"

"No."

Ash's head was beginning to hurt. Lasi must have cut through too many layers of brain.

Ash looked back at Lasi and remained silent. Eddie had his head down.

"Is there anything else?"

Yes, thought Ash, *I'd like to get up, seize my chair and throw it at your head. I'd then like to grab you by the hair and repeatedly slam your head against that damn keyboard you keep typing on when you are supposed to be looking at me as I talk. And then I'd like to take that stupid mouse and...*

"Is there anything else?"

"No," said Ash resolutely.

While his thoughts had been comical, they were disturbing at the same time. What a great meeting, thought Ash.

"I'm so happy I flew out here," he said under his breath.

"Hang on," said Lasi, suddenly, "We're not done yet."

Oh no, thought Ash. Did I just, in my inability to control my silly sentiments, destroy my career? Ash stood still for a few seconds. He closed his eyes tightly and clenched his jaw. Time to face the music, he thought to himself. He slowly turned around.

"I don't want to hear any more complaining..."

Oh god, that was so stupid. Stupid. Stupid. Stupid.

"...about compensation for your junior people."

Ash was stunned with what he just heard. He had a partial sigh of relief. But then he had to begin another battle.

"Lasi, I have made comments about their compensation because I am worried they are going to leave. They have a lot of expertise and familiarity with our portfolio company investments. If David and Steven go, it would be a huge strain to get someone else familiarized. Furthermore, they work incredibly hard and should be rewarded."

Lasi held an intent interest with his computer again.

"Eddie, don't you agree?"

"No, Eddie doesn't agree," Lasi denied for him.

Ash noticed Eddie was going to move his arm down, but then brought it back up.

"You are one of us, now," proclaimed Lasi, "We can't have you speaking out against what the firm's decision is."

"Was there anything else?" asked Ash, too irritable to continue debating with Lasi. Beyond that he felt dejected and demoralized.

"No," said Lasi.

Ash walked out of Lasi's office. He went to his hotel room. He felt a sudden urge to take a shower. He felt dirty, unctuous, like he couldn't be in his own skin. As he stood there in his towel looking at the mirror, water running in the background, the words resonated in his mind.

"You are one of us, now."

The steam from the shower filled the bathroom. Like the smog in Los Angeles, it crept up on him from all sides. It covered the mirrors and blighted out the image of himself that Ash had been seeing.

CHAPTER 7

Ash continued to describe for Steven the saga with Project Emancipate.

"So we went another five rounds with the CCCP before getting a final approval," recalled Ash, "and even then, they established conditions. Relaying those conditions to Boas was another ordeal. I preferred to do it in person."

Ash narrated his call to Boas.

"Boas, it's Ash."

"How are things? I was just thinking about our last meeting."

"Are you having a negative knee-jerk reaction?"

"No, not at all. I actually really enjoyed spending time with you."

"Well that's great to hear. Perhaps you can prepare to spend a significantly more amount of time with me."

"Oh, really?" asked Boas.

"Yes, the deal got approved."

"Hey, that's great news. I am really excited! I was a bit worried with the series of questions you had kept asking me regarding my situation and our deal, so I am really relieved that it worked out."

"Well, I'll be honest, there was a fair amount of back and forth that went on," admitted Ash.

"I know," said Boas, "You told me you would call me six hours ago. And now your voice sounds so hoarse you seem like you were at a rock concert or something."

"Sometimes it's annoying how perceptive you are," Ash chided.

"You can hide *some* stuff from me," he responded, "But not everything."

Boas's practicality was awe-inspiring. He called it like he saw it, even if that meant being self-deprecating.

"Tell me Ash, how did you end up at Popular Capital? I hope you don't mind my saying it, but you don't seem to fit in," commented Boas.

Ash divulged the story.

"This would have been easier to relay to you over a bottle of wine," indicated Ash.

"That's true. Next time we will do that," suggested Boas.

Ash smiled to himself. He was testing Samuel's advice. It looked like Boas passed.

"And then," said Ash to Steven, "I remembered the conditions from The Commies."

Ash continued.

"Actually, Boas, we have a few items to clarify. I thought maybe we could do it in person. How is next Tuesday for you?" asked Ash.

"I was going to have a supplier come in, but I'll change that," said Boas.

"That'd be great. I have to be in Europe at the end of the week, so I wouldn't have much time."

"No problem," said Boas, "We'll make it happen. Oh, and while you are out here, I'd like you to have dinner with me and my wife," added Boas.

"That would be great," said Ash, "I'd love to meet your wife."

Ash's office phone rang. "Steven…," Ash started.

"I know. We'll continue later."

• • •

Ash was a bit sad as he took his very next trip to Munich. It would be one of the last times he would be going because GeldXpress was about to be sold. A buyer had the company under a letter of intent. Ash was negotiating with them to finalize the deal. This was an exciting milestone for Ash. He knew eventually that the company would have to be sold. The only reason companies were bought in private equity was to sell them for a gain at some future point. He had to admit he was feeling exhilaration for that.

It was also a vindication. His vision for the transaction had been proven true. The company had been purchased for two hundred fifty million, and it was being sold for four hundred million. During the time of Popular Capital's ownership, the company had paid down a significant amount of debt. Ash was looking forward to bringing a gain of two hundred million to the firm.

"Just like when you buy a house," he had to explain to David, "When you sell it, you get the increase in the market value and also whatever you have paid down of the mortgage."

He wondered if he might be able to expect a great payday. Perhaps receive some of this gain as compensation for himself. That is how it was supposed to work in other private equity funds. He then thought back to the conversation in Lasi's office.

Ash shook his head contemptuously. Perhaps seeing Lothar's company succeed, which he now, strangely, felt a part of, would have to be compensation enough.

When Ash arrived at GeldExpress's headquarters, he went into Lothar's office.

"Guten morgen, Herr Gyan," the receptionist and Lothar's assistant would both say to him as he entered.

Ash and Lothar chatted briefly for a few moments. The potential buyer arrived, and the men went into the conference room. Ash sat next to Lothar at the table, across from the potential buyer. The potential buyer was another private equity group. Popular Capital knew the buyer would have to borrow money to do the deal, and Lasi had insisted that Popular Capital by allowed to provide the funding. It was a key part of the deal from his perspective.

"Your interest rate is too expensive. We can get cheaper debt here," said one of the members of the deal team from the buyer.

"Well, that was a key part of our deal, that you work with us to provide you the loans," Ash commented.

There was discussion on their side. The buyer was from Sweden and neither Lothar nor Ash could follow what they were saying.

"No, it is not possible," said the buyer.

"Well, I'll have to go back to my people about that," said Ash.

"Maybe they should come to the meeting next time," the buyer suggested.

Ouch. That hurt, thought Ash. Unfortunately, Ash couldn't really argue with what the buyer was hinting at. On a key decision making matter, Popular Capital had incapacitated Ash.

"Why don't we proceed on other matters?" Ash urged.

They started going through a few other issues.

"You know," said Ash interrupted the buyer, "this would not be a problem if you had disagreed to it in the first place. I am fully capable of negotiating this deal. It's just that when I have communicated with my Partners to expect a certain transaction to transpire, then out of respect, I have to go back and inform them and make sure they are comfortable if and when that deal changes."

"That's fine," said the buyer.

"It's not like you are wasting your time here. I am

able to make big decisions," insisted Ash.

Lothar turned to look at Ash. He had a partial frown on his face. It exhibited part concern and part desire for Ash to stop talking. Ash stood up.

"Excuse me, I think I'll step out for some water," Ash explained.

He walked outside. What he couldn't stand was how true what they were saying was. He hated how decisions had to be handed down to him; it completely undermined his authority and his role as a Partner. It made him look weak and incapable of leading the charge. Ash hated this. His vision of private equity had been different. He had always dreamed that a Private Equity Partner was where you were an equal with your peers and a collective decision is reached and executed upon. If changes need to be made, they could be done on the fly. He knew Benson didn't enjoy that type of a set-up, but Max certainly did.

● ● ●

Ash needed to meet with the sellers of Project Flow in Tennessee to finalize some key terms in the purchase agreement they would be executing. When things reached this stage of the negotiation, and the sellers were going to continue running the company and be minority shareholders in the business, Ash liked to spend some time with them getting to know them.

"Who is traveling this week?" asked Eddie in the Monday gathering for that week.

"I'm heading to Tennessee on Wednesday," Ash proffered.

"What are you doing there?" asked Eddie.

"I'm going to be having dinner with the sellers on Project Flow. We'll also negotiate some of the final terms in the transaction," replied Ash.

"Do you really need to go out there to do that?" asked Eddie.

Sometimes, Eddie, you are as useless as the three clocks in this conference room.

"I have decided that I am going out there to do that," maintained Ash.

"Well then, I'll go with you."

"You really don't have to," said Ash.

Ash thought maybe he should begin pleading at this point. The last thing he wanted was for Eddie to go. Ash liked to build a rapport with people and Eddie was, quite frankly, a real drag.

"Oh, I'm coming," said Eddie.

Ash had arranged to have dinner with the two sellers, Ricky Bennett and Johnny Harris, at a restaurant where they had all been together when the transaction was first announced. Ricky and Johnny were honorable, Southern gentlemen. Ash felt a close affinity towards them. He was impressed with how they had built their business from scratch into a global player in their industry. The hard work and initiative they put into starting their business and the recognition in the industry they received today was awe-inspiring for Ash. They were good to their people; those people in turn had been loyal and worked diligently for them. These were real men in his opinion and they had every right to be proud of their accomplishments. Ash felt that they were entitled to the nearly one hundred million dollars each they would be earning as a result of their selling their company to Popular Capital. That net worth would make them as wealthy as Lasi. In Ash's assessment, Ricky and Johnny deserved it.

They started the evening with a few martinis each. At least, Ricky, Johnny and Ash did. Whenever Ricky and Johnny drank, they reminisced about their childhoods.

"My ol' man was a real son o' a bitch," Ricky announced.

You could see his eyes swell with emotion. They turned pink then red. Ricky was a tall, thin man. While his body frame was slight, his presence carried the weight of a man three times his size. He walked through that town in Tennessee with the earned pride of accomplishment. Some people who met him for the first time in recent years accused him of having a big ego. Those who had known him for many years, or long enough to know the man, knew he had earned it. People recognized that and acknowledged him. Walking down the street or entering a restaurant, they would greet him with enthusiasm. "Hello, Mr. Bennett, how are you today?" He enjoyed that. He would even randomly remember some of their names.

"He made me work fo' him fo' a whole year. He ne'er paid me a dime."

Ricky downed his drink.

"Told me he'd give me some o' dat comp'ny stock. Dat I'd 'come 'is pahdner," moaned Ricky.

It was a wonder, thought Ash. Alcohol, while diluting enunciation, makes accents more pronounced. Ash was having an increasingly more difficult time following what Ricky was saying. This was the fourth time he heard the story.

"Ricky, tell us about the time he abandoned you in Taiwan," prodded Ash.

Ash thought that at least he'd have a better time hanging on with a story he had some familiarity with.

Ricky put his hand on Ash's shoulder.

"You's a good man," Ricky gushed.

"We's both wen' o'er there in Taiwan. Back dhen it was run down, muhd everywhere. It weren't dhem tahl buildins' they got dhere today."

Ricky took another sip from his drink.

"I's dhere wid dat son o' a bitch and dhen dat monsoon arrived."

Ricky took another swill from his drink.

"Dat son o' a bitch hurd dat weatha 'port and he flew right outta dhere."

Ricky took another guzzle.

"Ne'er e'en tell me he's leavin'."

Ricky sipped again.

"I so stooopid, I went 'n' stayed. Couldn't find no food fo' two days in dhat mess. Everythin' all closed up."

Ricky gulped again.

"Dat son o' a bitch."

"The important thing is, you got even," Ash reminded him.

Ash toasted Ricky.

"I sure did."

"Boy, when I bankrupted 'is comp'ny by competin' wid him. Dhat wuz the proudest day in my life."

Johnny, who'd been quiet this whole time, seemed to be brimming over with experiences he was eager to relate as well. Alcohol was so good at fostering community.

These are the parts of the dinners I look forward to the most, thought Ash. This is where he got to know, really know, the people with whom he was working. There wasn't any buttoned-up propriety enforced by the confines of an office. People were real in this setting. Ash knew, once you get over this hump with people, the relationship assumed a new meaning. People graduated from business associate to friend. It was interesting to Ash how knowing someone's pains and struggles was the key to getting over that divide.

"I 'ad a stepfadher who wuz real mean to me," Johnny interjected.

Ricky turned to his partner and placed an arm over his shoulder to comfort him.

"Well, he'd beat on me," Johnny added.

He took another sip of his drink.

"I'm ahright. It'd be stupid stuff, ya' know. I'd fall 'sleep on da couch and he'd kick me. Tell me ta get my ass inta bed."

He drank again.

"I still can't geht ta sleep at night widhout my sleepin' pill," Johnny lamented.

Eddie remained quiet most of the evening.

"C'mon, Eddie, 'ave yourself a martini," encouraged Ricky.

"No, no, I'm okay," protested Eddie.

"Ash, you ain't gonna say no, are ya?" enquired Ricky.

"You can count on me," said Ash.

He and Ricky high-fived.

Johnny piped up, "'member the time we took dhat trip to China?"

He was facing Ash although he seemed to be looking towards Ricky. Ash thought he'd go ahead and answer.

"Yes, Johnny," said Ash, "That was only six weeks ago."

"Well, ya know, we fohrgot to visit one of dhem factories. Dhat dhere hose clamp manufactu'er. We ne'er went to see 'em," said Johnny.

He began to sway back and forth. Johnny was a large man. He was over three hundred pounds, and he was only five-feet-eight inches tall. When Ash had the application for his health insurance submitted, the carrier had raised the premium, citing an "unfavorable height-weight ratio." Johnny was a good foil to Ricky. He gave Ricky his space and let him enjoy his achievements. Johnny was a man Ricky knew he could trust.

They had a bit of the superhero – sidekick dynamic, Ash realized in his second trip to visit with them. Johnny deferred every time to Ricky. Given their physical characteristics, Ash would always conjure the image of Don

Quixote and Sancho Panza. But there were no delusional ambitions here. These were real men, of this time, who had accomplishments to their credit and had the right to be proud of them.

Currently, however, Ash was afraid Johnny was going to fall over.

"Yes, we did, Johnny," informed Ash.

"Nah, I dun dhink we did," Johnny refuted.

"We did, Johnny. His wife was the one who served us the fruit, remember?" asked Ash.

Johnny's face turned red.

"I...I...I dun 'member too much o' dat day," Johnny confessed, beginning to chuckle. His laugh was infectious. Or perhaps it was the sight of his whole body convulsing in perfect synchronization with his laugh that made Ash join him in the mirth.

Ash remembered back to that trip in China. At lunch that particular day, Johnny, Ricky, Eddie and Ash had all been ganged up against by the heads of five different factories with whom they had been meeting on their trip. The factory owners were trying to out-drink them. The group went through forty forty-ounce bottles of beer at lunch.

"All's I 'member is dat you hung in dhere like a champ, Ash," praised Johnny.

Johnny poked a finger in Ash's shoulder. Ash felt like he was being tipped over. It's a good thing I have this bar buttressing me, thought Ash.

"Ya even challenged Eddie ta drink when he wasn't drinkin' 'nuff," Johnny recalled.

Ash suddenly felt embarrassed Johnny had remembered that episode. Ash remembered thinking Eddie kept demurring having a drink with all of the other guys. He sipped his tea like the two ladies who were with them did.

Ash remembered slipping and announcing to the waitress that they wanted more tea "for the three ladies."

Ash had attempted to use what little he knew of Chinese with the waitress in an attempt to impress her. He thought he was saying two when he requested the tea for the ladies, but it turned out he was saying three. At the time he said it, the waitress giggled. Ash thought it was simply because she found it fascinating that this Hispanic / North African / Arab man was speaking Chinese. Ash had gotten distracted by Johnny cheering him again, so he didn't notice when the waitress held up three fingers. Unfortunately, Eddie did. The two ladies seemed to think it was a brave indictment of Eddie and they shared it with their boss, who shared it with Ricky and Johnny. The howling and raucous laughter spewing from Ricky and Johnny was embarrassing. It was only then that Ash realized his mistake. It was hard to get them to let it go at the time. His apologies and explanations to Eddie were met with a scowl.

And now, unfortunately, they reminded Eddie about it. Back when it transpired, Eddie had remained on edge for the remainder of that trip, after they got back and until today. Ash attempted to apologize for it constantly. Eddie seemed to forget. But Ash had also come to learn that Eddie was a man who kept his grudges, albeit in a closet most of the time, only allowing them to see the light of day when it was time for retribution.

All Ash could do was lean against the bar and brace himself. He began stroking his neck.

"Oh yeah," said Ash.

"Eddie, how come, ya never drank dhat day?" asked Ricky.

"I did drink," insisted Eddie.

"Eddie, ya know what I want ya t'get outta dhis here deal?" asked Ricky, ignoring Eddie's self-defense.

Eddie laughed, "No, what?"

Ash knew Eddie was thinking about the amount of money that could potentially be made for Popular Capital in this deal.

"I want ya to learn to lighten up," Ricky encouraged. "Ya just way too damn serious all da time," he added.

Ash looked at Eddie. Ash thought they would all laugh together. Ricky and Johnny were already howling.

Eddie had a serious expression, almost grave, on his face.

"Well what about Ash, what does he have to learn?" asked Eddie.

Ash almost spit out his drink. Oh my, he thought. Have we reverted back to kindergarten? *Did the teacher just scold you, Eddie? Are you being pushed around by the school bully and it's "just not fair"? Are you going to run and tell Mommy?* Ash conjured a mental image of Eddie as a kid, stomping his feet in the dirt in protest.

"Ah, ain't nuthin' wrong with Ash. He knows when ta be serious and when ta have fun," Ricky noted.

"Ain't dhat da truth!" Johnny seconded as he cheered Ash with his glass and winked at him.

Ash was gracious with Ricky and Johnny, but on the inside he was cringing. I'm going to have to pay for this, he thought to himself.

On the way back to the hotel, Eddie accosted Ash, "Why'd you pay for dinner?"

Ash was surprised. Oh, so this is how he's going to do it, thought Ash.

"Well, we usually pay for dinner when we take a management team out," explained Ash.

"Yeah, but they are getting so much money, they could afford to pay," said Eddie in a tone revealing his anger.

"I invited them to dinner," said Ash, "For me, if I do the inviting, that means I pay; if they extend the invite, they should pay."

"Well, that's not how we should do it," Eddie countered.

"I don't agree with you," said Ash.

"Well, you ought to pay for this one out of your own pocket, since you practically leapt at the chance to spend the firm's money. You really need to be more careful with Popular's money," proclaimed Eddie.

"Right, like going three years without a functioning clock," mumbled Ash.

"What are you saying?"

"That's fine, Eddie," Ash conceded, "I'll pay for it."

The following morning, Ricky and Johnny were joking with Ash in their office. Eddie was outside making some phone calls.

"Well, I had a wonderful time last night," said Ash.

"Yeah, we did too," said Ricky and Johnny, almost in unison.

Ricky looked at Ash. Ricky seemed more pensive this morning compared to Johnny.

"When ya gonna go do somethin' else?" asked Ricky.

Ash was taken aback by the query.

"Ya can't be enjoyin' workin' widh 'im," said Johnny, jerking his thumb towards Eddie's bag.

Ash blushed.

"We wuz talkin' 'bout you da odher day. You's a good man. Man can tell, you like people. You knows how to get along widh people. How ta understand 'em," Johnny added.

"Dhat guy dhere, he's a piece o' work," said Ricky.

Ash began stroking his neck. He managed to smile a little bit and even chuckle.

"Why dun't ya start your own pri'ate equity fund?" Ricky asked.

He said the last three words slowly and purposefully, punctuating them with emphasis. It was as if he was attempting to unleash the words with maximum impact. Ash could envision him saying immediately before making the comment – "stand back fellas, I'm lettin' her loose."

Ash was convinced it was their overt friendliness and liking of him that prompted them to make the comment. It was nice banter to share in a comfortable setting. An endorsement of the "we think you are swell" motif that colored their interactions lately.

"We'll back ya," he offered.

Now it felt like a different beast. Money where the mouth was? They would *show me the money*"? Ash suddenly felt like the sports agent from *Jerry Maguire* where he left a big agency with a single client. It was the only client he needed to get started. Ash couldn't shake the fact that he suddenly felt very comfortable. It was exciting to be sought after that way. He played the words in his mind again.

"We'll back ya."

Ash's mind began to race. He wondered about that possibility. Ash thought about it for a few minutes. And then several minutes. He had essentially checked out of the rest of the conversation. This had always been a dream of his, but he never thought that it could be now. Could it be now? If he had these guys' support, it could go a long way.

Ash mused about what it would take for him to launch his own private equity fund.

● ● ●

On the flight back from Nashville, Ash gazed out the window. He felt fortunate to have a clear view. He was impressed with the majesty of the Rocky Mountains. The view gave him a respite from the onslaught of thoughts flooding his mind. He had to admit, he had a bit of a headache, but there was such an excitement electrifying him at this moment. His thoughts were uncontrollable. At times they would occur to him with the grace of a ballroom dance. At other times it was like the sound at a Metallica or other heavy metal band concert. And then it was that same concert with all of the bands playing at the same time. Ash thought back to his recent meetings with Samuel and Boas. And then he replayed the words from Ricky and Johnny.

"We'll back ya."

And then it occurred to Ash. It must have been over Colorado. He knew what his first step in forming his own private equity group had to be.

CHAPTER 8

Ash drove up the hillside to the small cluster of buildings by the water's edge. When he reached the top, he had a wonderful view of the ocean. It was an idyllic setting. Two dominant colors – dark blue and light blue battling for real estate in that view, their struggle taking them to the outermost limits of human vision, ending at the line of infinity, the ultimate victor unknown – does the sea swallow the sky or does the sky evaporate the sea? He could only imagine what evening would be like, with the skies changing their moods. Wow, thought Ash, he wondered how any work could get done with magnificent scenery like that. Or perhaps it was an opportunity to be inspired to do one's best work.

Ash waltzed into Max's office. He had coordinated with Max's assistant earlier to be sure he was there and his schedule was free. It was during that plane ride Ash decided such matters were not handled over the phone. You had to go see the person directly. There was no other way to witness that initial reaction. Ash knew more would be revealed in the immediate aftermath of Ash presenting the idea through Max's body language and physical response than simply relying on his voice over the phone. Plus, if Ash could make Max feel more obligated because he was there facing him, well, then, that was just a ploy that Ash would have to get comfortable with using.

"Let's go to lunch. I'm buying," Ash declared.

They sat in the restaurant. It was full of beautiful people. People who were carefree and eye-pleasing to watch.

"It really is good to see you," said Ash.

Ash knew what he was doing - he was stalling. He was suddenly nervous. Ash became conscious of every sound from other tables, passers-by, the waitstaff. He looked around at the other people seated. Would they witness a victory today or would they all be laughing at him for his defeat? Ash wondered how many of them were there to discuss something monumental – a proposition, a separation, a confession. He envied those that were there casually. What if Max hated the idea? Or worse – what if Max really liked the idea but hated the idea of doing it with him?

"And it's really good to see you," responded Max, "Oh, where are my manners? Congrats on the promotion."

"Oh, thanks," Ash murmured, a bit sheepishly. Even though it had been over a month, he was still *under*whelmed by the event.

"Well," Ash averred, "I am ready to leave."

"Hey, that's great. Which firm is it?"

"Well, it's something I would like to start new."

Max's eyes widened. He leaned his head down and forward.

"Really?"

There was a dash of excitement in what was otherwise disbelief in his reaction.

"Yeah. And I need your help with it."

"Sure, anything, Ash. What do you need?"

"Why don't you, me and Benson start something together?"

And there it was. It was out there. Ash felt a sense of relief sharing it. There was no turning back now. It was out in the open. He couldn't un-pop the balloon, unsmoke the cigar or make her a virgin once again. It was done.

Ash watched with earnest Max's reaction. At first Ash sensed Max was surprised. That made sense. Max was silent for a few seconds. His eyes were darting across the room.

"Whoa, really?"

Ash could see some excitement blooming in Max's face.

"Wow, I just never thought of that as a possibility. I mean, I guess I did someday. I just didn't think about it being so soon," said Max.

"I know how you feel," Ash confessed, "I had the same reaction."

Max's response was a pensive excitement. That was exactly what Ash wanted. Ash knew if he had been over the top excited from the get-go, he would have been putting on a show and in his heart he would have already discredited the idea. This reaction was perfect – it meant Max was envisioning himself doing it.

"Ash, I think this is a great idea. I love it. I need time to let it sink in, but I love it!"

"It's great to hear you say that. I was so worried that you wouldn't find it interesting."

"No, it is *very* interesting."

"Now we just need to get a hold of Benson," said Ash.

Both laughed.

"That might be as challenging as launching the fund," Max surmised.

● ● ●

After Ash left him that day, Max called his father. Ash had predicted he might. Max was fortunate to have had mentors at his work guiding him professionally and a mentor to guide him through his life.

"So what do you hate about the idea, Dad?"

"I am most proud of you son! You finally going to work for youself!" exclaimed Mr. Chu. His voice still carried an accent.

"Well, I am in a way, working for myself now, Dad. I am a Partner."

"No, no, this is better! Now you don't own youself. Soon you will be 'big boss.' This very good. Very good! I 'big boss' for many year. Is better."

Max started, "Dad, I am a partial...." And then he stopped.

"You are right, Dad, I think this is something I need to do."

"You *must* do, son, you *must* do. I give you blessing. You *must* do."

● ● ●

Ash knew he needed to speak with Samuel. He had mixed emotions about talking to him. He had been hopeful he could have more pieces of the puzzle solved before he approached Samuel, perhaps even more concrete answers. He knew Samuel was a master at focusing in on the inconsistencies or the problems of an approach, an argument or a solution. It gave Ash a sense of joy when he could respond well to those queries of his. And at times when he couldn't, Ash knew the question Samuel had raised bothered him a great deal and that it was precisely his inability to surmount that issue that brought him to Samuel in the first place.

"I'm going to launch my own fund," beamed Ash after sitting down in Samuel's garden with him again.

"Bravo," Samuel praised. "This is an important step."

"Yes. I feel like the time is right."

"But you've only just made Partner."

"I know."

"Are you applying the golden handcuffs rule?"

"The one where you try to get out and try something entrepreneurial before you are making so much money that you no longer have the desire – or the will – to leave?"

"That's the one."

"I'm not sure Popular Capital is capable of golden handcuffs. You know what they pay."

They both laughed.

"I always worried about you since the time you told me you were going there," Samuel admitted.

"Well…"

Ash could sense the gush of disappointment swelling inside of him again. Some days he wished he could start all over and never make that decision. That was useless, he thought. This is where I am now, and I have to move forward from this point.

"…thank you, Samuel. I know you have been concerned for me."

"Now," said Samuel, "a traditional private equity fund is a much better place for you to be."

"I'm glad to hear you say that."

"It won't be easy to get there."

"So I hear."

"But you've never been one to back away from a challenge."

I suppose it is true, thought Ash.

"Do you think I am being sensible?" asked Ash.

"Rationally speaking, what you are saying makes perfect logical sense. Three people, Partners in their respective firms, indicating that you have achieved the highest level of your profession, coming together to start a new fund doing the same thing, makes a lot of sense. It happens in law and medicine all the time.

"However," Samuel continued, "the path is not smooth."

"The people making a decision to provide you with

money are not, strictly speaking, rational."

Ash thought there was irony in that. Finance had so many people who were not, as Samuel said, rational.

• • •

Despite Eddie's protests, Ash knew he needed additional manpower. Since Eddie was the head of the office, he was supposed to have ultimate say in terms of the number of people they had. Ash devised a clever way to get around him, the only way it could possibly work – go straight to Lasi. Lasi loved having people working for him whom he perceived were capable of expanding his vision. If Ash could get Lasi interested in a potential candidate, Eddie would be powerless to put an end to it.

Ash found that candidate in Patricia Kim. Patricia was Asian-American. She was bright, experienced and had a great rapport with people. It helped that she was young and attractive. Nobody complained about having to spend time with Patricia. Unfortunately, that also made her the target of lascivious banter from her male colleagues when she wasn't around, which basically stemmed from everyone else in the office, as she was typically the only female. Ash wanted to hire her as a Vice President.

Ash felt relieved he was able to convince Patricia to join. It was hard to entice any candidates of any caliber join them. Each time they attempted to hire, they would extend offers to a range of five to eight people before one agreed to accept. When asked candidly why they declined employment, they would most often cite the abysmal compensation as their chief reason for looking elsewhere. After that were issues such as reputation, type of deals they would be working on and rumors they had heard from their friends and colleagues at other firms about how difficult and unwieldy The Commies could be to deal with. Enough people had done transactions with Popular Capital at that point that the company garnered a lackluster reputation in the market.

Ash felt slightly conflicted in hiring Patricia. It was a conundrum – should he be honest about what transpires there or should he cover up to paint the best picture. The question was moot in many ways; there had already developed a significant reputation in the marketplace for Popular Capital, so there was no reason to lie. He also worried about potentially leaving and whether that was deceitful. He convinced himself that it was okay because she had been interested in the position before she had interviewed with him and she would meet everyone and have to be comfortable with the whole group.

Ash recalled prior discussions to hire people. After hiring Jason, they had considered a few other possible additions before Eddie decided to not spend any more money. At the time Eddie had instituted a practice of openly discussing each potential candidate. While Ash was not averse to soliciting opinions from the group – who knew what someone else could pick up on - he didn't feel like a democratic process was the best way to make ultimate hiring decisions. Ash knew that the likes of the ELVES would not be likely to hire someone who would threaten their positions. But Ash knew why Eddie did this. His allies outnumbered Ash. He had the opportunity to have Ash's views outvoted. Except for this time.

They all entered the conference room for their meeting. Ash was met with that horrible musty smell as he walked in. He looked up at the wall. Yes. It was still seven thirty-three pm.

"I found someone I'd like to hire as Vice President. I think she is smart and capable, and I'd like to have her on the team," Ash pronounced.

There were a few seconds of silence. Bob was muttering something under his breath that was producing laughs from others sitting next to him.

"Anyone else have comments?" asked Ash, upset.

Ash knew not to direct it at Eddie. Eddie was always the last to offer his opinion. "I don't know" was always his favorite expression during conversations like this.

David spoke up, "I think she'd be a good addition to the team. We certainly could use the help."

"Thank you, David," said Ash.

"Anyone else?" asked Ash, "good. She is here now and I want everyone who hasn't met her to spend time with her. Oh and by the way, Lasi wants us to hire her."

Eddie looked up.

"Lasi has met Patricia," declared Ash looking straight at Eddie.

Eddie stood up. Ash noticed that he wasn't holding his right hand where he usually kept it.

"What?" asked Eddie.

"That's right," said Ash.

"What did Lasi say?" enquired Eddie.

Eddie's face was turning brighter and brighter red.

"He said we would need a damn good excuse not to hire her," said Ash, "he also commended you Eddie, on your choice of candidates."

Ash smiled broadly. Ash knew it was the only way to strong arm him and his cronies.

They re-assembled in the conference room after everyone had met Patricia. Ash never informed Patricia about how he had to work through Lasi to be able to hire her. He felt embarrassed that it would take such an extreme measure. Ash pretended that it was all normal course.

There was silence. Nobody said anything. Ash was growing impatient.

"Well?" appealed Ash to the group.

"I think she'd be good," offered Steven.

There was another sneer from Bob.

"Why don't you share your comment with the

group?" Ash put him on the spot.

Bob looked at Eddie and then stared at Ash. While returning the look to Eddie, Bob said, "I said she has a nice rack."

Half of the room laughed.

"I'm sure human resources would be interested in your views," said Ash.

"Whatever," said Bob, looking at Ash and shrugging his shoulders.

"Well if nobody has anything meaningful to add, I'm going to give Patricia her offer letter," declared Ash.

Ash looked at Eddie. There was no movement and no response from him.

Ash walked over to him, opened his wallet, pulled out two twenty dollar bills and threw them on the table in front of Eddie. Ash briefly contemplated throwing them at Eddie's face, but he decided not to.

"Let's fix that damn clock," demanded Ash.

Eddie didn't say a word. He took the two twenties and placed them in his pocket. Ash walked away, disgusted.

Thirty minutes later, Eddie came by Ash's office. Ash expected him to comment on the clock stunt.

"Can I see the offer letter you extended to Patricia?" Eddie requested. His tone was very soft.

"Sure."

Ash shuffled through some papers and then pulled a file from his desk. He handed it to Eddie.

"Whoa, her compensation is fifty percent higher than Bob's. They're both VPs."

"Yeah. That's what it takes to get the right talent."

"This isn't fair. If Bob finds out, he is going to be really upset."

"Yeah, well, Lasi approved it."

Eddie walked out of the office. His arms were at his side.

• • •

It took almost a month to get a hold of Benson. Max and Ash coordinated their efforts to double team him. They thought that by leaving messages that said "Max and I need to talk to you desperately" it might quicken his response. They were wrong.

They finally ambushed him at his home one night. He had an enormous house he recently purchased in the Hollywood Hills. There was a dramatic drive up winding roads to get to his house. When they got there they faced a broad grid-iron gate. They had to alert Benson as to their presence via a video monitor. When they walked down the path to the front door and rang the doorbell, Benson showed up in his boxer shorts. He had poured himself a glass of Scotch. The television was on in one room. There were boxes everywhere. No dining table. Several pieces of furniture were covered in cloth.

Ash felt the urge to ask him, more so to punctuate the response, as he already knew the answer, "So, when did you buy this place?"

"It's been over a year," grumbled Benson, annoyance in his tone. Ash couldn't tell if it was directed towards him or if it was a personal reflection on the fact that it looked as if he had just moved in.

"Benson, you look like you have just been with a woman," Ash observed.

"Let me guess," said Max, laughing intentionally, "Did you charge her batteries? Did you upload data from your stick? Is she emitting a soft glow that is illuminating your room, right now?"

Benson snarled, "Piss off, you guys."

Ash thought to himself, I don't know why Benson thinks he is British. He was born here.

Max disappeared. He came running back.

"I found her!"

There, in his arms, was Benson's laptop.

"You guys suck."

That was more like it, thought Ash.

"We have a plan for you Benson," Max enticed.

"Yeah, instead of doing these financial models, you'll be able to do a *fashion* model," quipped Ash.

"Not funny," Benson protested.

"I don't do models anyway, my insubordinates do," defended Benson, "I just review them.   I am a Partner, you know!"

"Ohhhh…." said Ash and Max together.

"A little sensitive there, are we?" Max asked as he play slapped Benson.

Ash and Max both knew that he was.

"Guys, I've got a flight in the morning," said Benson.

"Ohhhh….." said Ash and Max again in unison.

"A little high and mighty, don't you think?" challenged Ash, "Now that they stopped flying the Concorde your going to have to settle for regular first class.   I'm so sorry.   I know it's going to be a tough transition.   Is your ass going to adjust?   We feel for you.   We'll be the ones screaming from coach."

Ash and Max could be this way with Benson.   They had been with him for most of his emotional ups and downs. They figured since they had lifted him up from his own vomit, they were entitled to a certain amount of encroachment in his life.   He understood the rules.

"Don't be such a whiny little bitch," Max jested, as he tried to grab Benson's shorts to pull them off.

It worked.   Benson finally laughed.

"Pour us some scotch," directed Ash.

The three sat poolside.

"Benson, have you even gone swimming here?" asked Ash.

"No."

"Didn't think so."

"So you guys are gonna help me find women?" asked Benson, trying to get back to the topic.

"Benson," started Ash, "We need to start a private equity fund together. The three of us."

Benson was quiet. After the last few minutes, he seemed to be waiting to see if they were joking or not.

Ash sensed that.

"Oh no, we are *not* kidding," Ash assured.

"It's true," said Max.

"You've got to be kidding me," said Benson.

"No, we're not."

"You blokes are serious?"

There it was again, thought Ash. This time Ash shot a glance to Max whom he noticed was also trying to restrain a smile.

"Yes, we are," Ash assured.

"Wow," said Benson.

He looked up at the night sky. He looked down over the city. There was a fantastic panoramic view of Los Angeles there. It looked like a dark computer screen with a few individual pixels lit orange, green, white and red.

"I think that it's a great idea," he finally agreed.

Ash was thrilled to hear him say that. Max looked relieved too.

"Guys, I'm exhausted," Benson confessed.

Ash and Max looked at him. Ash felt pity for his friend. He did look burned out, disheveled to a certain degree, a beached whale.

"You know, I'm supposed to be a Partner, but very few decisions are actually rendered by me. It's all about the guys who started the damn place. And they have such huge egos, bigger than the states of New York and California combined. We are always just pushing for the next biggest deal. We also seem ridiculous whenever we club with others to get a deal done, you know?"

Actually Ash and Max didn't; they didn't work on the deals in the double-digit *billions* Benson was working on.

"Our investors give us a hard time – they say that every firm that worked on that club deal claims credit as the deal lead or deal originator and that the others were brought in at the eleventh hour and basically only wired money."

"That happens?" Ash asked.

Ash had, somewhat naively he realized in hindsight, thought that everything was so rosy at the industry's top firm.

"And the politics and the backstabbing are just really getting to me."

"Well," said Max, "We think we have a solution that will get you out of that."

Benson started nodding his head in slow motion. He then smiled.

"You chaps are all right."

CHAPTER 9

Ash walked into the Connoisseur Wine Shop. It had recently opened and was billed as the fanciest wine store in all of Los Angeles. It had also been ranked in *Food & Wine* magazine as one of the top cellars in the city. Ash was immediately drawn towards the fine mahogany wood throughout the store, used for shelving, cabinets and racks. There was burgundy velvet everywhere – hanging from ceiling to floor throughout the space, as lining for several of the shelves holding wine and as a makeshift curtain that opened to the central counter and cash register. As he entered, he overheard a female voice from behind that curtain. There was someone she was helping who hovered over the counter. He was a big fellow, and Ash could not get a good view of who was talking. Her voice had a sonorous mix to it that was simultaneously commanding and sweet. I would welcome this woman yelling at me, thought Ash. The timbre of her voice had a lyrical quality that was equally matched by a weight of authority. Her accent was French, but it had evaporated to a degree, a telltale sign she had been in an English-speaking country for some time.

Ash positioned himself to be able to get a glimpse of her. Her beauty had a subtle, ephemeral quality to it on first view that was also everlasting in the imprint that it left in his mind. He had this urge to possess that view, own it somehow, but he couldn't make it his and then simultaneously he couldn't get it out of his mind or be rid of it. Her soft, almond-shaped eyes – each flash of her eyelids a whisper, chiseled nose and high cheek bones illustrated a perfectly sculpted face. Her wavy, almost loosely curled, shoulder-length hair exuded a golden hue. Audrey Hepburn meets Catherine Deneuve. Juliette Binoche meets Gwenyth Paltrow. Her cheeks had a tint of cranberry and her lips had the appeal of blood red oranges – not the skin – but the fruit beneath. He could just taste her. As a cocktail she'd be a cosmopolitan – made with Grey Goose – and a splash of Grand Marnier.

His interest was piqued. Ash took a bottle of a 2003 Margaux from Chateau d'Yquem, a fabulous first growth wine. He approached her with it. She hadn't looked at him yet, as she had become occupied counting cash once the prior customer left. As he neared, he watched her lips move. Her upper lip had a slight overhang that seemed to come to a subtle, delicate point. Every time her lips moved up and down, it was like a bird pecking at seeds. Her apron hugged her contours like a tight rubber glove. They revealed, or artfully concealed rather, her shapely full figure. It was enough to get the blood of any man, or a woman with those tendencies, excited.

"Hello," said Ash. He was deliberately slow and patient.

"Yes?" she asked. Her lips were still moving, and she had yet to make eye contact with him.

"Whenever you're ready," said Ash patiently.

He wanted her to stop what she was doing and interact with him. He wasn't looking for a half-concentrated response.

He could see her cheeks get rosy. "I'm sorry," she offered, blowing out a breath forcefully. "It is just that, this needs to get done," she said.

"No problem. I'll wait."

Her "o"s were spoken with a perfect rounding of the lips, her "g"s had a soft j tone to them and her "th's" had an intoxicating, faint, hint of a 'z' sound. Every time Ash heard that 'z', it was as if he were crystal, his heart resonating in pitch with the sound. She sounded like she was singing to Ash.

She tilted her head to the side as she counted the last pieces.

"Okay, sorry," she repeated from a distance as she looked up.

When she looked at Ash, he smiled. She walked closer to where he was standing, only the counter separating the two of them.

"I hate competing with money," said Ash.

She laughed.

"I'm sorry about that," she reiterated

Ash kept smiling at her. Oh those precious 'z's thought Ash. She smiled back and then lifted one eyebrow and tilted her head to one side.

"Yes," said Ash, and without looking down, he asked, "do you have this from 2000?"

"Wow, excellent taste," she complimented.

Ash increased the broadness of his smile. He loved hearing that.

"But, I am sorry, I cannot oblige your request," she said leaning her head forward momentarily as she said "cannot" for emphasis.

"But what I do have which would be just as nice..."

"...would be a '99," Ash completed.

"Why yes," she said with a broad smile.

Ash loved how this was going.

"Why don't you show it to me?" he suggested.

She walked from behind the counter, swinging her hips around the edge of the countertop in a manner which seemed intentionally slow. She kept making eye contact with him, turning back frequently as she walked.

I could follow her anywhere, thought Ash. He was sad

when she stopped.

"Here it is," she presented.

As she handed the bottle over, he deliberately touched her fingers as he took the bottle from her.

She was watching his face as he surveyed the bottle. He was watching her from the corner of his eye.

"Looks lovely," he said looking up at her.

She smiled coyly.

"So if the 2000 is Beethoven's Ninth Symphony, what would the '99 be?" asked Ash with a devilish smile on his face.

"The '99 would be the Seventh Symphony, bold and strong, but it won't sing for you," she replied after only a second's pause.

"And the '03?" asked Ash, ecstatic with her response.

"The '03 is more subtle. It would be like Beethoven's Violin Concerto in D," she clarified, "Its intensity sneaks up on you and leaves you with a zesty finish, making you crave more."

Ash was floored. He worried about making the initial comment, not knowing if it would be considered too over the top and too esoteric to be considered cool. He was relieved when she responded positively.

She walked back to the counter with a bounce to her step, triumphant, as if she had passed some difficult exam, aced her tennis court opponent or scored the match-winning goal.

Ash paid for the bottle, thanked her and left.

He came by the next day. When she saw him enter, she finished helping her prior customer with a smile on her face.

"And how was it?" she asked.

"It was wonderful - just as you described - exactly like the Seventh," said Ash. "I even listened to the Seventh while I drank it."

"Ohhh..." she giggled.

"And it turned out to have a bold finish, just like the Seventh," said Ash with a smile.

She made the same motion with her raised eyebrow and tilted head.

"There is a wine tasting I would love to go with you to," he said to her.

She smiled warmly.

"It's tomorrow," continued Ash.

She nodded her head in agreement.

Ash gave her the address and they agreed to meet there.

"I'm Ash."

"Sophie."

• • •

Ash, Benson and Max got together again to settle some additional details and to get the ball rolling.

"Okay, we need to have a book," said Benson.

"Oh, we are going to be writers now?" joked Ash.

"No, it's the Confidential Information Memorandum, aka the Private Placement Memo, the Offering Memo or the 'Book,'" Benson defined, "And here are some samples of what they need to look like."

Benson handed out some samples.

"Damn, these things are thick," Max noted.

"Yup," Benson agreed, "Over one hundred pages and the best thing is that nobody reads them."

"What?" asked Max and Ash together.

"It's true," said Benson, "Nobody reads them. But every potential investor that we speak to will require us to have one. It's like a measure of professionalism. If you spent the effort and the time to get one done, you are a little more legitimate."

"Great," said Ash, flipping pages.

"Well, some people will look at parts of it," Benson revised, "They will look at the table of investments showing our track record of performance – i.e., how much money we have made from doing deals in the past, and they will read our bios."

"Well, that's better than not reading anything at all," said Max.

As they continued to thumb through it, a silence befell them.

"Okay, guys, I know what you are thinking," said Max.

Ash and Benson knew better than to refute their thoughts.

"I'll take the lead in writing this since I am less busy than you two," offered Max.

Ash and Benson both smiled.

"There's more," Benson amended.

"Oh great," said Ash.

"Once the Book is done, we need to do a slide presentation," Benson proffered.

Benson handed Ash and Max some samples.

"It's basically the Book in slide format that we will talk people through," he added.

"So how about when Max finishes with the Book, you and I tackle the presentation?" Ash suggested.

"Sounds good.　Don't tell Max the presentation should only be around fifteen pages," said Benson, amplifying his voice.

"You guys suck," said Max.

"Hey, think of the greater good here," said Benson.

"Yeah, yeah, spare me the tear-jerker rhetoric," said Max.

"Actually, the presentation tends to be as useless," said Benson, "They get to page three and just start asking questions."

"You know, I have noticed the same thing with management teams of potential targets I bring in to meet The Commies. We get to page three, and they start asking questions," Ash recalled.

Max and Benson were well aware of The Commies. Not only had they heard Ash complain about them numerous times, they had also heard it from people not working for Popular.

"But if you show up with three pages, they'll think you are unprepared," added Max.

"Sounds like a lot of smoke and mirrors, doesn't it?" Ash posed.

"Yes. So, we need to have it," concluded Benson.

"From there we can begin to set up meetings and get the story out," said Ash.

"Yes," said Benson.

"We need to take the greatest care in building our initial circle of support," cautioned Max, "I don't want word to get out widely so that we have problems with our existing jobs."

"You are absolutely right," Benson affirmed.

"I guess we should stage this where we talk to a few people who are most likely to support us from the onset, and once we have an initial target amount, we cut the cords at our respective jobs, and we can launch the fund to do deals and continue to fundraise," suggested Ash.

"Sounds like a good plan," said Max.

"We should also make sure we have a Placement Agent before we cut our 'proverbial cords,'" said Benson.

"A what?" asked Max.

"They are like an agent or manager for an actor or musician. They have relationships with a bunch of money sources. We are the 'talent' that they shop around to see if we can get more investors," Benson outlined, "Getting one of them to sign us up is going to be key in raising money beyond our friends and family."

"Yeah, I don't see that we can make it with just capital from our friends and family," said Ash.

"Not in a way that we would like," added Max.

"Right," Benson concurred.

● ● ●

"I heard what you did in securing me this job," said Patricia. She had been working at Popular for over a month.

"Well," said Ash, "you definitely deserved it." Ash thought for a moment. "The truth be told, what I did has more to do with how our company is and the way the people are versus anything else." Ash rubbed his chin. "Boy, you find out about things around here. How did you discover this anyway?"

Patricia smiled knowingly. "David told me."

"Little runt. He should learn to keep his mouth shut."

They both laughed.

"There is something I need to tell you," said Patricia.

"What is it?"

"It has to do with Bob," she said.

"What – he doesn't like me? That's no surprise," said Ash, chuckling.

"No, it's not that."

Ash grew serious.

"What is it?" asked Ash.

"He has grabbed my ass on several occasions."

"What?" asked Ash, his jaw low.

Ash was stunned over what he was hearing. Bob had made that immature comment in the meeting to discuss Patricia's candidacy, but what Ash was learning now was ridiculous. The guy was married, and he had a child already.

"Has he done anything else?" asked Ash.

"He has reached for my chest a number of times," said Patricia.

"W-w-what?" Ash was stunned. "When has this happened?"

"Oh, during group dinners with others in the office," said Patricia.

"Is anyone else involved?"

"No."

"What did the others say who were there?"

"David and Steven kept trying to make him stop. Jason was laughing."

Ash rolled his eyes. It didn't surprise him.

"I'm very sorry to hear that that happened, Patricia," Ash apologized for the vulgar behavior.

Ash began stroking his neck.

"You don't deserve this behavior." He then turned to Patricia. "Are you prepared to report this?"

"Yes, I am actually a bit sick of it."

• • •

Ash cornered Steven by his cubicle.

"Let's go into my office. I'll pretend to be on the phone and let's just get through the rest of my telling you the history on Project Emancipate," pitched Ash.

"Deal," replied Steven.

Ash started describing as they walked to his office.

Ash, Boas and Wendy, Boas's wife, proceeded to dinner. They decided to eat at the restaurant of the hotel where Ash was staying.

"Wendy, I'd like you to meet, Ash."

"How do you do?"

Wendy was as tall as Boas. She had a thin frame, but there was evidence of child bearing in her mid-section. She wore glasses. Her brunette hair was shoulder length and had a natural curliness. There was a sort of artistic disarray to it. It was clear she had conceded to its unruliness and only managed it enough so that it didn't look unkempt. She had a broad smile and a focused gaze when she spoke or was speaking with someone else.

"It's nice to meet another one of Ash's colleagues," said Wendy.

"Well, I think we still have to qualify it as 'potential' colleague," said Ash, "Boas is still deciding whether he wants to work with me or not."

"Yeah, as if it all boiled down to that," quipped Boas.

"Tell me about your children," asked Ash.

"Oh," said Wendy, "You must have seen the photos in Boas's office."

Ash tried to think. Yes, I suppose his office did have photos. Just don't ask me what was in any of them.

"We have three kids," Wendy started, "Aged seventeen, fifteen and twelve."

"Wow, Boas, you don't look old enough to have a child about to graduate from high school."

"Well, we started early," Boas offered. "We were married between our junior and senior years of college."

Wow, thought Ash. I can't believe they identified their life partners so early on and have made it work all of these years. Ash was in awe.

"You must be eager to know the origins of Boas's name," stated Wendy.

Ash was about to tell her that he and Boas had discussed it, but when he looked up at Wendy, he detected a childlike sparkle in her eyes that showed her enthusiasm and excitement at being able to relay the story to Ash. He decided to indulge her.

"Boas's father was an anthropologist. He loved the study of man, and he loved people from all over the planet. Boas, the famous anthropologist, was, and is, his hero."

"You have followed in your father's footsteps," pronounced Ash while facing Boas.

"That's kind of you to say," commented Boas. He winked at Ash. Ash could tell that Boas appreciated Ash's letting Wendy share the story of his name. Ash smiled and nodded his head gently in response.

"So how did you guys meet?" Ash quizzed.

"Well, my father happened to be a professor of anthropology at the college Wendy and I both attended," Boas explained.

"I took all of his father's classes," added Wendy.

"And she would show up for all of his office hours," Boas recalled.

"Oh, yeah, I forgot about that," Wendy said, blushing.

"So she was always around, and I was always around. Sometimes Dad would be busy with another student or on the phone. She would ask me some questions because I was there, and I knew a bunch of the answers since I grew up with it," added Boas.

"One thing led to another and here we are," Wendy gushed.

That's a great story, thought Ash. Sometimes it's nice to get behind the business plans and financial statements and see that there is *life* in these companies. There are real humans, with real emotions and real experiences behind them.

How could Ash possibly relay that to The Commies?

"So, Boas, you never wanted to become an anthropologist?" Ash delved back into the conversation.

"I always wanted to become one. And I still am," answered Boas, "It's just that it is a hobby for me."

"Julia, our oldest, says she wants to become an anthropologist," commented Wendy.

The pride with which Wendy spoke was palpable.

Ash wondered what it would be like to have a family.

"How about you? Are you married? Is there someone special in your life?" asked Wendy.

Ash thought briefly.

"Well…" Ash stammered.

"Come on, don't be shy," encouraged Wendy.

"Honestly, my time has been really occupied with work," said Ash.

He hated the way that sounded. Did he really want to be that guy? The one who was married to his job?

"I have been dating, I would say, opportunistically," added Ash, "But nothing is in, what I would call, advanced stages yet."

Ash kept looking up and around the room as he spoke.

"You see, Wendy, he is longing for someone and wishes he had a person to describe," commented Boas while laughing.

"Is it that bad?" asked Ash managing a laugh.

"Oh don't mind him," said Wendy, "He always gets this way with people."

The rest of the meal continued with similar pleasantries. Ash was surprised when the time passed as quickly as it did.

"You know why I asked you to dinner and decided to include my wife, don't you?" Boas queried when they had finished the meal.

Ash enjoyed the get together so much he hadn't really thought about any other agenda.

"Wendy reads people really well. Sometimes better than I do," he explained.

"I find it hard to believe that anyone can be more astutely attentive than you," laughed Ash.

And then Ash got worried. He tried to re-play the evening in his mind. Did he blunder at any point?

"If she responded well to you, I knew we would work well together," he added.

"How did I do? Did I pass the test?" Ash questioned.

"We're still talking, right?"

"Got it."

They were walking to Ash's hotel lobby.

"Oh, there are two other things I forgot to mention," said Ash.

Boas looked fatigued.

"Can this wait until the morning?" he asked.

"Sure, let's wait until then."

Ash didn't sleep well that night. He wished he had mentioned what he needed to tell Boas prior to the dinner. He suddenly worried about how Boas might react. He didn't want him to feel jilted in anyway.

"Although you had your pension scheme before with your parent company," Ash mentioned to him the following morning, "we won't be able to continue with that."

Boas was quiet. Several seconds passed before he said anything.

"You're cutting the pension?" Boas finally asked. His voice had the hint of betrayed trust.

"There's more. We are no longer going to subsidize all of the healthcare insurance," Ash said. "Now, we will only pay a portion of it."

"I don't think we can do that," said Boas. Boas's tone was firm. He looked directly at Ash. He didn't squirm in his chair. Ash didn't completely understand.

"What do you mean?" asked Ash.

"I'm walking away from the deal, is what I mean."

"Please don't do that," Ash urged.

"Look, I know you are just the messenger, but I can't do the deal without those two stipulations."

Boas put his hand forward. He was offering it in a handshake.

Ash was stunned.

"That's it?"

"Don't get me wrong, I like you a lot," said Boas. "I just need to have this," he said, "It's for my people. They see the healthcare coverage, and they really like that."

Ash listened intently to what Boas had to say.

"Many of them have also been here for twenty years. They were attracted to the jobs because of the pension benefits. There is significant value there and they won't – or at least they shouldn't – be asked to abandon them."

Ash looked at him ruefully. He was searching for something to say.

"But, Boas, you have such a lucrative deal on the table for yourself. It's a package worth a lot of money," Ash reasoned.

As soon as he said it, he regretted it. He recalled Boas's earlier words – "you will know what is important to me." Ash knew what he had just said was not the highest priority for Boas. Ash felt strangely conflicted. He admired the stance Boas was taking, yet he knew it was killing a transaction Ash had worked so hard on to get to the point where they were.

Boas seemed to sense all of what Ash was going through.

"I know this puts you in a tough spot," assured Boas.

Sometimes I wonder if he is too perceptive. Am I not left with any more private thoughts while interacting with him? he wondered.

"I'll see what I can do," Ash recalled saying.

Ash got up from his chair. He and Steven had been in Ash's office for an hour.

"And that's when we had to go back to The Commies again. It would have been the seventh time. If I didn't really love the deal, and quite frankly, appreciate Boas as much as I did, I would have given up much earlier," Ash admitted.

"Good thing that doesn't happen on each deal," said Steven.

CHAPTER 10

Ash began noticing Eddie and the ELVES were spending quite a bit of time in the conference room. Sometimes they would be in there all day. Ash wondered whether they all hated their respective offices or something was truly wrong.

Ash decided to invite himself into one of those sessions. As soon as he walked into the conference room, all three looked up at him. Ash saw Jason turn down his laptop computer screen and flip over a stack of papers in front of him. Ash noticed the words Project Elba on one of the documents he flipped over. Ash heard Lasi's voice on the speaker phone.

"Hey, Lasi, don't mention any names...uh... the door is open," indicated Eddie while looking at Ash.

"How did this information get to them? Who leaked it to them? If the public finds out we are in ENORMOUS trouble," Lasi demanded without acknowledging Eddie's request.

"Well, it wasn't me. It was Bob's fault," Eddie accused.

Ash was taken aback. I'd hate to be Bob right now, he thought.

"I thought I was leaving it in his capable hands, but he screwed it up," Eddie continued.

"Don't you think you ought to apologize to Lasi for making a mistake, Bob?"

"I'm sorry," said Bob in a sour tone. Ash didn't detect much remorse. It sounded much more like embarrassment.

Bob looked like he was close to tears.

Eddie put the phone on mute as he whispered Jason a question.

"What are you doing here?" Bob asked Ash.

"Checking the time on the clock," remarked Ash. Still seven thirty-three pm.

Ash continued to rub his chin.

● ● ●

"Managing these damn portfolio companies is such a nightmare," Benson bemoaned to Max and Ash.

Benson poured another round of drinks for the three of them. They were all at his house again, doing their kick-off planning meeting.

"We are supposed to be the paradigm of efficiency compared to the public markets, but there is so much absurd posturing and ego-goosing. Everything is governance by committee. We waste so much time producing these documents that go back and forth. The Board meetings are always so convoluted and elongated. It would be better if they just let one firm take the lead and do what they want. Every time one buyout fund wants to do something, the other contests. The first one goes and blows $125,000 on a consulting study to bolster their position and the competing private equity firm spends $200,000 to defend theirs."

Benson stopped for a second to take a sip of his drink. He was still moving his hand while he took a sip, indicating that he wasn't done.

"Everyone needs to be right, and because of that, no one is in control. In the end, we never get over the impasse and we start arguing about another project that will never get off the ground," he concluded.

Ash half expected steam to be rising from Benson's head. Man, we thought he had it great, but all this while, he has been nearly as miserable as us. Ash then looked around at Benson's place. Well, not nearly as miserable.

"And for that reason, I don't want to go into this thing with the expectation that we are going to partner with other groups on every transaction. I think we have been doing this enough that we can do it ourselves," Benson indicated.

Ash and Max agreed with him.

"It is much better to be masters of our own destiny," Ash declared.

"Yeah, my father has been real keen on extolling the virtues of being able to control our own lives in this new venture. If we give it up by joining forces, it won't be as enticing," offered Max.

Benson's phone rang.

"I'm sorry, guys, I gotta grab this."

Max polished off his drink.

"You're in a good mood," Ash noted.

"Yeah, I just talked to my dad. He's really stoked about this."

"That's great," said Ash.

Benson came back.

"Sorry, guys. Where were we?"

"You know, I have seen some interesting venture deals lately," offered Max.

"Yeah, but we can't show such a lack of focus," said Ash.

"You're right," said Max.

"It's a very different type of investing anyway," said Benson.

Benson's phone rang again.

"Cheerio!"

Ash and Max couldn't contain themselves. They almost fell over with laughter. Benson had to leave the area in order to answer the call.

Benson came back.

"Stop it, Limey," Ash said to him.

"What?" Benson asked in disbelief.

"Let me guess, you've been spending a lot of time in London lately?" asked Max.

"Oh right, is it that obvious?"

"You need to cut that crap out," Ash admonished, "You sound ridiculous. You have no ties to Britain except as a tourist."

"Right, right," said Benson.

"Anyway, to get back to what I was saying, venture capital is like going to Vegas and laying down twenty bets. You know that with each one you are trying to hit it big, looking for a payout of twenty or thirty to one. So as long as one hits, even if the others tank, you are golden," said Benson.

"Right, and our investing leaves little room for that. You really have to go in with a well articulated plan of attack," said Ash.

"Right," said Benson, "to contrast with hedge funds, they are gambling with blindfolds on. They don't get to see any information until it's too late when they invest in market-based assets. That's why they have to resort to hedging, shorting, futures, swaps or other derivatives to protect their investments regardless of where the market goes. For them, it almost doesn't matter if the market goes up or down, so long as it moves. Naturally, if they predict it they do better, but they just love volatility. If markets are moving, they are making money. Static markets are bad for them."

"You know," said Max, "...and by the way, thanks Professor Wong,...the common element to what we have been doing has been buy-and-build strategies."

Ash and Benson were considering this as they thought

through their own deals.

"Hey, you are right," Ash agreed, "Some of my best returns have been where I led the deal to acquire a platform company and we bought anywhere from two to eight other businesses to bolt on to that platform. We ended up with a much bigger company that got sold off for a premium."

"I've done a few of those as well," Benson offered.

"Well, there we have it, we are going to be a buy-and-build strategy fund," said Max.

"Right," said Benson, "Do you guys use one hundred day plans?"

"Come again?" asked Max.

Ash shook his head no. "What are those?" he asked.

"In our shop," said Benson, "we come up with these one hundred day plans. It is supposed to be for the first one hundred days after the deal closes. It is supposed to be a game plan for all of the changes we are going to make during that time period."

"Does it work? Do you guys stick to it?" asked Max.

"More stuff gets done from that list versus any other or from any initiatives presented post-Close. Since it's been floating around for a while, people know what's on it. Sometimes there are executional snags we hit, disagreements on how things should get done, but for the most part, most items on that list happen. It doesn't all happen in the first one hundred days, but it happens," said Benson.

Ash was amazed.

"We just never have any time to be thoughtful like that on anything. I wish I could sit and articulate all of the initiatives I'd like to pursue to make my companies better. I'm always just too busy putting out fires, dealing with the pressure to keep doing more and more deals or spinning my wheels responding to silly requests and inquiries from The

Commies. And then, inevitably, something goes wrong somewhere and that takes the lion's share of my time for the week, leaving no time for anything else reactive, let alone proactive. It's a shame; I think that is what our shareholders are expecting of us, and we fall so short. "

"It's also a great marketing tool," said Benson.

"How do you mean?" asked Max.

"We use it when we are fundraising. It's a way to show that we are proactive. Since our LPs have the list of things we said we were going to do, we are kind of required to follow through on it."

"I like this idea," Max admitted, "I think we ought to implement it in the new fund."

"I agree," Ash concurred.

Ash finished his drink.

"Let me ask you guys, how many portfolio companies do you manage?"

"I got five, and I'm dying," said Benson.

His phone rang again.

"I have three, and I think that's a good number," said Max.

Benson came back.

"I kind of agree; three is an ideal number," said Ash.

"That would be great," said Benson, "So three a piece, we'll do nine deals in our first fund."

"Geez, I have ten deals I'm managing right now," said Ash.

Benson's eyes opened wide and Max nearly choked.

"They're killing you," said Benson.

"Yeah, now don't ask him how little he gets paid," teased Max.

"Hey, guys, what about a name?" asked Ash.

They all looked at each other. They began to laugh.

"Ooops," said Max.

A few seconds passed as they were lost in their

thoughts.

"How about Negociant Capital?" suggested Ash.

Max and Benson looked at him quizzically.

"You give me crap for sounding British, and you are coming up with this French rubbish?" rebuked Benson.

"Okay, good point."

"What does it mean?" asked Max.

"It literally means 'trader,' but it is a term from the wine industry. It refers to a vineyard that will buy grapes from smaller growers and winemakers and make wine that he sells under his own label. Generally, the people he is buying from are too small to make wine on their own or don't have the muscle to distribute broadly. Since we plan on buying platforms and adding on to them by acquiring other businesses in a similar area, it seemed to fit thematically," presented Ash.

Max and Benson looked at each other. Smiles were creeping up on both their faces.

"By jove…" started Benson.

"Hey look, I'm glad I sold you on it, but don't even start with that!" said Ash, heaving a pillow at his friend.

"Does this mean we can only do deals in Europe?" asked Max, "We've got our Anglo-phile, our Franco-phile – I guess I oughta focus on Italy."

• • •

Ash approached Eddie.

"Eddie, we have a sexual harassment problem," Ash annunciated.

It took Eddie more than five seconds to look away from his computer towards Ash.

"Say that again," said Eddie.

His manner was lethargic. Ash wondered how he would react. He could see how Eddie would be reluctant to make ripples about this.

"Well, I don't think it's a problem," said Eddie after

Ash repeated himself.

"Eddie, that's absurd.   We need to report this to human resources.   This is a hostile work environment," said Ash.

"Oh come on," said Eddie, his tone getting more aggressive, "She invites that behavior.   You see the way she is so flirtatious with all of them."

"First of all, she is not flirtatious.   She engages with people, she shows interest and concern and she responds. There's a big difference between that and being flirtatious. Only a moron couldn't tell the difference.   Regardless, I don't care if she prances around in her lingerie," Ash countered, "Bob is not excused from behaving that way."

Eddie's phone rang.   It was Lasi.   Ash knew he would postpone their discussion.   Ash walked out of Eddie's office without uttering another word.

● ● ●

"These all say the same thing," said Max to Ash and Benson.

The three had arranged to do a conference call over the phone to monitor progress on the making of the "Book."

"I can just cut and paste," said Max.

"Well, since they don't really read it," said Ash.

"That's fine.   Just take out the best parts, alter the wording for good measure, and slap it in.   In a way, it's good if our material for Negociant Capital sounds like other more reputed firms," said Benson.

"I should be done in a few days then," said Max.

● ● ●

When she arrived, she was dressed in black.   A silk scarf perched delicately around her neck.   It sectioned off her head from the rest of her five foot six inch frame in a way that made it a showpiece.   He could pick her out of any crowd.   Her stance and body movements were as graceful as those of a swan.

"Tell me about yourself," Ash encouraged her.

"Well, I have a Ph.D. in art history, but my passion is wine," she started.

Ash felt suddenly fortunate he passed his time while studying finance taking a few art history classes. There was that one graduate student teaching assistant – Catherine Bourgogne - who was perhaps most responsible for his desire to take the classes. I'll have to remember to send her a bottle of wine as thanks later, he thought to himself.

"And where did your interest in wine come from?" asked Ash.

"My family had owned a vineyard in the Bordeaux region for generations, but my grandfather had to shut it down during WWII," Sophie shared.

Sadness had a hard time penetrating that face. Ash had to rely on the slight quiver in her voice to understand her sense of loss.

"I'm so sorry to hear that," offered Ash.

He knew it was a token, but it would be too early to embrace her at this point or engage in any other form of more intimate physical contact. Not that he wasn't dying to do it.

"My father missed it terribly, and although he was a professor of sociology, he attempted to start a wine shop in France."

"When you say attempted, do you mean things didn't work out?" Ash pressed.

"He ran it for ten years and then lost it in a family dispute with his brother."

"Oh," said Ash.

As he fumbled to think of something else to say, the sommelier at the wine tasting called everyone's attention.

In a maneuver that made Ash's heartbeat hasten, Sophie leaned into him while holding his arm, "He was my inspiration to start the wine store," she whispered.

She let go of his arm. Ash was saddened, but he knew to hold on to it would be awkward. Ash couldn't wait for the wine tasting host to finish, as he was eager to get back to chatting with Sophie. The sommelier went on and on about themes, expression, growths, varietals. All of which would have been fascinating for Ash had he not been overwhelmed with the desire to do something else.

They began with the first selection. They both sipped it. Ash turned to Sophie.

"Well Dr. Matthieu, it tastes like a Matisse – it limits itself to a few flavors, all of which are very bold and it has a strong, lingering finish," Ash assessed.

Sophie dropped her jaw in disbelief and let out a little laugh. She touched his arm again – almost as if she needed support to prevent falling over. Ash held his smile.

"That was *very* clever," Sophie said.

Ash responded by broadening his smile.

Another wine came around, and they both sipped it. Ash turned to face Sophie and raised his eyebrow in invitation of her critique.

"This one is more like a Picasso - very complex, seemingly confused with competing flavors, but they give way to a dominant theme that holds at the finish," said Sophie. She marked the end of her comments with a hearty laugh while looking up briefly as if she were in awe of her accomplishment.

"Well done," Ash praised her, "Well done."

He let the moment simmer. They shared a glance that deliberated for a few moments.

"I don't know why people rely solely on fruits and vegetables for their comparisons," said Ash.

"They shouldn't be so limited," added Sophie.

At that moment, they overheard a couple standing next to them discuss the black currant tones of the Cabernet Sauvignon. They both laughed together.

When the last wine of the night came by, they both sipped, frowned and look at each other.

"Edward Munch," Ash declared.

"Oh yes, 'The Scream' all the way," added Sophie.

They both threw out their contents together.

"The evening has been very inspiring," said Sophie.

Ash didn't want it to end.

"Can I take you to a late dinner?" asked Ash.

"That would be lovely."

As they sat at the restaurant, and the hours progressed, they graduated to more intimate details of each other's lives. The two empty bottles of wine were great catalysts.

"Tell me about your past relationships," urged Ash.

"I just ended a long one," she said.

I suppose my timing is good, thought Ash.

"He was also in art history."

"Oh," said Ash, "So you met while working together and things got awkward when you broke up?"

"Exactly like that. I just kept seeing him at conferences and in reviewing papers. It was just too hard."

"That must have been a challenge," said Ash.

"Our profession is such a small world," Sophie recalled.

"I felt like I needed a change," she added after a brief pause.

"Well, I'm glad that you felt that way," said Ash, smiling as invitingly as he could.

"It was no fun going through that," she commented.

Ash felt embarrassed, "No, I'm sorry, of course not, I didn't mean to make light of it."

Ash placed his hand on hers.

"What exactly went wrong?" Ash asked.

"He didn't make enough time for me. He thought too much about himself. His work was always prioritized above me or my work," she lamented.

"It's good that you ended it," decided Ash.

This provoked a coquettish smile from Sophie.

"And how about you?" Sophie probed.

"Relationships?" asked Ash.

"Tell me something. I still don't even know what you do," she protested.

"Well, I don't feel like talking about it," said Ash, "Let's just continue with our evening."

"Oh," said Sophie, "Sounds very intriguing."

She gave him a coy smile.

"Well, lest you think I am a drug dealer, let me just say that I am a Partner in a private equity firm," said Ash.

"Wow," was Sophie's response, "That is quite a buzz word these days."

"Yeah, I guess," said Ash, "Would you like to try a dessert wine? There is a Muscat I noticed on the menu."

"Sure," said Sophie, graciously.

• • •

Two days passed and Ash didn't hear anything from Eddie, as Ash had suspected. Ash approached Eddie to resurrect the topic.

"Oh, that thing again," said Eddie.

"What are we going to do about it?" demanded Ash.

"Look," began Eddie, "She's not as innocent as you think she is."

"I don't care about how you interpret her behavior. What Bob did is unacceptable."

"Well, we have determined that she lies frequently," Eddie revealed.

"That's absurd," said Ash.

"Well it's true," said Eddie.

Now more than ever, thought Ash, he wished he didn't have to deal with Eddie and his cronies.

"How did you find out about her lying?" Ash asked.

Eddie hesitated for a few minutes. Ash moved about while awaiting a response to the question.

"A few people brought it to my attention," said Eddie.

Eddie stood up to walk to his bookshelf. Ash noticed his right arm was in its usual position.

"Nobody has brought it to my attention, and I work with her more than you do," said Ash.

Eddie remained silent.

"I'd like to have some names," Ash demanded.

"Well...for example, Jason came by..." Eddie began.

"Jason? Our Jason?" asked Ash in disbelief, "You mean the guy who is desperate to be a Vice President and has had a chip on his shoulder since we hired Patricia? *That* Jason? How can you take his comments seriously?"

Eddie was mute.

"That's quite an accusation," said Ash, "And before we conclude that it's true, we ought to ask around. We owe it to Patricia."

Eddie reluctantly nodded his head in agreement. His arms were at his side.

● ● ●

"I've got 'em," proclaimed Max.

"Really? How do they look?" Ash interrogated.

"They're beautiful!" said Max, "Hang on a few minutes, and I'll bring them by."

"You can't bring them here!" exclaimed Ash. Ash was standing in his office at Popular Capital. "Meet me at Starbucks on the corner."

"Got it," said Max.

"Did you try Benson?" asked Ash.

"Yeah, he's in London, again," said Max.

Ash walked out of his office towards the elevator. He passed by Eddie. He had his right arm in position.

"Hey," said Ash.

Eddie just looked up at Ash, didn't say a word, but had a slight smirk on his face.

"Any resolution on those matters?" asked Ash.

They were in the hall, so Ash couldn't be specific.

"Don't worry yourself about that," said Eddie in a dismissive tone.

"Well, I am troubled by it. I'll speak to you when I get back," said Ash.

"Are you going to be gone long?" asked Eddie.

"No, I'll be right back," Ash promised.

"These are gorgeous!" said Ash, "I don't feel like touching them.   I am afraid to damage them."

Max had just brought the books from the printers.

"This is great," said Ash, "Just looking at this makes me feel accomplished."

"Well, we still have an uphill battle," Max reminded him.

"I know," conceded Ash, "Benson and I are almost done with the presentation."

"That's great!" said Max.

"Yeah, we need to start scheduling meetings now.   I'll try to get us hooked in to some private placement groups – the 'agents.'   We should also talk about hitting up our friends and family.   I have a few guys in mind," said Ash.

Max looked pensive.

"Hey," proclaimed Ash, "Your dad probably has a bunch of contacts with his entrepreneur buddies who would love this."

Max had a look on his face like he had just been caught stealing.

"Uh, yeah, that's true," said Max.

Ash waited for a few minutes.   He was troubled Max didn't seem more enthusiastic.

"Why don't we do a few other meetings first and then we can try and think of those guys," Max suggested.

"Sure," replied Ash.

"It's just that …well, they are my dad's friends and I don't want to look stupid in front of them.   You know, it would get back to my dad.   I have to make him proud by making him look good," Max explained.

Ash was relieved. Thank goodness Max isn't having cold feet.

CHAPTER 11

They had set up their meetings in the inverse order of their interest. They had scheduled a meeting with a private placement group in San Francisco. This group had a mix of clients – some were seasoned private equity groups that had been around for twenty years and were raising their fifth or sixth fund, some that were trying to get a second or third fund and some debut funds.

"We like emerging managers, but debut funds receive the most scrutiny," said Ross, the most senior guy they were meeting with. He was one of two people from the firm.

They had reached page three of their presentation, just like Benson had predicted.

"We anticipated as much," said Benson.

"But we believe we tell a credible story. We have each been in finance for ten or so years and are each Partners in our respective firms," added Ash.

"We have a well articulated game plan. We are going to focus on the types of deals where we have a cross-section of expertise," indicated Max.

"And what area is that?" asked Ross's sidekick.

"The platform build-ups…that's why we are called Negociant Capital…it was on page one," said Max, sheepishly.

Unfortunately, he sounded like a sailboat with the wind stopping. The sail came tumbling down. Ash felt it too. By the look of Benson's face, he was in no doubt a part of the dive.

"Have you guys done any deals together?" Ross asked.

"Well no," said Ash, "We have our individual expertise we are going to forge together. Combine best practices from each group."

Ross looked at Ash.

"You're the debt guy," he stated, "What private equity best practices do you know?"

We have a subtle one here, Ash thought to himself.

"Well, while the mainstay of Popular Capital's business is providing financing, there are a large number of private equity buyout transactions that we do," Ash attempted to clarify.

"Really?"

"Yes, I personally have been involved with a handful. They are indicated on our investment summary," Ash pointed out referring to the Book.

Ross reviewed that page and thumbed through the rest of it.

"I am Chairman of three companies," said Ash.

He wanted to go on to say that it was more than Benson and Max combined, but he decided not to. He didn't want it to seem as if there was any internal competition.

"Your biggest problem is going to be that you haven't worked together yet," Ross surmised, "People will worry that you guys won't be able to get along, and it will kill the performance of the fund."

"I see," said Benson.

"Most funds successful in raising money have been working together for a while," said Ross.

Thanks for stating the obvious thought Ash.

"How do we get over that hurdle?" asked Max.

"We have been friends for a very long time," indicated Ash.

"Doesn't the fact that we can bring diverse perspectives to the table help us? Isn't that a useful point of differentiation?" asked Benson.

"Not really. You really need to make yourself like other groups that have been successful."

"I thought that investors wanted some kind of differentiation, something that makes us unique. If we were exactly like other groups, it would be hard for us to craft an argument that they should invest in us, right? They could just go and invest in that other fund – why would they bother investing with us?" asked Ash.

"They do want something different, as long as it has been done before," Ross explained.

Ash looked at Benson and Max.

"So they want something different, so long as it is the same?" asked Ash.

"Exactly."

"Oh, well that clarifies everything. Thanks so much for being so elucidating," stated Ash, his sarcasm coming across like a frying pan being struck to the head.

"Er...don't mind our friend," Max apologized.

Max put up his hand towards Ash. Ash put both of his hands up to indicate that he understood and wouldn't utter another word.

"So, other than that, does it look pretty good?" asked Benson.

"No. I said that it was going to be your biggest problem. Your next problem is going to be the fact that your experience is lopsided across the three of you."

"We are all Partners," said Benson.

"Yeah, but he...what's your name...Ash is it?...he doesn't have real private equity experience."

Ash's eyebrows arched.

"Any other comments you might have?" asked Max, quickly trying to cut Ash off from saying something.

"What kind of a screwed up name did you choose?" asked Ross's assistant.

"We thank you very much for your time," said Benson, in a rushed tone.

"Hang on a second," Ash interjected.

Benson and Max had distraught looks on their faces.

"Is there anything you actually *liked*?" asked Ash.

Benson and Max gave out a collective sigh of relief.

"The book looks nice," Ross complimented.

"Thank you again for taking the time to meet with us," said Benson, in the same hurried tone he had utilized earlier.

"Yeah," said Max, "It was a pleasure meeting you both."

"Thank you," said Ash.

Ash was the first one to get out of the door.

"What the...." asked Ash when they were downstairs in the lobby.

"It's okay," said Benson.

"Yeah, so that one didn't work out. We've got others," said Max.

Ash mostly stayed quiet the rest of the trip.

"Take care, you guys," he said to them both with minimal energy.

"Hey, the next one is coming up in a week. We have to meet them in London, however," said Benson.

"Why?" asked Ash.

"Well, that's where they are based."

"Okay."

● ● ●

"Charles, I closed on that medical instrumentation company," said Ash.

"All right, congratulations," said Charles.

"It would be great now if you could begin sending over possible transactions," said Ash.

"Send them to you?" asked Charles.

"You know what, why don't you just send them to Boas directly. He is a great guy, on top of his game and really keen to work on acquisitions."

"Will do."

• • •

Ash walked into Patricia's office.

"Ash, how are you?"

She was surprised he came to see her.

"Hey, everything is fine." Ash was pensive. "Do you know what is going on with Eddie, Bob and Jason?"

She leaned in a little bit. "I hear one of their portfolio companies, Project Elba, tanked."

"Tanked?"

"Yeah, as in about to file for bankruptcy."

"Oh great," said Ash sarcastically.

This usually spelled trouble for Ash. He would need to work twice as hard now in order to get the same benefit since his deals were always mingled in with Eddie's deals to determine the office's overall performance.

"What went wrong?" asked Ash.

"I don't know, but I think one of the Operating Partners is involved."

"You mean to try and clean it up?"

"No, as in, he was the one who caused all of the problems."

"And Eddie just stood back and let it happen?"

"Well, you know him," said Patricia, "The man is spineless."

• • •

They arrived in London for their second meeting.

"Are you okay?" asked Benson.

"Oh absolutely," said Ash.

He had been feeling guilty about how visceral his reaction had been.

"I'm sorry about that, guys. I overreacted a bit."

"Hey, it's okay. They really seemed to have it in for you in that meeting," Benson observed.

"Yeah. Don't worry though. We'll raise the money and rub it in their faces," Max promised.

Max signaled a high-five for Ash. Ash felt good. He was proud and happy to be trying to get something off the ground with these guys.

"Man, my back is stiff," complained Ash as he tried to stretch himself, "I got stuck between two large people on the flight over. They don't give enough room as it is in coach."

"I got lucky, I had an empty seat next to me," said Max.

Ash and Max looked at Benson. He was looking a little embarrassed.

"How was your flight, Benson?" asked Ash.

"Uh...fine...I slept the entire way," he responded.

"Hey wait a minute," said Max, "Did you fly in first class?"

Benson nodded his head yes.

"You know you're not going to be able to do that for awhile once we launch the fund, right. You may as well get used to it," said Ash.

"What do you mean?" asked Benson.

"Well, we're not going to have a lot of cash at the beginning. We have to fly coach for a while," illustrated Max.

Benson looked sullen. "How long do you think that will be?" Benson inquired, a little nervously.

"I don't know...ten years, maybe," indicated Ash.

Benson seemed troubled.

This time they met with three guys. None of them looked older than forty. They went through their round of introductions and handed out business cards.

"So, are any of you Partners in the firm?" asked Benson.

"No. Sylvester is the closest. He's probably four or five years away," said Todd.

Oh this is great, thought Ash.

They started the presentation. They made it to page three.

"Do you guys have your bios in here?" Mark questioned.

Ash could tell from his accent that he was from the US.

"Uh, yes..." said Max who was speaking at the time, "We have it later in the presentation."

Max was about to continue.

"What page is it on?"

"Twelve."

This time Max waited.

"How come your ages aren't here?" asked Mark.

"Well, we know we are on the young side," said Benson, "So we thought it might create a knee jerk reaction against us."

"Yeah, we figured we would get people to know us a little bit and our experience before we sprang that on them," Ash added.

"You gotta have your ages in here," Mark declared. He looked at Sylvester. "They gotta have their ages in here." His attention returned to Ash, Benson and Max before reiterating, "You *gotta* have your ages in here. Hang on, let me show you."

Mark got up and left the room.

"I guess we should wait until he returns?" Ash suggested.

"Yeah, that's a good idea," said Todd.

Mark came back in the room. He had five books in his hands. They looked like the book that Ash, Benson and Max had written and the samples that Benson had shown to Ash and Max.

Mark flipped through the first one. He got to the bio page, opened it and laid it on the table in front of Ash, Benson and Max. He repeated the exercise five times. A full fifteen minutes had passed since he first asked about their ages.

"You see, everyone does it," Mark said, "After your name on the bio page comes your age in parentheses."

Ash was dying to ask him if he had another example.

"Well, we are all in our mid-thirties," said Benson.

"That's going to be your biggest problem," Sylvester surmised.

"I see," said Benson.

"We were told that our biggest problem would be that we had never worked together," quipped Ash, hoping to make light of the situation.

"Oh, that's really bad, too," Todd agreed.

"Also," asked Sylvester, "You say here that you have a combined forty-five years of private equity experience. However, haven't you been doing debt?"

He was looking at Ash.

And then Benson and Max looked at Ash.

To all of their surprise, Ash was smiling.

"Actually, I'm just a bank teller," Ash wisecracked.

"Well, thanks for the feedback, guys," said Benson, hurriedly.

"Hey, yeah, anytime," said Todd.

"We still have some time to kill, if you want to go through anything else," Mark encouraged.

"Yeah, I have a question," Ash piped up.

He could tell Benson and Max were nervous again.

"Is there any chance you would represent us?"

"Well, why don't you work for another ten years and we can take a look at it again," said Sylvester.

"Thanks," said Ash.

"What kind of things should we focus on over the next ten years?" asked Benson, "What do you look for when you look to represent a private equity fund?"

Ash was impressed with Benson thinking quickly. It's was actually a great question to be asking.

"Generally, you really need to find a way to differentiate yourself," said Sylvester.

Ash, Benson and Max nodded their heads. Max began to speak first. Ash knew it was because he wanted to cut Ash off.

"Actually, we have been hearing that a lot of investors are a little hesitant to try something new."

"Yes, that's absolutely correct," said Mark.

Ash couldn't be stopped now.

"So they want something different, so long as it is the same?"

"Exactly," said Sylvester.

"So, what did you guys do before moving to the private placement side?" asked Max, hoping to make some light conversation and steer the topic away from Ash.

"Oh," said Sylvester, "We were all at private equity funds."

"What happened? Were you all at the same one?" asked Benson.

"No. Different ones. None of them were able to raise second funds."

"Is that popular to make the switch?" Ash quizzed.

"Oh yeah, just about everyone at this firm used to be in private equity. We try to use that as our main selling point," said Sylvester.

"Fascinating," said Ash.

When they were alone together, Ash turned to Max

and Benson.

"That is so screwed up. You couldn't help yourself raise a fund when you were in private equity, and now you are going to make a career out of trying to raise money for others," laughed Ash. "Don't they see the irony in that?" he asked.

"I think they miss the irony in a lot of things," said Benson.

"Don't ever let me become one of those guys," pleaded Ash to Benson and Max.

"Don't worry, this will happen," encouraged Benson.

"Well, we are zero for two," Ash tallied.

"I know," said Max.

"We'll keep going," said Benson.

"You know, I have heard that comment before somewhere," said Max.

"Which one?" asked Benson.

"The 'so they want something different, so long as it is the same' comment," said Max.

"You probably heard it from one of your Partners," said Ash.

"No, that's not it," said Max.

"Okay. Well, next we have that meeting in New York," Ash recounted.

● ● ●

Ash continued to recount the Project Emancipate deal history for Steven.

"I had to call Boas back to inform him of the results of our going back to The Commies to try and make a deal work," Ash indicated.

"Well, I have some mixed news," Ash offered to Boas at the time.

"Okay, why don't you go through it?" suggested Boas.

"Well, the pension thing is a no go," started Ash.

He worried how Boas would react. He decided that it was best to be as honest with Boas as possible. If things didn't work out, they wouldn't work out. All he could do was try to bridge the divide in the thinking.

"I see," said Boas.

"But I have an alternative suggestion."

"I'm listening."

"Ultimately, the goal is long-term financial security. The Commies argue that pensions are for the largest of companies only and that small companies rarely have it."

Ash paused for a moment to catch his breath.

"They aren't wrong," reacted Boas, holding true to his being fair-minded.

"Yeah, it's an accurate statement. I have to give them credit," said Ash.

"But since the employees are interested in long-term financial stability, I suggested we create a very pervasive option plan that will go several layers deep into the organization. If things go well, those who had the largest of the pensions will be pretty well off."

"I have to say," started Boas, "That's a rather good way to approach it. I knew my wife was right about you."

"On the healthcare side, they agreed not to pay in full, but to pay seventy-five percent and asked that the employees pay twenty-five."

"I see," said Boas.

"Boas, you know you have full discretion on people's raises up to a limit of fifteen percent," Ash reminded him.

"Hmmmm...I see what you are getting at," said Boas.

"Yes," said Ash, "The net impact would be ten percent, which is not so severe."

"I won't lie to you. I think I can sell it."

It occurred to Ash that there was so much posturing Boas could do, so much gaming to try and cut a better deal. But he was being genuine and straightforward. Ash almost felt guilty for representing the side he did.

"And that was it," said Ash to Steven, "We funded the deal and I made Partner later that day."

CHAPTER 12

Ash met with Sophie for dinner again.

"I know that you hate talking about work, but I need some advice," she requested.

I love those 'z's thought Ash.

"Sure, go ahead," he invited.

"I am having some cash flow problems. Some corporate customers, restaurants and caterers, are taking time to pay me. I think I will apply for a loan," she told him.

"Good idea," said Ash. He thought he was done.

"But now they are asking me for a business plan."

"Makes sense."

"Can you help me with it please?"

Ash smirked. "So, all this time, you have been after me for…"

Sophie's face changed. She was about to launch into an animated protest.

"…my calculator?"

They both laughed.

"Sure, I'll help you. I hate numbers, but I'll help you."

Sophie laughed again. But Ash hadn't joined her.

"What? You're serious?" she questioned.

"Yeah. Hate numbers, hate the analytics, and gosh, I hate building financial models that go into business plans."

Sophie had a look of disbelief.

"It's tedious and it doesn't tell the story. How do you show in a business plan to some bank your passion for what you do, the inspiration from your father and grandfather? I know it serves a purpose and has its place, but people make too much of it. I'd just as well pay someone else to do it so I don't have to," Ash explained.

"But you are *un financier*!" Sophie exclaimed in protest.

Ash thought about correcting her. But that killer French accent stopped him. It sounded so noble and sophisticated when she said it.

"Say it again, what am I?"

"UH fee-NAHN-see-YAY"

"Again," Ash insisted.

She threw her napkin at him.

• • •

The transaction with Project Flow was continuing apace. Ash was finding Eddie's involvement meddlesome. What a nuisance, Ash would think to himself.

They began negotiating the finer points of the transaction.

"I'd like to use Finkel and Weinstein for the deal. I really like Peter Strumm over there," said Ash.

"No. We should use McCarthy."

"I don't like using McCarthy. That lawyer thinks he's a business guy, and he always negotiates and questions the wrong things. I like guys who are smart, aggressive and stick to what they know," Ash persisted.

Eddie shrugged his shoulders.

Several days passed.

"Eddie, I forgot to tell you, I turned the first draft of documents on Project Flow," Ash told him while he was in the hall.

"Oh, I should probably look at those," Eddie said.

"I already sent them out."

"Next time, be sure to let me look at them."

"Okay," Ash acquiesced.

You're going to make meaningless changes just to get your hands into it aren't you?, thought Ash.

"You used McCarthy, right?"

"No. I used Finkel and Weinstein."

Eddie walked away without saying another word. He moved away too quickly for Ash to get a view of where his arm was positioned.

The following morning, Ash received an e-mail from Lasi.

"Modify counsel on Project Flow to McCarthy."

How do I argue with this guy? Ash wondered.

After a week, comments came back from Ricky and Johnny's lawyer. They scheduled a conference call to go over the comments and react to them. Ash sat in the meeting.

"We see your comments on the escrow dollar amount," Joel stated, the lawyer from McCarthy, "We are okay with it."

"Uh, this is Ash. No, we are not."

"It looks reasonable to me," said Joel.

"Oh, you are going to argue with me on this? This is a business matter. And, by the way, you are my lawyer. I am paying you. You do what I tell you," instructed Ash.

"So we'll leave the escrow amount open," Joel proposed. "Next, we go to the deferred purchase price amount. We are fine with that."

"Eddie, aren't you going to say anything?" Ash pressed.

Ricky and Johnny's lawyers had changed it so that they got the deferred purchase price in one year instead of five.

Eddie looked at the document. He didn't say anything.

"Don't you think that is aggressive?" asked Ash.

"Joel, what do you think it should be?" asked Eddie.

"Why would Joel know?" Ash hissed, "We are the ones who would know because we are the ones negotiating stuff like this all of the time."

Joel stayed quiet.

Ricky and Johnny's lawyer piped up.

"Just so you guys know, we find this terribly entertaining."

Ash walked out.

Over the next few weeks, Ash let Eddie and Joel negotiate the docs. He would review them afterwards and comment to Joel accordingly. It was frustrating to let the two of them run amok with the documents, but Ash found that this created the least amount of brain damage for him.

When the deal finally closed, Joel introduced himself to Ash.

"Hey, I just wanted to clear up any hard feelings," Joel said.

"Does Eddie always let you make the decisions on business matters?" asked Ash.

"Oh yes, that's how it has always been with us."

"Care to be a Partner in a private equity firm?" prompted Ash.

"Who? Me?" asked Joel.

He had a surprised look on his face which turned into a bit more eagerness than Ash had anticipated.

"I've always thought about making the switch. Do you think I'd be good at it?" queried Joel with bountiful energy.

"I'm just kidding," said Ash in disgust.

● ● ●

Project Flow finally funded. David went to great lengths to lay out the various wires that needed to be transmitted to close the transaction. The most important wire, of course, was to get Ricky and Johnny their money. As this was a joint transaction, the deal teams were integrated. At some point, David lost the managerial oversight of the funding memo and Jason had taken it over. Eddie had forced David to relinquish control and Ash had not been around. Several hours later, it was Ash who had given the order for the wires to be initiated. He called Ricky at the time they were sent.

"It should take about two hours for the money to reach your bank," he advised them.

"Ahright, we's is gonna wait for dhat money to arrive," said Ricky.

Three hours had passed, and Ash never heard from them. He decided to give a call to them to see what was wrong.

"Is the deal closed? Can we file the change of ownership with the Secretary of State?" Ash asked.

This time it was Johnny with whom Ash spoke.

"Do what now?" asked Johnny.

"Has the money arrived?" Ash recapitulated.

"We's got some money, but it ain't da whole amount," indicated Johnny.

"How could that be?" asked Ash.

"Well it's a coupah mill'n short," declared Johnny.

There was silence on the phone.

"Uh...well," started Johnny.

"It's okay, Johnny, go ahead," encouraged Ash.

"I jus' sure do hate neg'tiatin' widh folks I like," shared Johnny.

"It's okay, I understand."

"Uh... I 'ope ya don' mind...if we don' consider the deal closed 'til we get all our money," requested Johnny, cautiously.

"That's fine. Of course," Ash assured, "I am just troubled about what happened to it."

Ash called Joel.

"There shouldn't be any problem," insisted Joel.

"I'm going to initiate a trace with the banks, to see where the money went," Ash indicated.

"Uh no, don't do that, I'll just do it from here," insisted Joel.

"Fine," agreed Ash.

The groups: Eddie, the ELVES, David, Steven and Ash had been camped out in the interim inside the conference room, trying to go through each individual wire, at Ash's insistence. Eddie kept answering his cell phone and going in and out of the room.

It took about two hours for Joel to get back to Ash.

"Well we didn't send out enough money initially, so we are going to send another wire to finalize the amount," stated Joel.

"How can that be? I spoke with James in treasury and he quoted me the right amount," said Ash.

As soon as he said that Eddie got up and as he left the room he was making a call on his phone.

"Ash, I gotta grab my other line," said Joel.

Ash hung up. He called James.

"Let's run a trace ourselves to see where the money went," requested Ash.

"Did you alter the instructions?" Ash asked Jason.

Jason's first response was a simple no. While Ash was waiting for James to call back, he asked Jason a second and third time. Jason became increasingly more agitated.

"I told you already, I didn't alter them!"

"Then how did we start with enough money, but not end with enough money?"

"I don't know." He grumbled and walked away.

Ash's cell phone rang. He thought it would be James.

"Hey bud, we's got our money. Congrats we's pardhners in biz'ness now," said Ricky.

"Thanks guys, congrats to you too. Let me call you in a while," Ash said.

"Eddie, did you approve the second wire?"

"Yes," admitted Eddie.

"My name is on this deal. It's going to look like I did that on the system."

"Well, you were busy."

"I've been standing right here," said Ash.

Ash's phone rang again. This time is was James.

"Ash, it's funny, I see the amount we sent was the full amount and I can confirm some of the accounts that they were sent to, but the bank says the instructions were changed at the last minute," indicated James.

"Thank you James."

Ash walked out of the room. He felt like he was about to complement the existing hole in the wall with another one.

● ● ●

Ash arrived at Sophie's place. It was a second floor walk-up. She lived in Manhattan Beach, walking distance to the ocean.

"Lovely place you have here," Ash commented.

"It's nothing special," she offered.

From the outside, she was right, it didn't look like much. But she had done a fabulous job with the interior. Ash felt like he was walking into a photo shoot for *Home & Garden* magazine. The rugs matched perfectly with the sofa cushions which had elements of the prints on the walls. It was tastefully and efficiently decorated. There was a modern touch to it. The sofa and dining table were set low to the floor, creating a sense of high ceilings. The legs of the sofa and the dining table had the same metallic finish. She had placed mirrors on a strategic wall that gave the impression of a space double the actual size. Ash felt very comfortable.

Sophie was putting the final touches on the meal. Ash made himself busy setting up different tasting stations of the wine he purchased. He was careful not to show her the bottles' labels. He wanted her to be surprised.

Ash handed Sophie the first glass.

"Like a Monet," she said.

"Ah yes, very true," agreed Ash, "The flavors are not really crisp. They sort of blend together in a bit of a mush." He gave her another glass.

"Oh, your hands are full," he noted.

Ash went into the kitchen, took a glass from the cupboard and filled it with water. He brought it to her and held it to her lips while she drank.

"You must clear your palate a little," he directed.

She drank from the second one. Ash did the same.

"You go first," she said, looking at him coyly.

"Van Eyck. Almost a perfect contrast to the Monet. This one has very distinct flavors to it that are well articulated." He took another sip. "It's a very precise wine."

"Right you are, *monsieur*. And I have the perfect cheese to go with this."

She brought out the cheese and fed Ash a bite from her hands.

"Now drink," she instructed him.

"Yes, you are right. A perfect pairing."

"Let's do the others after dinner," Sophie suggested.

After the meal, they sat on the sofa together. Ash brought the two bottles that he had not yet opened. They tried the first.

"This is a Van Gogh," Sophie stated.

Ash sipped it again. He rubbed his chin. He tried it once more. And then another time. He adopted a sheepish expression on his face.

"Well, I hate to admit it, but I'm at a loss to feel it," Ash said. "How do you mean a Van Gogh?"

Sophie had a devilish smile on her face.

"Did you trick me?"

Sophie's smile broke into a laugh.

Ash started shaking his head. "I can't believe you tricked me," he laughed.

Sophie turned to face Ash. She sat on his lap facing him.

"I didn't trick you," she said. "I just didn't tell you everything."

"Starry Night. By Van Gogh," revealed Sophie.

Ash smiled broadly.

"Hmmmm....I get it. A glimmer of hope," affirmed Ash.

"*Exactement.*"

Ash moved his head forward. The two kissed.

"Did you want dessert?" Sophie asked.

"No," said Ash, "But I do want you to try this last bottle. I saved the best for last."

Ash retrieved the bottle and came back to the sofa where he reassembled himself with Sophie. He had a single glass with him. She took her sip first, and then he took his. Ash set the glass down.

"Hmmm…just like I thought…," said Ash.

"…a Botticelli," said Ash, running his hands through her hair, "Subtle, delicate, beautiful."

They kissed again. This time Ash carried her off his lap and into her bedroom.

CHAPTER 13

"So, the buyers don't want to use our loans," informed Ash to The Commies. He was reporting back on the GeldXpress sale process.

"Forget it, the deal is off," Lasi vetoed.

Ash decided to stay silent for a while. Nobody else said anything.

"We would be sacrificing an over two hundred million gain because we can't put a hundred million dollars to work? I'm sorry, but I don't follow the logic there," said Ash.

"WHO DO THEY THINK THEY ARE?" demanded Lasi.

"Lasi, imagine if you were in their shoes. Wouldn't you do what is best for you? Wouldn't you look for the cheapest debt possible? When someone buys a house, they look for the lowest interest rate possible on a mortgage."

"They are changing the deal on us," Lasi huffed.

"Yes, but they have a valid reason," argued Ash.

There was a brief pause.

"Look, we either match the lower rate they are getting or we forget about providing them the loan," continued Ash.

"We can't bring the interest down," said Jake.

"Why not?" asked Ash.

"We have to borrow at a certain level. If we don't earn at least that, we can't give the money out as a loan."

"Doesn't it fluctuate the way it does for banks, so that there is always a spread of profitability?" asked Ash.

"No, we don't get the benefit of that. Ours move based on the broader market, and we have done so many of our deals with fixed rates. Hence, when interest rates go up, our profits get squeezed to almost nothing," Jake explained.

"So, wait a minute – and I realize this is off topic – if interest rates spike, we can actually lose money because we have loaned at a fixed rate?"

"Oh yeah, if interest rates spike we are screwed," Jake assured.

Oh great, thought Ash. This damn place where I am working so hard is nothing more than a house built of toothpicks – without any glue.

"We should make them pay more," piped up Lasi.

"What?" asked Ash.

"MAKE THEM PAY MORE. Now that they are getting cheaper debt, they can borrow more and pay us more," Lasi reasoned.

"A two hundred million gain is not enough for you?" asked Ash.

"We need to get even with them for altering the deal."

"I need some credible reason to ask for an increase in price. I can't just go in there and say this is our revenge deal point," resisted Ash.

Ash was getting exasperated. Under his breath, he said, "I wish you still negotiated deals. I'm sick of this ivory tower crap."

Come to think of it, thought Ash, half of The Commies had never even negotiated deals in their careers. The others had been removed from it for so long, they had become delusional in their expectations.

"So what's it going to be?" inquired Ash.

"Ask for twenty-five million more," demanded Lasi.

There was the sound of a click and the line went dead. Ash shook his head as he listened to the dial tone.

● ● ●

Ash called The Commies once again after two days.

"The buyers of GeldXpress are ready to walk away from the deal."

"Why are they being so myopic?" asked Lasi.

That's what they are asking you, Ash pretended to tell him.

"Look, I can see their point of view," Ash theorized, "I didn't think it was a particularly well founded approach."

There was silence on the other side of the line.

"Look, why don't we go back, offer a slightly lower interest rate on the debt – not to match the offer they have – but something lower. And then maybe we can make the fees lower than the bank so that it looks to them like they are getting a reasonable deal."

"FINE. Go ahead with that," said Lasi.

After two additional weeks, the deal was back on track. Ash remembered getting the call from James.

"Congrats Ash," said James.

"You have just recorded the biggest gain in Popular Capital history! We just got the wire for two hundred two million three hundred forty nine!" he exclaimed.

Ash felt more relieved than accomplished. He didn't have to deal with The Commies anymore on this transaction. Ash wondered how much of the gain he would see for himself. I hope I don't have to settle for forty-nine dollars he thought to himself and laughed.

He wouldn't even get that amount.

● ● ●

A few quarters had passed already and Ash didn't have a chance to listen to the shareholder calls. Patricia had been diligent about listening to them and she had informed Ash that they were beginning to heat up quite a bit. Lasi was getting a lot of pressure.

"We had another strong quarter where the number of deals we did was at a record pace. We put a lot of money to work. Our profits and earnings per share are in line with earlier guidance," stated Lasi.

The operator came on the phone.

"We have a question from Mr. Dennis Wilkinson of Claymore Investment Advisors."

"You guys put a lot of money to work again, beating your budget for capital invested by over fifty percent. But your profit and earnings per share remain the same. What is going on? Where is all of the increased fee income and income from interest going?"

"Thank you for your question, Dennis," said Lasi.

"Just answer it please," demanded Dennis.

"Well, we have pursued a number of initiatives to bring more services in-house. We have established an in-house accounting team, an in-house operations team and an in-house legal team..."

"So you are building an empire at the expense of the shareholders?"

"We are doing this so that we can better create value for our shareholders."

"It's good to hear that you think about that. Because all of the investments you have made have either been flat or they have declined in value. None of them have increased in value the way you have been promising. And I don't see how these in-house teams are going to help you create that value," specified Dennis.

"We did have the example of the sale of GeldXpress. That provided us with an over $200 million gain," Lasi pointed out.

Oh great thought Ash. *Glad that my hard work helps you out.*

"Yes, but then you offset losses at six other investments against that. You were at a net $0," pointed out Dennis.

How very communist of you Ash thought to himself. No wonder I never got paid any money. Why was that fair? Why should I be carrying other people for their mistakes? I could understand that if I had a vote, or a say, in whether those investments were made, then yes, I would have to shoulder some responsibility. But all of these decisions were handed down. This felt very unfair to Ash.

"Well, the operations team will review ways to increase value at each portfolio company and..."

"How can you say that and not laugh at yourself? What kind of private equity are you practicing over there? You have one hundred investments and six operations guys. That's over sixteen companies per person. What are they going to do, spend two-and-a-half hours a week with each one? How are they going to get anything done? I suspect you are only using them to review new deals, so you can avoid the landmines you have stepped into in the past."

"Our portfolio has been steady and strong. I ASSURE YOU, we work hard to align our interests with management teams. They think of us as their partners. They respect us because we look out for them. We all aspire to get rich together."

"Yeah, you can't BS the numbers. How's Project Elba doing?"

Ash was stunned. Did everyone know about this except for him?

"We have that situation under control. Operator, next question please," requested Lasi.

The operator came back on the line, "We have a question from Mr. Ray Snyder of Robinson Capital."

"You don't seem to pay your employees very much. Aren't you afraid that they will leave?"

"NO. That is a situation I DEFINITELY have under control," Lasi avowed with authority.

"Would you care to elaborate?"

"LOOK, my job is to ensure I get the employees to work the hardest possible while paying them the least amount possible."

Lucky us, thought Ash.

"So people won't leave?"

"Those who do leave are expendable."

"I hope none of them are listening to you now," said Ray.

That day, the stock market punished Popular Capital fifteen percent.

• • •

Ash hadn't seen Sophie in weeks. He had been traveling extensively. He apologized profusely to her. She maintained her sullen mood.

"I know I was supposed to help you out," admitted a sheepish Ash.

"It's okay," muttered Sophie.

"Things are getting really crazy at work. I am actually getting quite sick of it," Ash declared.

"Why don't you just leave if you hate it so much?" Sophie prodded, trying to understand.

They sat on her couch in her apartment. His head lay in her lap. They were enjoying a nice Pomerol.

"It's just a matter of time," explained Ash.

"Once we get Negociant off the ground, things will be much better," Ash assured.

"My clever little *financier*," Sophie cooed as she ran her hands through Ash's hair.

It's true, thought Ash. Nobody knows what I do for a living. And then another thought occurred to him.

"Remind me to tell you more precisely what I do. I don't think I've done a good job of explaining it."

She bent down. The two kissed.

• • •

Ash approached Eddie in his office.

"I asked three people with whom she has interacted," he told Eddie.

"None of them have indicated the same as Jason."

"Hmm..." said Eddie.

"What has the result been of your inquries?" Ash probed.

"Well...." said Eddie.

"Come on," said Ash, "I bet they couldn't substantiate it either."

Eddie didn't respond.   Ash didn't need him to.

"I think we ought to take disciplinary action against Jason."

Eddie didn't react.

"This needs to become a part of his review," Ash pointed out.

Eddie shrugged his shoulders.

Ash walked out of his office.

● ● ●

"You're not comparing apples to apples."

Ah yes, thought Ash. The hackneyed phrase employed by people in finance. Ash wondered how fruit became the convention.

"Why do they keep saying that?" asked David.

"Well, David, the phrase typically means one of two things. One, you have genuinely tried to compare two different beasts. This usage is rare. More often than not it means the speaker doesn't understand what you are saying because you are relying on a finance or accounting concept that is way over his or her head, they refuse to acknowledge that and instead try to make you look bad," explained Ash.

"You're just not comparing apples to apples," insisted Ted.

"Right now, we are getting a bowlful of the latter," said Ash.

Ash put the phone on mute again, getting tired of

hearing The Commies' voices.

"There are a handful of other terms, 'at the end of the day', 'net net', 'cut and dried', etc.," explained Ash.

"Those meanings are pretty obvious," sensed David.

"Yes. You can't go a day in our business without hearing one of these phrases thrown around."

• • •

Ash arrived in New York for their third meeting. His heart was heavy at this point. He was finding it difficult to temper his reaction in the meetings. He had such a strong desire to realize the dream of launching a private equity fund. If it didn't come through, he was nervous now, he didn't know what he was going to do.

They ended up meeting with the founder of the firm.

"It's really great you are taking the time to meet with us," said Ash.

"Yes, we really appreciate it," said Benson.

Max hadn't arrived yet. Ash and Benson knew they had to stall for time.

"Well it's my pleasure," said Dylan, "You have a really fascinating story and an interesting mix of talents."

"I apologize for our friend being tardy," said Benson.

"It's no problem. It's not even two pm yet."

"So which one of you had the idea first?" asked Dylan.

"Well, that was me," said Ash.

"How'd you come up with the idea?"

Dylan seemed really gregarious. He was in his mid-sixties. He showed a genuine interest in them and their story. It was almost paternal how he interacted with them. It put Ash at ease. He began to feel hopeful that maybe they could pull this off.

"Well, it was actually suggested to me by two founders who started a company we bought recently," said Ash, "They would like to be investors as well."

"Was that Popular's first business they bought?"

"No," said Ash pausing out of surprise, "They have done several."

Oh brother, here we go again, thought Ash.

"Have they really? That's great. I have a friend over there. Jake Roberts. He told me a while ago that Popular was going to try and do more typical private equity buyouts."

Oh no, thought Ash. Jake was one of The Commies.

"They wanted to raise a fund through us, but it wasn't going to work. Doesn't your founder have a communist background or something?"

"Something like that," Ash admitted.

Boy, *his* past is making me look bad. How do I defend myself now? Ash thought.

"Yeah, don't kid yourself, guys, pedigree is super-important to these investors. They don't like stuff like that. That's why we could never raise a fund for them," he said.

Benson and Ash listened intently. Ash felt spooked. He thought it was odd that he was, in a strange way, following Lasi's tracks.

"It's probably as bad as running for office," he said.

Max finally arrived. He came into the room.

"Dylan, this is our third Partner, Max."

Dylan remained seated and extended his hand in what seemed like a lackadaisical manner.

There was an awkward silence as Max sat down when Dylan didn't say a word to him. Dylan began turning pages in their book.

"So you were saying about pedigree, Dylan," Ash attempted to resume the conversation.

"I guess I didn't read through the bios fully," said Dylan.

"Your last name is Chu?" He looked at Max.

"Yes," said Max, "Do you know my father?"

"Should I?" asked Dylan.

"Oh," said Max, "I thought maybe you recognized my name."

Ash was taken aback too. What happened to happy, father-like Dylan?

"Look, fellas, you have a nice background, you've done well in your investments, you even have some diversity in that you have some debt lending experience," Dylan recapped motioning towards Ash, "But if it's just the three of you, I don't think it's going to fly."

"I don't understand," said Ash. He thought to just let the debt comment go.

Dylan took a deep breath.

"Think about the most successful private equity funds. The ones you admire the most. Even consider the entire universe of private equity funds."

They all began nodding their heads.

"How many have an all Asian set of Partners?"

The simplicity with which he said it mirrored the simplicity of the sentiment. All three sat speechless, motionless and without emotion as they absorbed the comment. None of them had thought about this.

"Remember what I said, it's like running for office."

They continued to grapple with what he was saying.

"Look, having some of the Partners be of Asian ancestry is fine and is even looked upon favorably with all of the deal work through outsourcing involving India or China. I just don't see how this configuration will fly."

Ash, Benson and Max were lost in their thoughts. They hadn't expected this.

"Listen guys, don't be so sullen. This is a progression. Thirty years ago, your fathers could never have been the heads of leading consulting firms or investment banks the way your peers with a similar ethnic background are today."

"If you guys had built your track record in Asia, I could find you three hundred million there."

"Compare it to politics. Could you imagine an Indian-American or Chinese-American President? Members of Congress sure, maybe even a Senator or Governor, but the time isn't right yet for a President."

"Have heart, guys. Your kids will be well positioned."

"What if we found someone with the 'right profile' to join us?" asked Benson, "What should we be focused on in order to try to be successful?"

"What you need is a way to differentiate yourself," said Dylan.

Ash, Benson and Max looked at each other.

"Let me guess," said Max, "While being the same as others?"

"Exactly."

It was a quiet ride in the elevator down to the lobby floor. Each thought about their lives, what this endeavor had meant, but most importantly, all had the quintessential question on their minds – where do we go from here?

"You guys wanna grab a drink?" Ash suggested.

They walked into the nearest bar they could find. It was in the lobby of a hotel.

Ash ordered a martini with Benson and Max following suit.

"Can I also look at your wine list?" asked Ash.

"Is it that bad?" asked Benson.

"Are you gonna double-fist it?" asked Max.

"No," laughed Ash, "I just like to see what they have."

The laughter helped break the tension.

"So, I figured out where I heard that comment before," said Max.

"Which one? The 'something different so long as it is the same' comment?" asked Ash.

"Yeah," said Max.

"I dated a screenwriter for a while. She would always say that in thinking of ideas, she wanted to follow the adage of Samuel Goldwyn from MGM, you know Metro-Goldwyn-Meyer. He would always say – 'give me the same thing – only different,'" retold Max.

"So when they find a formula that works, they hate to change it or take a risk on something new," said Benson.

"That's great for us," said Ash sarcastically.

"Ok, where do we go from here, guys?" asked Benson.

"Before I respond, I'd just like thank you on behalf of myself and Benson, for not referring to us as 'mates'," said Ash.

They all laughed. Again.

"Guys, I think I bring you down," Ash noted.

Benson and Max turned to face Ash.

"No way," Max denied.

"Yeah, forget those guys. They'll eventually figure it out," said Benson.

"No," said Ash, "You guys have a great background. You don't need me. If you guys want to find one or two guys with the right *profile* and no debt experience staining their backgrounds to give this thing a go, I won't be hurt or offended. Seriously, if you guys have a chance, I'd want you to go for it."

"It's not going to happen," Max stated.

"Not for me," said Benson.

They each raised their respective glass and said cheers.

"I guess it's back to the status quo," said Max.

"Yeah," said Benson, blowing out a deep sigh.

Ash was silent.

"Are you all right?' asked Max.

"I'm not sure," said Ash.

After a few seconds pause, he added, "Let's order another round."

The crowd was beginning to fill in around them. They were managing their umbrellas and overcoats. One man bumped into Max with his soaking wet bag, leaving water droplets on Max's suit.

Gradually, the conversation regarding work, their careers and their future ceased. They talked about their other goings-on in their lives. Ash reflected on how much he had enjoyed this endeavor, chasing after a dream with two guys he admired. It had been a real pleasure. He didn't like thinking about the status quo. He preferred to think about Sophie.

Max looked agitated after a while.

"You guys?"

"Yes, Max," said Ash.

"Are you all right?" asked Benson.

"Yeah, I just feel like I need to let you know something."

Ash wondered if he was about to come out of the closet.

"The thought of working with you guys was the most exciting part of this project," he said. He was silent for a few seconds.

"That was the thrill for me as well," Ash agreed.

"Yeah, that's what got us all jazzed up," added Benson.

"No, there's more...." He looked really uncomfortable. "The only reason I am sad that this didn't work out is because we won't be working together. Otherwise...." He took a deep breath. "...I'm actually a bit relieved it didn't work out."

Ash was stunned to hear this.

Max looked at Ash.

"It's just that launching this fund was more about me trying to fulfill my father's dreams, not necessarily mine."

Suddenly, Ash understood.

"I was doing it more to get his approval." Max let the comment sink in. "I am actually really happy where I am right now. I'm not so sure that I want to change it."

Ash could understand what his friend was telling him. Now that he said it, it actually made a lot of sense for Max.

"I'm sorry, guys," he said.

"Don't be," said Ash, "You gave it a try, we tried to make it work and look what we've discovered."

"I suppose I have a confession too," said Benson.

Are *you* coming out of the closet?

"I mostly did this because I am burned out," he said.

Ash had to reflect. That made sense as well.

"I'm so sick of going back and forth between LA and Europe three or four times a month. All of the time on an airplane is killing me. I need a change, some kind of change," Benson said.

He was sporting a goofy smile, "I also wasn't looking forward to the idea of not being about to fly first class."

They all laughed together. What made the comment really funny was the fact that they all knew how honest Benson was being. When the laughter stopped, the three were lost in their thoughts for a while.

"Truthfully, I thought this would be what I want, but now I am not so sure," Benson added in a more serious tone. "I don't know exactly what I want yet, but it is something different."

Ash couldn't help but feel the same way.

"I suppose we owe it to ourselves to figure that out," said Ash.

The three of them were consumed by their thoughts for an even longer while.

After a few hours, they made their way outside. The rain had been replaced with a slight mist, an infant fog. They walked through it, making their way to their hotel.

● ● ●

Patricia called Ash on his cell phone.

"How's it going," asked Ash.

"Badly," she responded, "I just found out that the money that was supposed to go to Project Flow went to Project Elba instead."

Ash was trying to recall the situation, "So that second funding that they did was extra, to cover up that the money went elsewhere in the first place."

"Uh-huh," affirmed Patricia.

That's why Eddie insisted we use Joel, the lawyer from McCarthy Ash realized.

"How did you find this out," asked Ash.

"Because they are trying to scramble for more money. Eddie, Jason and Bob are on the phone now with The Commies."

Ash was silent for a while. He understood now why Eddie wanted him to think Patricia was a liar.

"Ash?"

"Yeah"

"You know that the system records show that you approved the second wire, right?"

CHAPTER 14

Ash drove straight to Sophie's place from the airport.

"You let too much time pass before you see me again. Don't you miss me?" Sophie questioned after he took his coat off.

She knew just how to be irresistible.

"The dream is over," Ash said after he opened a bottle of wine and sat down with her on the couch.

Ash appreciated how she refrained from any other comments about not seeing her enough or her business the rest of the evening. She just doted on him. It was just the nurturing that Ash needed.

• • •

All Partners from Popular Capital got together for their annual off-site in Hawaii. Ash thought it was a bit ironic how they would complain constantly about not having money to pay junior people, but they could spend on an extravagant off-site for the Partners. Although he was a Partner, he had little say in how money could be allocated.

Ash had been looking forward to the event. He thought it was going to be a victory lap for him. Plenty of "attaboys," high-fives and slaps on the back. He had just earned the firm its highest gain on an investment. Ash had invested forty million of the firm's money and returned over two hundred million.

During the kick-off dinner, there were a number of people recognized.

"And our award for the highest fee earner, goes to

Walt Tilghman of our Dallas office," said Lasi.Everyone clapped.

"Our award for the largest deal size goes to Doug Weitz of our New York office," indicated Lasi.

Everyone applauded yet again.

"And now our award for the largest gain in our firm's history. This is what we work towards everyday that we do deals, everybody. We look for that smart investment, we work it hard and when we sell we hope to win big. This year we sold GeldXpress. It was a banner transaction. Eddie Cache from our LA office, come on up and get your award!" said Lasi.

Did Ash hear that correctly? He had to re-play the words in his mind. People began to stand all around him and clap voraciously. Ash felt each clap. Each sound of two hands coming together was a slap on Ash's face. They were standing, no less. This was a deal that Ash had conceived, fought the resistance to complete, had spent hours fostering a relationship with management and now Eddie, of all people, was going to take credit?

People around him started to chant "speech, speech, speech." Ash looked on in amazement. It felt like an out of body experience. He didn't feel like he was there. It felt like he was watching the events unfold as if it was a movie he was watching on the screen.

People were high-fiving Eddie. They were slapping him on the back. He took the microphone. Ash noticed how he held it with his left hand. His right hand was where it typically was, tight-fisted, parallel to the ground. If there was a sling there, Ash thought, he just might have used it to strangle Eddie.

"Thank you to everyone. You know I couldn't have done this without the help of..."

Are you kidding me? Ash mouthed. The last thing Ash wanted was to be recognized in this pejorative fashion.

Ash began walking towards the door.

"…everyone in the LA office."

Ash walked even faster.

● ● ●

He found a bar that was a bit isolated.

"Can I take a look at your wine list?" After scanning it, he said, "I'll try the 2000 Haut-Medoc from the list."

"Glass?"

"Bottle."

He reached for his cell phone. He called Sophie.

● ● ●

The next day, it was tough for Ash to get out of bed. He made it down to the sessions, however. The first person he saw in walking to the conference room was Eddie.

"Hey, Ash, we missed you last night."

"Did you?"

"What happened to you?"

Ash looked at Eddie for a few seconds. Ash's disbelief precluded him from saying anything. He then kept walking.

They began their discussion of best practices in the amphitheatre. Ash noticed how just about everyone had their laptops open and was banging away on their keyboards.

"Always speak to your portfolio company Presidents three to four times a week," said Lasi. "It is important for them to know that you are always there, watching over their shoulders."

"The last thing you want them to feel is any sense of leeway or deviation from the set plan," said Henry.

"Also, call them at odd hours of the day. Make it seem like you are always working so they should be too," Lasi added.

"I call each of my Presidents of my portfolio companies at 5:30 in the morning on their mobile phones. I then go back to sleep," said one of the Partners from San Francisco.

"I call them at 10 pm at night," said the Partner from Chicago.

"The best is when they don't answer. Call them in the office the following day and give them a hard time," said another Partner.

"The best is actually when they say that they are with their family. And they use that tone as if they want to get off the phone and they try to make us feel guilty for violating the sanctity of their personal time. I always get a kick out of that one. I just bulldoze right through it like I didn't hear a thing," another Partner countered.

"A few other ideas," said Lasi. "Never give them a raise unless they ask for it, when they say they are going on vacation, seem really disappointed and let down by it. Make them feel guilty for not thinking of the business twenty-four hours a day seven days a week," he added.

Ash left to go to the bathroom. It's a shame it's so early he thought to himself, that bar had a nice 2003 Graves that had caught his eye. Ash walked about for a few minutes. He then went back into the room.

There was a debate about not sweating the details and trying to focus on the *material* issues of a transaction.

"I think it is always good to keep an eye on expenses," Eddie opined to the group.

The hair on the back of Ash's neck stood at attention just by hearing the sound of Eddie's voice.

"Like keeping a nonfunctional clock up for three years?" confronted Ash.

Ash heard stirring from the other Partners. Eddie didn't comment back. Ash didn't want to come across as childish, so he modified his approach slightly.

"Well, I don't find that material," Ash refuted.

Ash thought he heard a gasp from the crowd.

"Well, what you find is material may not be what I find to be material," attempted Eddie.

Ash couldn't help himself.

"I think that is immaterial."

Several people laughed. Eddie didn't know how to respond. It should have made Ash feel a little guilty, but today it did not.

"How about some other best practices?" Lasi asked, making it clear he was trying to set the direction of the conversation.

"When you travel for portfolio company business, always charge them twenty-five percent more than the price of your travel," said another Partner, "That way you can start accumulating a bit of a slush fund for your office."

"Wait, how does that work?" asked another Partner.

The first Partner turned to face him.

"Let's say your first-class ticket to Europe costs $10,000. Charge them $12,500 and set aside the difference. You can use for anything you want."

"I have a question," Ash raised, trying to get to more serious matters, "How do we do a better job of retaining our employees and in attracting new talent?"

He was getting a little tired of the whole exercise of everyone passing around their cheat sheet.

"Don't worry about them," said Lasi, "The junior people are expendable. We get thousands of resumes a week from guys who are so desperate to get a job that they will do anything."

There it was, encapsulated in their pearls of wisdom, "capture naïve guys."

Ash looked at his watch. Twenty-nine hours of torture left. It felt like a prison-sentence.

"Another best practice that I'd like to discuss has to do with looking for add-on acquisitions," Lasi said.

"The key here is looking for synergies. And by that we mean mostly headcount reductions. How many people can be laid off by bringing these companies together? You will end up with huge cost savings that will help drive the returns on our investment."

"Let's keep going down the list, if there aren't any questions," he suggested.

"Next topic is outsourcing. This is a dirty word in the US, but, boy, does it save us bundles. I mean think about it, no Environmental Protection Agency, no Occupational and Safety Hazard Agency, no Child Labor Laws. It's America in the 1920s! It's great!"

I'm not sure Karl Marx would agree with you, Lasi thought Ash.

"Another best practice we are going to start to roll out is the consolidation of our insurance purchases for health insurance, life insurance, business insurance, worker's compensation, whatever it is, so that we can get more competitive rates."

Lasi looked at Ash while he spoke.

Does he know I have checked out of this mentally? Ash wondered. I really need to step out. He got up and went to the bathroom. He took another walk. And then he proceeded to pass time by pacing in the hallway. He started out with his arms folded, stroking his neck and then he rubbed his chin.

Lasi was leaving the amphitheater when he saw Ash there.

"Ash, I wanted to talk to you," he said.

Ash couldn't help but roll his eyes.

"Yes?"

"We really need to get into the swing of using our Operating Partners," Lasi said.

"I thought they were creating problems at our portfolio companies," responded Ash.

Lasi crossed his arms.

"Isn't that the reason why Project Elba is having

problems?"

"You don't know anything about that, UNDERSTAND?" Lasi insisted.

"I don't?" tested Ash.

"YOU DO NOT," Lasi persevered.

Suddenly Lasi changed his demeanor.

"Look, we have a few more Operating Partners joining, including a guy from a snack company," Lasi indicated.

"I thought we could use him at Capricorn," he added.

Oh-no, why is he after all of my well running portfolio companies?

"You know, that Company is running really well with a highly capable management team. Maybe we ought to leave well enough alone."

"Why stop there? Let's maximize our value. That's what we should focus on."

"Shouldn't we try to use them in places where help is actually needed?"

"Sure, absolutely."

Lasi remained standing there. Ash decided to remain quiet and just look at Lasi. Ash was curious how long they could go like that.

"Deal?" inquired Lasi.

"That's fine," conceded Ash.

"Great, we'll get Phil Short on the Board at Capricorn," determined Lasi.

"On the Board? Why does he have to be on the Board?"

"Just a formality. Make him feel good. You'll still be Chairman, so don't worry," said Lasi.

"You know, it's specifically when you tell me not to worry that I actually worry," retorted Ash. Ash thought for a few seconds. "How do you know this guy, Phil?"

"Oh, we go way back," said Lasi, "I've known him

for decades."

"What exactly did he do at the snack company?"

"He was in Operations."

Why is he being so elusive? thought Ash.

• • •

Ash walked into his office and was surprised to see Lasi.

"Hello, Lasi, I wasn't expecting to see you here," said Ash.

Ash shook Lasi's hand vigorously.

"Well, I had some meetings with shareholders out here, and I thought I'd swing by to say hello."

"Great. How'd your meetings go?"

"They went well."

"Can you and I talk?" asked Lasi.

"Sure."

"I think we have been treating you unfairly," said Lasi.

Ash felt like he needed to bang his own head in order to wake up.

"Uh-huh," Ash muttered.

"I know you have been concerned about your compensation," said Lasi.

"That's one way to put it," Ash responded, being very tentative.

It's probably the most stupid way, Ash thought. I have been bitching and moaning about it for years. This is beyond concern.

"We're prepared to offer you a handsome seven figure package."

Ash was floored. Could it be? Might he make as much as Max and Benson?

And then Ash understood.

"Did Jake hear from Dylan?" Ash asked.

"Yes."

Damn, cursed Ash. Everybody is lousy. Ash decided to remain quiet. He always knew this might be a risk. He would face the music. Although, the way Lasi was talking, it didn't seem like he was laying the groundwork for letting him go.

"It's okay, we all make mistakes," said Lasi.

Yeah, but my mistake was coming to work for you in the first place, thought Ash.

"We are willing to turn a blind eye," Lasi smiled as he spoke.

I don't think I like him this smarmy, thought Ash. No, actually, it's just that I don't like him at all.

"How come I never got paid for the sale of GeldXpress?" asked Ash.

"Now look, I'm not being petty, I don't think you should be either," Lasi suggested.

It must be easy not to be petty when I made you over $200 million richer and you control every penny of it thought Ash.

"We are just going to need you to do a few things for us," Lasi offered his compromise.

Oh, here it comes, Ash braced himself.

"Like additional portfolio companies?" Ash asked.

"Something like that. Eddie will keep you informed and approach you at the right time," Lasi said.

Eddie? Something really didn't feel right about that. I wonder how he has hidden his horns, thought Ash.

"And let me guess, there will be consequences if I don't follow through?" asked Ash.

"Let's not talk about unpleasant outcomes."

"No. Let's."

Lasi smiled. It was creepy, felt Ash.

"We may even have a place for you as head of our Asian operations," hinted Lasi.

Are you sure I'm the right guy? Don't you think Eddie

would be thrilled to do it? Ash thought to himself.

"What Asian operations? Popular has no presence in Asia right now," Ash pointed out.

"I have to go now. Remember, seven figures."

CHAPTER 15

Boas called Ash.

"I haven't heard from you in a while," indicated Boas.

"I'm sorry. I've been meaning to stay in touch, but things have been chaotic for me," Ash explained.

"I understand. I won't take up much of your time. I got a call from Barbara Landers at Popular Capital headquarters. Said she wanted the contact of our health insurance. Anything for me to worry about?" asked Boas.

"Not sure," replied Ash, "let me get back to you."

Ash asked Eddie about why headquarters was enquiring about health insurance.

"Oh, they are trying to see if they can consolidate health and other insurance across all of our portfolio companies so that we get the cheapest rates," Eddie explained, "we went over that at the off-site, don't you remember?"

"I've been trying to do my best to forget the off-site," Ash retorted.

He surprised even himself with that comment. He felt relieved to not just relegate his true feelings to inner monologue. What a stress relief to get it out.

Ash explained to Boas what was happening.

"Oh, okay," said Boas.

It sounded like Boas was going to hang up.

"Boas?"

"Yeah?"

"Do you think I should stay at Popular?"

"Well don't leave now, with whom am I going to relate?"

"You're right," said Ash, "people like you are the reason to stay."

Ash sent an e-mail to Lasi.

● ● ●

Often times transactions that Ash and Eddie were reviewing would come from investment banks. Investment banks would be hired by companies to, among other things, run a sales process for the business. This was the mergers and acquisitions activity that Ash became effective at describing while interviewing and only began to understand once he had gotten the job.

Eddie had gone about town telling all of the major investment banks to send all the deals to him. Initially, it didn't bother Ash so much. Ash had always been busy with his existing portfolio and in proactively soliciting deals, which he found more engaging and, he had to admit, more fun. In many instances, Ash had a chance to avoid auctions and bidding wars that were the hallmark of working with investment banks, thereby side-stepping an artificial raising of the purchase price.

In one instance, the investment banker presenting a deal was his good friend Warren Stolsky. Warren ensured Ash saw the information memorandum or the "Book" directly. The Partners at Warren's firm insisted on sending directly to Eddie, as per stated instructions. Hence, both Eddie and Ash ended up with a Book. Now there was a question of which one of them would pursue it.

On the very next nationwide Monday morning call, although he was having trouble opening his reluctant eyes at seven in the morning, Ash noticed Eddie had entered it onto a list of deals that Lasi used to monitor everyone's activities. He had called it Project Retro. Eddie had only put his own initials on the list.

"Why don't I take the lead on this?" offered Ash, later that Monday when both were in the office.

"No, it's okay," said Eddie.

Is that all you have to say? thought Ash. Ash would have expected some further explanation, some faint detail of why that made sense, some rationalization for approaching it that way, even if it were false.

"Well, I have this friend at the investment bank that presented the deal. We get along well. I think he can be helpful to us if we decide to pursue the deal," explained Ash.

"Okay, good," said Eddie.

Eddie looked back down at his computer screen. Ash deliberately waited several seconds, standing there, awaiting some kind of different approach or further explanation. It never came.

"I'm going to add my initials to the list as well," declared Ash, "that way I'll be kept in the loop and I can help you along the way."

Eddie was silent. Ash walked away.

Popular placed its initial indication of interest and the price range it was willing to pay for the company.

Warren called Ash, "You guys are embarrassingly low in your valuation. We can't get you a meeting with the Company."

Ash rolled his eyes. He and Eddie had argued about this. Ash indicated Eddie's range wouldn't allow them to get to the next round. Eddie insisted. Ash decided he didn't love the company enough to fight for it.

"Between you and me," offered Warren, "if you still want in, I can accept another range from you."

"I really appreciate that," Ash confessed, "I'd like to go with my initial valuation range. I will e-mail you a revised proposal letter."

"I look forward to getting it."

"And, Warren, thanks again. I know that you are

under no obligation to do this for us."

"No worries."

Ash augmented the letter and sent it over to Warren. Warren e-mailed back saying they had made it to the next round.

Ash felt like he should inform Eddie. Part of him felt like being devilish and not letting him know. Ultimately, however, he didn't think it was the best, or the most fair, approach.

Eddie wasn't in the office. Ash sent him an e-mail asking Eddie to call him as soon as it was convenient.

Days passed, Ash had never heard back and the two were not in the office at the same time for the rest of the week.

On the following Monday, Lasi prompted Eddie about Project Retro.

"We haven't heard anything," proclaimed Eddie.

"Yes, we have," Ash corrected.

"Go ahead, Ash," said Lasi.

"We had to up the bidding slightly. It's more in line with where comparable companies have been selling. We are still in a comfortable range where the numbers pan out well. We have been invited to the next round."

"Great. Good work," congratulated Lasi.

Ash hated that he liked receiving that praise. It made him feel shallow and vapid. But boy did he love it. He didn't want it to end. He tried to come up with something else to say where he would get another positive stroke, but he couldn't come up with anything in time.

When Ash got to the office, Eddie sent him an e-mail. It indicated there would be an office meeting starting in forty-five minutes, once all of the junior people had arrived.

Ash wondered to himself why he just couldn't have opened his mouth. *I just passed by your open office door thirty seconds earlier, saying good morning.*

Ash surveyed the pathetic clock when he entered the conference room. It's still seven thirty-three pm in Los Angeles.

In the meeting, Eddie accosted Ash. He did it Eddie-style. He had his computer open, and he pretended to be doing something with it.

"Why did you proceed on Project Retro without me?" he asked without even looking up.

"Eddie, the banker called, I tried reaching you and you never responded."

Eddie pretended to be half-listening to Ash's response. Ash stood there and stared at him. He didn't budge. He was getting increasingly more agitated with Eddie. After several minutes, Eddie finally looked up.

"Are we good?" asked Ash.

"Yeah…I guess…"

"The meeting is next Thursday. We should decide whom we are going to have at…," indicated Ash.

Before Ash could even complete his sentence, Eddie cut him off.

"We need Jason and Bob there."

Bob high-fived Jason.

"Do we need both of them?" asked Ash.

"Yeah…" Eddie confirmed.

"Why, what's your problem?" asked Bob.

"Why don't you tell me yours first?" challenged Ash.

Bob squirmed in his seat. He exchanged a glance with Eddie. He stayed quiet.

"No?" asked Ash, looking at Bob, "Then you don't get to hear mine either."

Ash turned back to the group.

"I'm bringing David…."

"Of course," mumbled Jason.

Ash chose to ignore him.

"…and Steven."

"That's a lot of people," said Eddie.

"Yes it is," said Ash, without looking up from his pad.

The meeting took place at Warren's firm's offices. The six from Popular walked in and there were introductions with the management team.

Eddie quickly sat down and opened his computer.

"How was the flight in?" asked Ash of the President.

"Oh it was okay, not too bad," he responded.

The President looked at Eddie and then at Ash. He looked down at the business cards he had in his hand, shuffled through them quickly, paused for a few seconds when he had arrived at the card he was seeking and then stuffed all of them back into his pocket.

"How long have you lived in LA?" he asked.

And the light conversational banter continued.

Warren initiated the meeting. Bob had not yet arrived. Jason sat down and opened his computer as well. Ash, David and Steven sat with only the presentations that Warren had passed out in front of them.

When the President got to page three of his presentation, Bob stumbled into the room. He made a lot of noise as he sat down. Ash watched Eddie. He didn't even acknowledge Bob's entering the room. The President and the rest of the management team looked at Bob and looked at each other. They then looked at Warren.

"Sorry to interrupt," Ash said to the President, "This is another member of our team, Bob."

The President brought around his business card to Bob. He lingered a few moments to receive the reciprocating gesture, but Bob kept fumbling with his laptop and bag. After a few seconds had passed, the President walked back to the front and continued.

Bob opened his computer. The President continued. He didn't have the most engaging voice. Ash had to get up to take some coffee. The President's voice with the three of them – Eddie, Jason and Bob – typing away on their computers made for a sleep-inducing environment.

Ash noticed how as the President spoke, he would look at their side of the table, make eye contact with Ash, look over to the computers and look back at his board. He did this numerous times.

"We showed some more detail in the book we sent you that we don't have here in the slideshow," the President amended as he worked his way through his presentation.

Steven opened his laptop at that point. Ash looked over and saw it was an electronic version of the book they had received from Warren he loaded up onto his screen. Ash wrote something on a piece of paper and passed it to Steven.

"Turn it off and put it away. You can review the book back at the office."

Steven quickly did it. Ash noticed a smile on the President's face.

After another forty-five minutes of keeping the volume of his voice above the racket of the machine-gun typing that Eddie and his ELVES were engaged in, Ash could detect the President was getting more and more agitated. It was becoming a contest, a virtual test of wills. The sound of the keys being struck was a deterrent, a barrier, almost as if stones were being thrown at the President. Eddie and the ELVES were a resistance force not allowing the President access.

After continuing to watch the President's discomfort, Ash sat there and stroked his neck.

"I'm sorry to interrupt you again," said Ash, "But maybe we can take a restroom break."

He saw the noticeable look of relief on the President's face.

"Eddie, I don't think the President is enjoying all of your typing. Maybe you guys could close your computers for the rest of the meeting."

Eddie shrugged his shoulders.

Ash stood motionless for several minutes. He then sat down. He felt like he needed to apologize to the President. *I am sorry that my colleague is such a brute; please forgive him. I'm not sure where my colleagues' manners are, please don't let it bother you. Eddie wasn't loved enough as a child, spent all his time in front of video games, you know the type.* That was odd, though, thought Ash. Why should I be sorry for Eddie?

They continued the meeting. The President's tone, as much as it was in a military zone, was sounding more and more like a lullaby.

"What could possibly be so important?" snapped the President.

Ash was shocked back into the situation. Did the President just shout "*CLEAR!*" Ash's thoughts had wandered a bit.

"Why do you have to do that now?" he demanded.

He was now waving a finger at Eddie and the ELVES. Warren stood up.

"Perhaps it's time for another break," Warren suggested.

"Look, I'm sorry," said the President emphatically, with a deep intake of air, "I didn't mean to lose control. I'm sorry."

He nodded his head in the direction of Eddie and punctuated a nod towards Ash with a tiny smile and proceeded to sit down. Warren brought the President water.

"Why don't we jump forward to the financials and then come back to this?" Ash suggested. Ash knew the Chief Financial Officer would deliver that part of the presentation, and it would give the President a chance to rest.

Ash looked over to Eddie, but Eddie refused to make eye contact. He also refused to put his computer away. He kept his laptop open, brining the screen down to a forty-five degree angle or so. He let his arms dangle by the side of his chair. The ELVES followed suit.

When the management team finished their presentation after another hour, Warren stood up.

"Perhaps you could spend a few minutes talking about your firm's background and a little bit about the types of deals you look for," Warren suggested.

Ash was about to start, but Eddie cut him off.

"Well, we have a pretty comprehensive website, so check that out at www.popularcapital.com."

Ash was shocked with what he was hearing. This was the chance to make your firm stand out as a potential suitor. *We are competing to buy this Company Eddie*, thought Ash. *You know, we need to make a good impression to get a date.* Ash wondered if this was how Eddie attempted to get a girl to go to the high school prom with him. Ash thought of a young Eddie with a nasal voice saying over the telephone – 'well you can see my yearbook photo' when a girl indicated she didn't know who he was. Ash then realized that such an event likely didn't occur. Eddie never would have made the phone call. Ash thought it would be best to let Eddie finish; Ash would then try to talk to the management team directly on a personal level afterwards.

"In terms of deals that we look for, we try to be a little different than others."

Ash was wondering where the hell he was going with that. It couldn't be farther from the truth. Nothing different or unique would ever make it past Lasi.

"What does that mean? You are looking for non-traditional investments now?" asked Warren.

Attaboy, Warren. You grill him thought Ash.

"No, we are still doing the same types of deals we have

always been doing."

"So it needs to be different, so long as it is the same?" clarified Warren.

"Uh, yeah," conceded Eddie.

Ash was struggling to contain his laughter. He really appreciated his friend, Warren.

Eddie and the ELVES said their perfunctory goodbyes with their spiritless handshakes and left. Ash lingered for a while, attempting to engage in some conversation with the management team. They seemed tired; no doubt it was related to the President's outburst.

As he was leaving, he caught a few moments with Warren outside of the conference room.

"Do you see now why you guys are disliked so much?" asked Warren.

"Yeah, I certainly get it," said Ash.

"Don't get me wrong, every private equity group waltzes in here and does the occasional check on their computer or the glance at the BlackBerry for wireless e-mail, but this was just too much. I was getting pissed myself after a while. I couldn't imagine having to talk over that."

"Oh, I completely know how you feel," Ash sympathized.

"Anyway, I'll be in touch," said Warren.

"Thanks, man. Oh, and thanks for making space for us to fit in. I appreciate it. Sorry that even after all that it was such a difficult meeting."

"No worries," Warren assured, waving from the end of the hall.

After a few days, Warren called and asked to speak with both Ash and Eddie.

"Well, it's down to you two," said Warren.

Ash thought this meant trouble.

"Our client wishes to do some due diligence on the two resulting firms. Can you provide some references?"

asked Warren.

Uh-oh, thought Ash. Sure he knew he could get the likes of Boas to provide a reference. Ash wasn't afraid about what they would say about him. He was concerned about what they would say about working with Popular.

Later that afternoon, Warren called Ash directly.

"I have to tell you, Ash, they are going to go after some unsolicited references as well. They've already started calling around, and we had a conference call this afternoon to discuss status. Popular has a really nasty reputation with its portfolio companies," Warren disclosed.

"Well, yes, you know how it is, when you upset somebody, they hold a grudge," said Ash.

Ash felt awkward defending the firm. He had grown tired of doing it. Why did he have to continue this uphill battle, attempting to prove to everybody his worth or the worth of the firm?

"I think you guys have a real long shot of winning this one," warned Warren.

Ash had resigned himself to such an outcome. He decided he was okay with it. He thought about his workload as well and felt that perhaps it was for the better. He also smiled to himself as he thought about how he could avoid having to work with Eddie.

"The only way I could see it working," Warren proffered, "was if you, and you alone, with some junior people, went and had a dinner or meeting with these guys directly."

Ash thought about this. "I shouldn't take Eddie?" asked Ash. He was half-teasing. He chided himself for being so juvenile. He just wanted to hear the response repeated back to him.

"No, don't take Eddie. I think the management team has seen more life from the rocks outside their headquarters lobby door. They just moved them a few weeks ago, you see."

Warren laughed as he relayed the last sentence.

"Thanks, Warren."

"Anytime. If you really want this, I want to try to help you."

• • •

Eddie approached Ash in Ash's office.

"We should really try and get Project Retro, you know the one where we went to the meeting," he said.

"You mean the one where the guy blew up at you because you, Jason and Bob were all on your computers?" asked Ash tauntingly.

"The one where your friend is the banker," indicated Eddie, attempting to avoid Ash's comment.

"You know, they are leaning towards the other group. They have called around to ask about us, and they have not heard good things," clarified Ash.

"What do you mean?"

"They have heard things like how difficult The Commies are," said Ash.

"That's not a big deal," protested Eddie.

"Sure it is. They know that anytime a portfolio company needs anything, going to the Partners in the fund alone is not enough, as it would be in a regular private equity firm. They know they have to go through the CCCP and everyone knows how difficult and random they can be."

"Why don't you see if your friend can get the Company for you?" Eddie asked.

For me? wondered Ash. They way you are asking, it doesn't seem like it would be for me.

"Do you even remember what the Company does?" Ash challenged.

"Sure I do. I was at the meeting."

"So you were paying attention at that time?"

"Just get the deal."

CHAPTER 16

Ash and David flew to Michigan to visit with Diversified Metal Industries. David, the low man on the totem pole, drove the car. It was understood *he* would be the one doing it. Ash sat next to him and tried returning some phone calls.

When they pulled up to the company, they saw an orange Lamborghini parked in a space designated "President's Reserved Parking."

"Someone has some money," Ash commented to David.

"Hi, I'm Dick Reed," said the President to Ash and David precisely as they walked in.

His voice was a bit more high-pitched than Ash would have liked. He spoke with a Jim Carrey-esque broad smile.

"Hi, I'm Ash. This is David. We spoke on the phone."

"Hey, fellas. Did you get in okay?"

Dick hit a wide tonal range when he spoke. When he started a sentence, it was really high pitched. It softened as he concluded. Dick had his arms folded across his chest. He kept shifting his weight from left foot to right foot. He spoke with an undying enthusiasm. Ash kept feeling like he had to say, "No, I'm not interested." He was a tall man, over six feet tall. Very thin. He had worn a suit today.

"Yeah, no problems," said Ash hesitatingly.

"Well, that's good. Boy, nothing spoils my mood more than travel SNAFUs."

He snapped his fingers as he spoke.

"Would you fellas like a refreshment to wet your throats after the dusty trip?"

Dick held his face in a smile as he asked the question. When did we enter an old Western movie? wondered Ash.

"Uh, we're good," Ash declined.

"Well, come on back, throw your stuff down and let's have ourselves a little tour," Dick invited them, and made a swinging motion downwards with his arm.

I wish he would slow down in his speaking, thought Ash.

"Did he just say SNAFU?" whispered an astounded David to Ash.

"Yes, while snapping his fingers," Ash added with equal astonishment.

Dick began taking them through the plant. As they passed by employees, each one would turn and smile at Dick and say, "Hello, Mr. Reed." Either this guy had a ton of respect or he had instilled the fear of God in all of his employees, Ash had determined.

They donned hard-hats and safety goggles and walked into the plant. It looked like they were entering a maze – the facility was compartmentalized into seven or eight zones that seemed like various sized building blocks randomly positioned together. Ash had a hard time understanding the order of the building or the rationale for its layout. The ceilings were forty feet high in one zone to accommodate tall machinery, half as high in another few zones and twelve feet high in the remainder. It also felt like they were walking into an echo chamber. Dick never stopped talking throughout the tour. There was one period for fifteen minutes where neither Ash nor David could hear a thing he was saying, as they walked close to the machines. Ash tried to inform him of that, but every time Ash screamed, "We can't hear you, Dick!", Dick would laugh boisterously.

When they got back to Dick's office, Ash pulled out his file.

"So, it looks like you lost the Healthy Living Juice Company account for making aluminum cans for their drinks for about three months, but you were able to get them back," pointed out Ash.

"That's right, Ash. I went over there and I straightened those guys out. I told them 'You'd better buy from us again.'"

Dick waved his finger at Ash and David for emphasis. Ah yes, an effective sales technique, so very intimidating, thought Ash. Ash felt like he was being spoken to by a game show host. *Tell me, Dick, did you threaten to create a SNAFU if they didn't comply?* Ash thought he'd better return to the meeting.

"But it looks like the profits came down on that account after you got them again. Did you have to price it below a competitor?"

"Boy, nothing gets past you! Yes siree, that's exactly what we did. We brought our prices down, and they came running right back."

"Dick, did you start out in sales?" asked Ash.

"Why, yes. You clever fella. How in the world did you guess that?"

"Just a hunch. You know, Dick, in looking at the financials, revenues came down but your cost as a percentage of sales went way up. Also, when I look at the overall cost divided by the number of units, that figure has been pretty constant over the last few years. That would suggest that you weren't able to get any leeway from your raw materials suppliers."

"Right you are, Ash."

Dick made a makeshift gun with his index finger and thumb and pretended to fire a shot at Ash.

"You hit the bull's eye," Dick added.

Dick hadn't stopped smiling since they arrived. Isn't his face tired? wondered Ash. I wonder how many injections of Botox he needed to hold that smile up. Why doesn't he recognize that we all know it is fake?

"In looking at your list of suppliers, it seems like there is only one supplier of aluminum. Have you thought about expanding the suppliers you have been working with? Maybe have a few of them compete on price to win your business?"

"Well, our supplier has been very good to us," said Dick.

Dick suddenly relaxed his smile.

"Where are they based?"

"They're here, nearby. A local company."

Dick's on-screen persona seemed limp now. He was losing his pizzazz.

On a hunch, Ash asked, "Can we go visit them?"

"Oh, well, I'm sure you are too busy for that," said Dick.

"No Dick, we're not. Anyway, I've never been in a Lamborghini. I'd love to experience it," said Ash.

When they got downstairs, Ash turned to David.

"You ride with Dick, I'll follow."

"No, it's okay, you go," protested David.

"No, it's okay. It only seats two. I want you to have the experience."

When they pulled up to the building of the supplier, Ash couldn't believe his eyes. The sign read "Diversified Metal Supply."

"Dick, who owns this company?" asked Ash.

Ash saw Dick gulp and watched as his Adam's apple moved down and retreated.

"I do."

Ash felt like he had just solved a mystery.

"And *that's* why you don't want to use any other supplier. And *that's* why the profits went down recently. The Company lowered its prices to its customers, but you kept the supply price the same, hence there were big losses for the Company. In essence, you kept your profits high here at the expense of Popular Capital's Company," clarified Ash.

"Hey, I'm not doing anything illegal. You can't prove that!"

"I didn't say you were, Dick."

• • •

"That guy, Dick Reed, has been fleecing you," Ash informed The Commies, "he owns the company's sole supplier of aluminum and has been maintaining his profits at that business at the expense of our Company. Prices have gotten more competitive with the Company's customers, but the costs haven't come down. Not only does the Company have lower profits, but debt-service is going to be an issue."

"Okay," said Henry.

"So what's the request?" asked Jake.

"I want to get rid of him. He won't be hurting for cash. He can always live in his Lamborghini," sneered Ash.

"Can't do it," said Henry.

"Why not?" asked Ash, "it's like the guy is robbing you. This is definitely bad for the shareholders."

"Well, he has a relationship with a Board member," said Ted.

"That's enough," Henry cut him off.

Ash couldn't believe it. He put the phone on mute.

"David, pull up our annual report. See who is on the Board," instructed Ash.

Based on the names Ash could remember, he couldn't think of with whom there would be a relationship. David started to laugh.

"'We are pleased to announce that Richard Reed, Sr. has joined our Board.' This guy started six months ago," David reported.

"How convenient," said Ash.

• • •

Ash went to his first University Private Equity Network function after becoming a Partner. The group had high achievers from all categories. The valet line told a good story. There were BMWs, Mercedes, Bentleys and even two Ferraris. The invitee list was a Who's Who.

Ash attended a few of these when he was still in investment banking and even with his first two jobs in private equity. Since he joined Popular Capital, he had only gone once. The last time he went he wasn't too keen on the event.

"Hey, Ash, what are you up to these days?" asked Seth, his former college classmate.

"Hey, I'm doing well. Getting used to this city."

"That's great. Yeah, it can be fun once you know your way around."

"Which group are you now with?" asked Ash.

"Farleigh Group."

"Wow," said Ash. He was genuinely impressed.

"That's the one with all of the political connections, right? Don't you guys have the former British Prime Minister on your Board of Advisors? There is even a Bush, right? The first one?"

"That's right, Ash," Seth confirmed. As he spoke, a really wide grin appeared on his face. There seemed to be a smug vapor emanating from his mouth.

"Who are you with?" Seth asked.

Damn, thought Ash. The dreaded question.

"I just joined Popular Capital," said Ash.

"Who?" asked Seth.

"Popular Capital," Ash reiterated.

As he restated the name, Seth put his hand up in the air and waved to someone off in the distance. He began walking away. As he was leaving, he turned around and hollered, "Hey, catch you later."

Ash knew he should have stuck to topics where he could appear more in command – wines, single malt whiskeys or cigars. In a sullen state, he swirled the vodka in his martini. *Shaken not stirred*, he thought to himself. Good god. How far am I removed from anything related to *Bond*? I keep sliding further away from the image of that icon.

Ash took a sip from his martini glass.

He also spotted Ari there.

"Who are you with again?" Ari quizzed.

"Popular Capital."

"Why did you leave private equity?"

"I didn't."

"Oh."

Ash walked away from Ari. He now knew what it felt like for that actor in the movie where he shrinks himself to infinitesimal size. Ash remembered that that was a kids' movie. He certainly did feel childish.

As he was leaving the event, Ash saw Seth get into his Bentley. Ash waved. Seth never responded. Ash decided he probably didn't see him. He rubbed his neck.

Bad memories thought Ash today. He had waited nearly five years before going again. Ash thought that maybe as a Partner, he would get a little more credit. Ash arrived and looked around. The same valet line was there as it had been years ago. This time there were more Bentleys and Ferraris, some Maseratis and a Rolls Royce.

He was wondering if he would see either Charles or Pedro. They always attempted to get together at such gatherings. They were never quite as discriminatory with the company they kept. While Ash thought, he began to rub his chin.

As he was doing so, Warren appeared.

"Ash, is that you?"

Ash turned.

"Hey, Warren, how are you?"

"I'm good, man. Good to see you. I hope you don't mind my crashing your party. I'm surprised you let an investment banker in to a party for private equity guys. I know I'm not as cool as the rest of you," Warren commented jovially.

Ash suddenly felt immature. Why do these events always make us rank our accomplishments? Stratify ourselves based on the caliber of the firm we are with?

"Don't sweat it," Ash said, and then after a brief pause he added, "I did the same years ago."

"Oh I tried many times to get into private equity, trust me. I was never able to leave investment banking, so I'm still slogging it out there," Warren laughed as he went on and on with his banter.

Ash's face brightened. Warren was a good guy and he had become Ash's friend.

"Wanna grab a beer?" Ash invited.

"Sure."

"Wanna go to a strip club?" offered Warren.

"No," said Ash. He had yet to understand the fixation that investment bankers had with going to strip clubs.

Warren shrugged his shoulders, "Okay."

As they walked inside, Warren asked the inevitable. "How 'bout you? How'd you end up at Popular Capital?"

"Well, I was at two other funds that had just started. I joined them when they were only a few years old," Ash said, "The firms simply didn't survive. They weren't able to raise subsequent funds."

"What's it like to be with a publicly-traded private equity fund? That's gotta be weird. There's so few others like you." Warren sought clarification.

Ash stopped in his tracks.

"You are right. It is weird. And the worst of it is, nobody outside of the firm really understands how it works. Come to think of it, I'm not sure people inside the firm understand how it works," Ash quipped.

"Yeah, we were all trying to figure it out."

"Well, guess what?" said Ash, slapping his hands together, "I get to show you."

Ash turned to the bartender.

"Two draught beers."

Ash surveyed who was around. It was full of some familiar faces and a lot of new ones. Five years is a long time to be hibernating, thought Ash.

"It's interesting how you talk about 'crashing this party', I myself am beginning to feel more like an outsider," revealed Ash.

"How so?" asked Warren.

"Popular Capital has such a negative stigma because we are publicly traded. You see, the investors of most private equity funds are a part of an elite, exclusive club of the world's wealthiest individuals and corporations. Access to them is challenging. Having them as investors means you have achieved something. Popular Capital has a pedestrian following. Anyone can buy Popular Capital stock. We are private equity for the proletariat," stated Ash.

Warren laughed. Ash reluctantly joined him.

"So you are falling off from the top of the hierarchy," stated Warren.

"That's right," said Ash with resignation.

"Well, you're not as far down as I am," assured Warren.

"Let's articulate what the hierarchy is," suggested Ash.

"Well, there are two broad categories – the service providers and those that control the capital, each with their own rankings," related Warren.

"Okay."

"Remember, service providers are less cool than those that direct the cash," reminded Warren.

"Right."

"At the bottom of the service providers are the accountants, then the lawyers and then us, the investment bankers. Senior lenders are at the bottom of the next category, you know the guys that provide the bank loans, then subordinated debt lenders and then you have private equity, which encompasses leveraged buyouts, venture capital and hedge funds," narrated Warren.

Ash stayed quiet, lost in his own thoughts.

"So you guys do a lot of lending of debt, right?" Warren asked.

Ash was disappointed.

"No, we are not just a bank or a lender," said Ash. His tone was a bit more aggressive than he had initially intended. It revealed his exasperation. He was finding it hard to maintain his patience.

Warren jerked his head back.

"Hey, man, I'm sorry. I know that. I was at the meeting for Project Retro, remember?" conceded Warren.

"I know, it's not you," said Ash remorsefully.

Ash raised his beer glass.

"Cheers," they said to each other.

Ash felt he needed to pick up the thread of the conversation.

"It's hard to fight against the stereotypical mindset," he opined.

Warren gave him a sympathetic look.

"I understand," Warren offered.

"Anyway," said Ash, realizing he wasn't trying to get a major gush of sympathy from his friend and thus far, the way he had structured the conversation, that was how it was coming across.

"So, yes, we are publicly traded," continued Ash, "and the way it works is that we take most of the money we raise from two sources. One, the public markets, and two, money we borrow, and invest it in the form of subordinated debt. The debt we invest in earns interest at thirteen to fifteen percent for us."

Ash hesitated for a second.

"It's called subordinated debt because it is *subordinated* to the debt that a company would get from a bank, called senior debt, where the interest rate is six to eight percent."

"I know," said Warren.

"Sorry," said Ash apologetically, waving his hand in an attempt to dismiss the comment.

He then paused for a second, "You know then that it means in a bankruptcy, the subordinated debt gets paid after the senior debt, right?"

Warren smiled.

"You're right," said Ash, "I'm really sorry."

Both of Ash's hands were in the air with a shrug of the shoulders.

"So anyway," said Ash after allowing a few seconds to pass so that his repentance could simmer with Warren a bit, "We pay interest of six to eight percent on the money we borrow, and we pay a dividend of eight to nine percent to our stockholders. Hence, when you break it down, we earn thirteen to fifteen percent and pay out roughly seven to eight percent to have the money to invest. The difference between the two allows us to pay for our expenses, salaries, rent, et cetera, and it also allows us to invest in lower yielding senior debt, roughly six to eight percent, and on zero current yielding equity."

"How much subordinated debt do you have to invest in for the balance to work?" Warren delved.

Ash smiled, his friend was getting it.

"About seventy-five percent of the capital." Ash continued, "Because of that, we do deals where we only invest in debt and we do deals where we buy the equity in a business where we can take control of the business and be the majority owner. When we do those deals, we will always do the debt in it as well."

Ash looked at his surroundings again. He thought about how difficult it would have been to have such a conversation in a strip club.

"So you are doing these equity deals, but aren't you guys just debt guys – all you care about is whether the business earns enough cash to pay your debt and you don't give a damn about growth, the way guys who are purely investing in equity do?"

Ash had to pause for a few minutes. It was not that Warren had quieted him, it was that he wanted so badly to be that growth focused, pure-play, private equity professional, and accordingly hated the stigma of being a debt guy.

"Because you know," continued Warren, "debt guys have a reputation for being myopic. People assume they are not smart enough to handle the growth issues. The reality is they don't get paid enough – either by the money they make or the returns that the capital they put to work gets – to give a damn."

What could Ash say? Warren wasn't expressing his own opinion; he was stating what the general community of professionals in their business felt.

Warren could see the expression on Ash's face. He became hypnotized by the path of its flight. Samuel's voice brought him back to the conversation.

"You know it's kind of funny what you guys do," described Warren, "It's like someone going to buy a house and then saying, 'okay, I'm going to be the mortgage lender also and pay myself interest.' That's screwed up."

Warren putting it this way made Ash lighten up slightly.

"Don't you ever feel schizophrenic?" Warren asked, "Hello, which Ash am I talking to? Debt guy or equity guy? Hello?"

Warren was waving his hands in Ash's face. His antics made Ash laugh.

"You oughta get to a traditional private equity group," offered Warren, his attempt to cheer Ash up.

"You guys are practicing no frills private equity," continued Warren, "The discount, bargain basement, off-the-rack version of private equity. No wonder everyone in the industry looks down on you."

No frills private equity, thought Ash.

"This is supposed to cheer me up, right?" asked Ash.

"Look, I want to see you at a better place, at a *real* place. You know, where you raise equity from private investors, *they pay you* two percent to manage it for them, you buy businesses for majority ownership, you jet set around from board meeting to board meeting, make grand decisions to shake up a business, make it grow, and then when you sell it, you get to split twenty percent of the gain you make for you and your Partners," outlined Warren.

Warren's attempts to cheer Ash up weren't working. Ash had already been through this ordeal with Samuel. Once was enough.

"Just like Max and Benson," said Ash.

"Yeah," said Warren, "Those guys have a great set-up." He paused. "Now wait, how does it work when you guys do equity?"

"Well," chuckled Ash, "we do go from board meeting to board meeting for the companies where we own the majority of the equity, we hear how the business is doing, make sure that the debt is covered, kill every growth initiative that the management team presents because it might put the debt at risk, and when we sell the business, we pray that Popular Capital overall did well so we might see a bonus."

"Hmmm, you're a debt guy in an equity guy's clothing."

Ash simply nodded his head slowly.

"And wait a minute, if you don't get any of the spoils, remember Max and Benson get twenty percent of the gain, what incentive do you have to actually make the value of the equity grow?"

"None."

"Why bother?"

Ash continued after a pause. "They try to give us options to emulate that twenty percent kicker."

Warren rolled his eyes.

Ash nodded in agreement.

"So if the business does well five years from now, maybe I'll get paid for value I delivered five years before," Ash shook his head in disgust.

"Hey, man, now you're depressing me," said Warren.

"Okay, okay," agreed Ash, a little sheepish, "I'll try to back off now. One of us in the pits is one too many."

Ash laughed a bit. He then raised his glass again and the two tapped their mugs.

"Cheers."

"To making things better," Warren stressed.

"To acknowledging that things *need* to be better," added Ash.

They both drank long gulps.

"How are things in banking?"

Warren went on to describe the various businesses he and his firm had been engaged in selling and how prices for businesses were going up and debt was getting easier to obtain.

Ash was lost in his own thoughts. Warren had re-surfaced many issues that Ash had buried when he yielded to Lasi's terms. Ash had tried to pretend, again, that the issues weren't real. Somehow, stating them like this with Warren made them hard to disregard. This was a problem.

"Kind of like the housing market," Warren said, "When house prices go up, mortgages are a lot easier to get."

Ash smiled.

Warren acknowledged his smile, "It's the only way to get Mom to understand what the hell I do for a living."

"It's sadly so true."

Both laughed at the situation.

"Warren, I am getting a lot of pressure to try and get Project Retro," said Ash, "What is the status of that? Is there something you can share with me?"

"Normally I couldn't, but since we are out together commiserating, let me tell you that it's not looking like it is going to be in your favor. The company really likes the other private equity group. They have had dinner with them three times, they have met each of the four Partners, and they like each one. With your group, they only really like you. The thought for them of working with Eddie is just not very attractive."

"That's exactly what I wanted to hear," said Ash. Ash had decided he didn't want to have to work with Eddie so closely.

● ● ●

Ash was missing his visits to Munich and the time he had been able to spend with Lothar. During Ash's last visit, both had actually been reticent, knowing that it was the beginning of the end of their more frequent and regular contact. They would always stay in touch, there just wouldn't be that excuse to communicate with each other three or four times a week.

Ash called Lothar to reminisce.

"Ah, halo, Ash. I was going to be calling you. I was visiting with a customer of mine, SLK Technologies," he started. "They are much bigger than GeldXpress, but they are interested in selling their company."

"Oh," said Ash, "Why?"

"The founder, *ein Genie*,...I mean he is genius engineer, is wanting to retire," said Lothar, accidentally slipping into German.

"I see," said Ash.

"His son is not involved in the business," Lothar added.

"What business are they in?"

"They are making electronic parking systems, yes? You are entering a parking structure and getting a ticket. When you leave, you are paying your money into a machine. They buy the cash acceptor device from us."

"Right, of course," said Ash, "This is a newer customer, right? You only began selling them a few months before the sale of the business."

"Ah, just so."

"I would like to have the contact person's name and number," Ash said.

"I send it to you, yes?" Lothar assured.

Ash called Albrecht Sturner, the founder of SLK Technologies, the very next day.

"Lothar tells me you are interested in buying companies but that you don't have a company yourself to combine it with," articulated Albrecht.

"That is correct. It's not like we are in the same or an aligned industry and we would buy your business for a strategic combination. We are what is called a financial buyer. We have a pool of capital that has been raised specifically for the purpose of buying companies, making them grow and selling them for a profit eventually."

"So, you will sell my business, you won't keep it?"

"Yes, after a period of ownership and improvement, we try to sell the business," Ash explained.

"Hmmm...I'll give it some thought," said Albrecht.

Ash could tell Albrecht was not enamored. He was an old school businessman and entrepreneur. He had tremendous pride in the Company he had built. It was evident from the care with which he spoke about it, the gentleness in his voice and his protectionist stance. Ash had engaged in conversations such as this before. Albrecht wasn't the type to take the money and run. He wanted to be sure the Company went into good hands and that it would be properly looked after.

Ash called Lothar.

"I could use your help. I don't think Albrecht is convinced of our approach in private equity. It would be great if you could call him and help him get over his concern," requested Ash.

"I think it might be better if I visit him, yes?" Lothar offered.

"That would be tremendous, but I don't want to take too much time away from you," said Ash.

"No problem at all. After all, I want to see us continuing to work together."

"I really appreciate it," said Ash.

● ● ●

After a few days, Lothar phoned Ash back.

"I think you need to pay him a visit. You fly to Stuttgart, yes?" suggested Lothar.

"Okay, no problem," said Ash.

"I think he is liking the idea. He is just nervous about the whole process. He is not knowing much about it," explained Lothar.

Ash could understand what he was going through.

"He said you sounded really nice and capable over the phone. He indicated he could see himself working with you, if that is what he decided."

"Okay great. I'll make my way over there," indicated Ash.

CHAPTER 17

Ash decided to head to Milan to visit with Triangle Cosmetics, one of the companies that he had "inherited" from Lasi.

Luciano Moretti, the President, met him at the airport.

"Eh...hello...welcome to Milano."

Luciano's arms went up and down emphatically as he spoke.

"*Grazie*," said Ash.

"Oh, *pahlo Italiano*?"

Ash started waving his arms in the air.

"Sorry. That's about all that I know."

"Oh...I eh thought that eh maybe you eh speak *Italiano*."

"No, that's about all I know," Ash confessed.

"Ah, no *Italiano*," Luciano attempted to clarify.

Luciano was shaking his head, while holding his index finger in front of his mouth as if he was telling Ash to stay quiet.

"No."

"But, just eh now, you eh say '*Grazie*,' so it eh make me think you eh know eh *Italiano*!"

I was there, my friend, I get it, thought Ash. Listening to Luciano talk made Ash feel like he was on a roller coaster. Or riding the sine or cosine function from trigonometry, the peak to trough making him feel like he was going to lose his lousy airline food.

"We eh wait for the driver," Luciano told him.

It was a warm September day. I wish they had more air conditioning here, thought Ash.

When the car arrived, Luciano introduced his sister, Cecilia.

"She eh make eh ahl of the choice for eh product."

One of the women in the car introduced herself to Ash as the translator. Ash felt a little relieved.

"Who do your products appeal to?" Ash solicited, by way of the translator.

Cecilia seemed to ask a clarifying question. After a few rounds back and forth between Cecilia and the translator, the translator turned to Ash.

"Everybody."

"Ah, of course."

He nodded his head in Cecilia's direction. She smiled and nodded back, saying something in Italian. I guess the translator doesn't feel it is important enough to translate that, thought Ash, as she stayed quiet. Let me try my question again, he thought.

"Is there a particular segment of the market you are trying to target?"

There was a further multi-minute back and forth between the two. Towards the end of their exchange, Cecilia kept moving her hand in Ash's direction, as if trying to encourage the translator to tell Ash.

"Everybody."

"Everybody?"

"Si, everybody."

"Is there a certain group for whom your products appeal to more?" Ash asked, trying to approach it a different way.

The same back and forth exchange occurred between Cecilia and the translator. When the translator turned to face Ash, Ash cut her off.

"Let me guess. Everybody?"

The translator indicated yes. Cecilia seemed excited by the exchange. She nodded her head in vigorous agreement, laughing and repeating "Everybody."

"Great, thanks," said Ash.

They arrived at the restaurant. It was a beautiful day under the shade of the cloth umbrellas. They sat in an open-air terrace overlooking a piazza. Ash enjoyed watching the passers-by. It was an enjoyable respite from his hectic travel schedule. He wished he could have been there with Sophie. Wine was served. Ash couldn't help himself. They had a lovely Brunello di Montalcino. Luciano was excited when Ash said how much he liked it.

At first, Luciano strained to hear him.

"*Molto buono,*" Ash offered.

Cecilia gave an animated response to Ash's comment.

"Ah! Just eh now eh you say eh no *Italiano*!" said Luciano.

Luciano called the wine steward over for another bottle.

"Why don't we wait until dinner? I'd like to get through a few things," suggested Ash.

"You eh no eh worry," Luciano assured.

"You eh Americans, you eh work too eh hard. Come eh from India o from eh other. You eh live eh America, you eh work too hard."

Ash could think of nothing more to do than smile and be gracious.

"I eh tell you what eh problem is," said Luciano.

He took a sip from his glass of wine.

"We eh sell the product, we eh no see money for eh twelve months. You company get eh upset, we eh never pay the *interesse*...."

He looked at the translator.

"Interest."

"...Interesst."

Ash couldn't believe what he was hearing.

"You let your customers have a year to pay you?"

Luciano looked at the translator, "Let?"

"*Permettere.*"

"No, eh they take. I no eh permit. They eh never send me eh the money. I eh have no eh choice. Everybody in eh industry is eh like that."

"EVERYBODY in the industry is like that?"

"Everybody," said Cecilia nodding her head yes.

How does she know what I am talking about? wondered Ash. Maybe she just really likes that word.

Luciano said something to Cecilia in Italian.

"Oh, *scusa*," Cecilia said.

"Eh yes, everybody in the eh industry eh they do like this."

"Wow. It seems so simple."

Ash was lost in his thoughts for a few moments. He took another sip of his wine.

"How come the guy before me didn't communicate that to my company?"

"Ah! He eh not eh so nice. I eh never eh tell him like I eh tell you."

Luciano thought for a moment.

"He eh no listen. He eh not so nice. I eh cannot talk eh to him. I eh never like him."

Luciano spoke in Italian to Cecilia and then smiled at Ash, "He eh never eh enjoy the Brunello."

Under his breath, Ash heard Luciano mumble something.

"*Bastardo.*"

Ash was quiet. I guess that means they like me, he thought to himself.

"Let me at least see the facility," suggested Ash.

"It eh is no eh problem. We eh permit you eh to see eh facility."

They drove to the facility. There were a series of two-story buildings at the end of a cul-de-sac. Each was labeled in Italian, but Ash was able to make out what they meant: "Raw Material Storage", "Production A", "Production B", "Finished Goods Warehouse". A steady flow of trucks was moving in and moving out. The guardhouse seemed efficient. There were no excessive delays. They walked through the front office. The space was well organized and arranged. There was a gentle buzz to the place. A throng of people scurried about, not panicked, just moving at a quick pace. Ash walked through the warehouse. It was the most immaculate he had ever seen. There was an electronic system in place that tracked every box. They had a robust computer system where they could track every box in their facility, and once it had left, track it during transit, through to its final destination. There were conveyor belts and computers moving product around. The warehouse was systematic and orderly.

Ash kept asking Luciano questions regarding the Company's finances and operations, expecting to find some manner in which there were other problems. Everything seemed to be running smoothly.

That evening, before he was planning on meeting Luciano for dinner, Ash went to his hotel and called Benson.

"Hey, you've looked at deals in Italy, right?" he asked Benson.

"Yeah."

"So how do the customers pay out here?"

"Remarkably slow. That's one of the challenges of running an Italian business."

"Can it be over a year at some places?"

"Not some, most," Benson clarified.

"Hey, thanks a lot, Benson. I appreciate it."

"No problem," said Benson.

"We ought to get together when I get back," Ash

suggested.

"Yes, good idea, let's do it," confirmed Benson.

• • •

Ash attended another board meeting for Capricorn Inc., an organic food company he had led the investment for three years prior. The Company had performed well during those three years, moderately exceeding their plan. There was an incredibly capable management team in place that had a lot of experience in dealing with selling to supermarket chains.

Ash enjoyed interacting with the President there, Glenn Eagle. He was always on top of his game. He sent out the monthly reporting package with financials precisely five days after the month closed, like clockwork. He would respond to e-mails within twelve hours. There wasn't a question Ash could throw at him that he didn't have the answer for. This was one of Ash's favorite investments. It ran on autopilot.

Typically, Ash would arrive in time for the Board meeting in the morning, they would have lunch together and Ash would be on his way. In this instance, Glenn asked Ash to come down the night before, so the two of them could have dinner.

"How is everything going?" asked Ash.

"Very well, thankfully. We've had some good success in launching various new product lines. It will allow us to further penetrate into supermarkets, gaining more of the shelf space," said Glenn.

"That will help with continuing to build the brand," said Ash.

"Exactly."

"That's great."

"There was one issue I wanted to ask you about," Glenn confided.

"Sure, go ahead."

Glenn pulled out a stapled document. It looked like

it had about five pages to it.

"We are running out of production capacity at our two plants. We could always try to outsource, but you know how I feel about our intellectual property being protected."

"Right," confirmed Ash.

"Unfortunately, there isn't a lot of plant capacity out there that we can lease."

"Okay."

Ash flipped through the pages. He saw a series of diagrams and floor plans.

"I figure we can either buy a larger one or build it ourselves," Glenn offered.

"And here are the possibilities?" asked Ash.

"Correct."

"Which one do you prefer?" questioned Ash.

"I like the idea of buying this facility near El Paso, Texas."

Glenn took the document Ash was holding and turned it to the appropriate page.

"How much would you need to make it happen?" inquired Ash.

"I estimate twelve million."

"So I'd better get you fifteen," laughed Ash.

"That would be great!" Glenn snickered a bit. "But I don't want to take on more debt than I have to."

I really like the way this guy thinks, thought Ash.

"Can you prepare a write-up, Glenn?"

"Sure."

"Since we are buying a building, we should be able to get a local bank in Texas to provide us with a mortgage."

"Right. The purchase price of the building is seven million. If Popular can come up with at least five million for a one-and-a-half million dollar down payment and three-and-a-half million to buy the equipment and industrial racking, that would be great."

● ● ●

"Go ahead, Ash," said Henry of the CCCP.

"Well, we have a few things to talk about," started Ash, "The process of selling my portfolio company Mayfair is going well. There were a few meetings between management and potential suitors last week. The deal could be done in two months."

There was chatter on the other end.

"However, I think we should pull the sales process," said Ash.

"What?" came the responses in unison.

I guess I have their attention now, thought Ash.

"The company just got a huge licensing agreement for a set of characters in the Spanish-speaking world. We have been investing in the infrastructure for the last three years. I think we wait nine months. Let them launch novelty products with these new characters, we enjoy some of the benefit, pay down more debt, increase the value of the business and sell then. We'll make so much more money," Ash advised.

"No can do," Jake nixed.

Ash put the phone on mute and turned to David.

"I hate when he says that."

"Don't you see the merits of waiting?" asked Ash.

"Can't do it," reiterated Jake.

"Why not?" asked Ash.

"No can do," repeated Jake.

Ash put it on mute again.

"Oh, I really love hearing that," he said to David.

Ash un-muted the phone.

"Guys, the management team has a significant pool of options here. They have been working their rear ends off to get this South American deal in place. And now that they are on the verge, we are going to yank it from them? If we sell to a company in the industry, which is likely, and not another financial buyer, they won't have a chance to have a huge cash out again. They have made a staggering amount of money for us. I think we owe it to them."

Ash thought he heard suppressed laughter on the other side. Suddenly he heard a beep and the line went silent.

"Did they hang up?" asked David.

"No, they put it on mute."

When they came back, Ash could still hear laughter in the background.

"Let's just go to the next topic," Henry ordered.

Ash was quiet for a while. He looked down. Several seconds passed. He looked up. He stood up. He began stroking his neck. Ash decided to move to his next topic, discussing Capricorn.

Previously, Ash had sent Glenn's write-up to David and asked him to augment it so it was in the correct format to send to The Commies.

"Who wrote this write-up?" Henry interrogated when they initiated the call.

"That depends," said Ash.

"What are you talking about?"

"If it's good then David wrote it, if it's crap, then I wrote it."

"What?"

"That's right," said Ash.

"Well, it happens to be good."

"Congratulations, David," said Ash, while winking at him.

"So it looks like we have a pretty straightforward transaction here," said Jake.

"I think so," said Ash.

"Are there any questions?" asked Lasi.

"I have one," Ted interjected.

"Where did they get the name Capricorn from?"

"That's your question?" confirmed Ash. "The Company was established over one hundred years ago selling fresh fish. The name of their first fishing vessel was 'Capricorn.'"

"Whoa, you know that?" asked Lasi.

"Were you trying to stump us?"

"Well, yes, frankly," Lasi admitted.

"Your deal is approved," Henry confirmed.

"Are you kidding me? That's it? Don't you want to know how it will be structured, what the payment scheme will be?"

There was a few moments of silence.

"No."

"You're sure," asked Ash.

"Yes, move on. Also, make sure you get Phil on the Board here."

Ash shook his head in disgust, put the phone on mute and turned to David and Steven, "We'd better send them an e-mail with all of the details. I don't want this to come back and haunt us."

"They don't get their money for over a year?" asked Lasi in disbelief when Ash began updated them on his visit to Triangle Cosmetics.

"How do they pay their bills?" asked Ted.

"Well, conceivably," said Ash, trying to suppress his laughter, "if the whole country is doing it, they can wait a year to pay their bills as well. I did point that out earlier."

David looked surprised with Ash's last comment.

"I think we ought to send some members of our accounting team out there," Lasi suggested.

"Why, to tell you the same thing I just did?" Ash fired back.

"Well, we ought to verify and confirm," Lasi said.

"I know how to read financial statements," said Ash.

David stood up and put the phone on mute.

"Ash are you all right?" David asked.

"Yeah, why?" queried Ash.

Ash turned the mute button off.

"Whom should we send?" Lasi asked.

"Hey, it's your company. Send whomever you want. We're going to go," declared Ash as he hung up the phone.

After two weeks, Ash received a call from Luciano.

"Why eh no eh come to Italy?"

"Well, I had already disturbed you, and I didn't need to visit you again," responded Ash. Ash was actually happy to hear Luciano's accent again. He had missed it.

"You eh – *como se dice* – college? Colleague?"

"Yes, colleague."

"He eh come here," said Luciano.

"How did it go?" asked Ash.

"Eh? Si, he eh go," responded Luciano.

Ash laughed.

"I mean how was his visit?" Ash clarified.

"I no eh like him eh so much. I eh don't talk so eh much to him."

Ah. Thanks for making my life more difficult. Actually it wasn't Luciano's fault, it was Lasi's.

After another week, he got a call from the accountant who had flown over.

"Not so friendly over there," the accountant said.

"Hmm…not my experience overall," Ash countered.

"Well, I got what I needed, eventually," He said, "You know, I have a bunch of ideas in my report about how to save the company."

"I wasn't under the impression that the Company needed saving," said Ash.

Ash was getting a little defensive.

"Well, I have a bunch of ideas on how to revamp the operations, alter the financing structure, maybe do an add-on acquisition."

"Are you trying to do my job?" challenged Ash.

"Now that you mention it, if you think the ideas are any good, and you feel there might be a spot for me..."

Oh please stop, thought Ash. He was becoming more agitated with guys overly keen to join them who didn't have real private equity experience.

"Sure. I'll keep you in mind," pretended Ash.

"That's great. Thanks. I'll forward you my resume."

Ash deleted the e-mail as soon as it arrived.

• • •

"Ash, I've been sending you a bunch of e-mails, but haven't heard back from you," Boas commented. Boas had finally been able to reach Ash on his phone.

"I'm really sorry," apologized Ash.

"Well, I also wanted to thank you," added Boas, "your friend Charles has been great about sending me all of these deals."

Ash was genuinely happy to hear that.

"I'm going to visit a few of these. I'll probably be hitting you up for some money soon," shared Boas.

Ash knew that he should be excited, but he truly had no desire to go down on his hands and knees in front of The Commies again.

"You're not happy," Boas observed.

"I'll be all right," assured Ash.

"Hey no heroics here, if you want to talk, give me a shout," urged Boas.

Ash would like nothing more than to open up with Boas. But how could he? He didn't feel right bad-mouthing Popular with him. Ash let several seconds pass without saying anything.

"Well, if not now, another time," offered Boas.

• • •

When Ash arrived in Stuttgart, he was greeted by Albrecht himself. He was an elderly gentleman in his early seventies.

Somehow he seemed to sense Ash's surprise about his age.

"I would work until the very end if I could," he said.

Ash was moved by that sentiment. He wondered what it would be like to love one's work that much.

"But my health is deteriorating," he commented, "I can't keep up with the pace. My wife thinks I will run myself into the ground if I don't slow down."

"Albrecht, I must say, you speak impeccable English," Ash complimented him.

"I studied at Cambridge in the UK. I had to learn the language well. It was only a decade or so after WWII. It was advisable to sound the least German possible. I even had people call me Alby for short, to be more unanimous," he replied.

Ash suddenly felt like things in his life had been tremendously easy compared to the struggles of generations past. He didn't think he or any of his peers could comprehend what going through a world war could be like.

"Tell me about how you started your business," Ash delved in.

Ash loved these background stories. After hearing Lothar's and Boas's, and even Ricky's and Johnny's, he was excited to hear as many as possible. This was fascinating to him. To hear about the spark through work was awe-inspiring.

"I started out in the printing business," he commenced. "I worked for the government press that made the Deutsch Mark in the Sixties and Seventies," he mentioned, "I was an expert at establishing their production equipment, working with the various presses and bringing them together in the most efficient manner possible."

"That's how I know Lothar has such a great product," he added as an aside, "Currency is tricky business."

Ash smiled.

"Ah, of course, you already know that," Albrecht commented.

Ash smiled even more broadly.

"From there, I joined an electronic identification company. They made the ID cards people use to gain access to secure parts of a building."

Ash listened closely.

"That's where I had the idea that parking meters for street parking and garage parking systems would go electronic, and I wanted to be at the cutting edge to make it happen," he concluded.

Ash was intrigued. This was the exciting part for him - seeing how ideas come to life.

"What made you have the spark to think about parking?" Ash asked.

"It's silly really. I was driving around in my car, and I was talking with my young son who was sitting in the front seat. I told him to imagine the car was like a person, and the other cars on the streets were the friends. Whenever we stopped at a traffic light, and the rear lights of the vehicle would turn on, I would say, 'hello, my friend, nice to see you.' My son would follow suit. That made me think about cars with ID badges, which made me wonder where it could be used, and I thought about reserved parking areas in a garage," he explained.

"A car with an ID badge," Ash repeated, his tone sounding mystified.

"That's right. From there it grew to printing for the parking meter and then issuing the parking cards and accepting payment via machines."

"Is your son in the business now?" Ash asked, although he recalled that Lothar had already indicated his son did not want to take over the business.

"My son is more interested in making movies than in

running a business," Albrecht lamented.

"Sounds like he gets his imagination from his father," said Ash.

The comment made Albrecht smile broadly.

"I know you are concerned with what will happen to your business once it is sold," Ash sympathized.

"Very much so," he confirmed.

"What if you were to remain on the Board of Directors after a sale? Perhaps even keep some ownership of the Company?" inquired Ash.

Albrecht's face brightened.

"You mean I could still be involved?" Albrecht clarified.

"Absolutely," said Ash.

"There is no way I could be as active as I have been in the past," he indicated, "I mean, that is the reason I need to consider a sale in the first place. I just don't have the energy I used to, and I am afraid of making a mistake."

"That's completely understandable. We can make it part-time. You come and work as much as you like," offered Ash.

Albrecht considered this for several minutes.

"This could be very interesting," he said, his smile as broad as it had been earlier.

Ash felt wonderful with the look of relief – which soon morphed into joy – that he could see in Albrecht's face. Whatever caution or pause he had approached the conversation with earlier was now replaced with more animated dynamics. He began using his arms and hands more to emphasis his points. His voice became more forceful. He appeared full of life.

● ● ●

"What's going on with this deal, Project Retro?" asked Lasi on the Monday morning call the following Monday.

"Ash is working on getting us that deal," said Eddie.

"No, I'm not. We have already lost it," said Ash.

"Oh God, what's going to happen to Project Elba?" panicked Bob.

"SHUT UP BOB!" bellowed Eddie.

Ash couldn't remember Eddie ever being that mad. What was this Project Elba business?

CHAPTER 18

Sophie and Ash were beginning to devote several nights a week to each other when Ash was in town. They would often stay at Ash's place, and on occasion, they would stay at Sophie's. It had gotten to the point where Ash began resenting traveling because he hated being away from her.

When Ash called Sophie this evening, he suggested she leave some toiletries at his place so she didn't have to carry items back and forth.

They ordered food in. They opened the obligatory bottle of wine. Ash brought out something exceptionally special. It was a Pauillac Chateau Mouton Rothschilds from 1986. Sophie recognized how monumental a gesture it was.

That evening, he delicately held his glass of wine while he negotiated the contours of her body. He kissed her neck. As he poured some wine onto her tongue, it trickled down her chin like he wanted. It made its way down her neck. She leaned back and her two copious breasts carved a perfect canyon for the flow. When the stream reached her navel, he added a few more drops from his glass. The sensation made her sit up. The wine then dripped, river-like, to her more private ocean below. A most inviting chalice, thought Ash. He didn't spare a drop. Like the great wine that silhouetted her body, Sophie peaked.

● ● ●

Ash was on his way to Sophie's place for dinner. He stopped by George's wine shop to pick up some bottles of wine. He wanted to surprise Sophie. He saw a man at the counter who looked like George, only younger. And with earrings, large muscles and ripped jeans.

Ash grabbed a few bottles and brought them to the counter.

"You must be George's son!"

"Yeah. You know my old man?"

"Very well. I come in often. I admire him very much," Ash said.

Ash extended his hand for a handshake.

"How is your dad doing?"

"Yeah, not so good. Had a heart attack a couple weeks ago."

Ash was shocked.

"I'm so sorry to hear that. Is he okay?"

"Yeah, he'll be all right. Pops is pretty tough. I told 'em to take it easy a lil' while. I'll manage things 'round here."

"Well, please give him my best," said Ash.

"Sure, I'll tell him you said hi. What's your name?"

"I'm Ash."

"Oh yeah, Pops talks about ya all the time."

"Really?"

"Yeah, he calls you some Indian or Arab genius 'bout wine or somethin' like that."

Sounds really endearing the way he says it, thought Ash.

"Well, please tell him I said thanks for the compliment."

"Hey, no problem. You take care o' yourself."

"Thanks. You too."

● ● ●

Ash met Phil at Capricorn's offices. He was a portly guy with thick-rimmed glasses.

"So what did you do at the snack food company

where you worked?" asked Ash.

"I ran their IT," Phil said.

"IT, as in information technology, as in computers, servers, et cetera?" clarified Ash.

"Yeah, that's me."

"Have you had any experience on the actual food side?"

"No."

"Wait here a moment," Ash instructed him.

They were standing in the reception area of the building.

Ash went to go find Glenn.

"Glenn, good to see you."

"Hey Ash, how's it going?"

"Look, I don't know what is up with this guy. He's not actually a real Operations Partner," said Ash.

"I'll keep him in the lobby for a while and figure out what is going on and what we can do with him."

"What's his background?"

"IT."

Glenn's eyes opened wide.

"Yeah."

"Can I keep him busy with your IT guys?" requested Ash.

"You want them to babysit?" Glenn laughed.

"Basically, yes," replied Ash.

Ash went into the lobby to get Phil. He was flipping through Capricorn's catalog.

"These foods are different from the chips and nuts at the old place I used to work," Phil offered.

"Yeah, the theme here is natural and organic foods, although the history of the Company started in fishing," explained Ash.

"Wow," said Phil. Phil looked up and around at the building. "My cousin sure has done well for himself," he commented.

"Cousin?" Ash asked, "You have a cousin who works here?"

"Lasi is my cousin."

Oh man, thought Ash. How did I become so lucky as to inherit all of these problems? Ash wondered what it was that he did to invite such headaches.

"Phil, can you give me another minute?" Ash had a pleading look on his face.

"Sure, are we gonna start the Board meeting soon?"

"Yeah. I'm sorry, I'll be right back."

"You know, I've never been on a Board before. This is going to be exciting."

Yes. It will be a real thrill thought Ash.

"I'll just be right back," Ash promised, attempting to leave for the third time.

He had to look in the factory to find Glenn.

"Change of plans, my friend," Ash advised.

As he explained the situation to Glenn, he stood with his arms folded, stroking his neck.

Glenn's phone rang.

"Yeah…yeah…what?…okay…yeah…tell him to call me."

Glenn hung up the phone.

"Looks like he found the IT department," said Glenn.

"How do you know?"

"My secretary just called. He fired our IT manager," said Glenn.

"Let me try Lasi again," said Ash.

This time Ash got through.

"Lasi, what am I supposed to do with your cousin? He doesn't really have food industry expertise."

"Look, just humor him, babysit him, whatever," Lasi said.

"Why didn't you tell me about him earlier?"

"Well, it wasn't an opportune time," indicated Lasi.

"He's creating problems already. He fired the IT manager."

Lasi started to laugh.

"Yeah, I'm sure it sounds comical from where you are sitting. But it is causing problems here."

"I'm sure you can power through it," encouraged Lasi.

"What about Glenn?" asked Ash.

"Glenn got his money for his building, DIDN'T HE?" demanded Lasi, "He got it without any scrutiny, RIGHT?"

"Lasi, I'm gonna go," mentioned Ash with an even tone.

Lasi hung up the phone. Ash wondered if that was why he would be cherry-picked to deal with such issues? Was it because he would "power through it"? Ash couldn't figure it out, but it was beginning to disturb him. He was beginning to feel like the proverbial fixit guy. That was a role he'd refuse. He wanted to do only the deals that he wanted to do. So long as he made money for the firm, everyone was happy, right? Such was evidently not the case, Ash was sad to realize.

Ash continued his internal debate. If I'm the fixit guy, how come they always seem to have their own agenda that they insist on following? They put me in places and I jump through a bunch of hoops just to do what they want to do, not what I suggest. This place is becoming so burdensome thought Ash.

Ash found Glenn. He was talking to the IT manager while Phil sat in the IT manager's office.

"So, you're planning to take over their IT department?" asked Ash of Phil.

"Well," he said, "things are in such a disarray here. I just had to get rid of that guy. He had to go."

"I tell you what," volunteered Ash, "Why don't we let him come back in here. You and I will go to our Board meeting...."

Ash watched as his face lit up.

"...and then one of your key initiatives can be to hire a replacement for this guy, someone who won't keep the place in disarray."

Phil looked around the office and then looked at Ash.

"Sound like a plan?"

"Okay," said Phil.

As they walked to the conference room close to Glenn's office, Phil began peppering Ash with questions.

"So what happens in a Board meeting? What do I need to bring with me? Is it okay to ask any question?"

"We'll get through a few of these, you'll get the hang of them and then you'll be a natural at it," confirmed Ash.

"Who else is going to be there?"

"Well, it'll just be Glenn and me," pointed out Ash.

"That sounds like a small board."

"Yeah, your cousin prefers it that way."

Ash sent an e-mail to Glenn, "Postpone real Board meeting until tomorrow. Let's just babysit Phil for two hours and pretend like we're doing the actual one now."

● ● ●

Since the potential transaction with SLK Technologies, Project Triumph, was larger than those Ash typically worked on, he decided to bring it to the CCCP. He decided he didn't want to have any headaches too late in the process. David had also been working extremely hard for Ash; Ash was eager to reward him and also to begin planting the seeds for David to be promoted to Vice President.

"When we present Project Triumph, why don't you give the pitch?" suggested Ash.

"Me?" clarified David.

"Yeah."

"You want *me* to do it?"

"Yes."

There was a few seconds of silence.

"Why?" questioned David.

"I just want you to increase your visibility with The Commies. It's important they become more familiar with your work and your contribution," explained Ash.

"Okay."

Ash could tell David was nervous.

"Listen, don't sweat it. You've been on countless ones of these. I'll be with you in case anything goes wrong. You'll be all right."

The morning of the conference call, Ash could tell David was out of sorts. Patricia, whom Ash had asked to join the deal team, voiced serious concern for him.

"I don't know if he is going to pull through," Patricia noted.

"Well, he'll have to get through it one day. Better when I can be there to bail him out in case anything goes really badly," said Ash.

They walked into the conference room. Ash took note of the clock. It was still seven thirty-three pm.

"You doing okay, buddy?" Ash asked of David.

He walked over to David. David looked pale. Ash massaged his shoulders as if he were a championship boxer about to jump into the ring.

"You'll be fine. Don't worry."

They dialed into the conference call.

"Hi, guys."

"Yeah, Ash, go ahead."

"Well, I thought I would give our colleague, David, a chance to present the transaction to you, rather than just me all of the time."

"Who?" asked Ted.

Ash cringed.

"David. He's been an Associate with us for…."

David held up three fingers.

"....three years now."

Ash paused for a while, "How come you don't know him? He's been on everything with me."

David put the phone on mute. "It's not worth it Ash. Don't worry."

"David, I'm going to un-mute this and you are going to talk," decreed Ash.

"Th-thanks for l-l-letting m-me speak," David stammered.

Ash became concerned. Maybe I pushed him too hard.

"W-we w-wanted to p-p-p-present to you...," said David.

Ash made a downward motion of his hands to David and whispered, "It's okay, take it slowly."

Ash saw David's eyes dart around the room. He looked like a drowning man. Ash quickly jotted something down on his notepad and put it in front of David.

"...a great investment opportunity that piggybacks off of our prior investment in GeldXpress."

Ash gave David a huge thumbs up and a high-five.

"Th-the c-c-company oper-, sorry, operates in th-the....," David struggled.

Ash threw the notepad in front of him again.

"...electronic parking systems space."

Ash sat down next to David and kept writing. David kept reading.

"Who would have thought that concrete parking garages would become bastions of cutting-edge technology laugh."

Ash hit his head with his palm. He quickly put it on mute.

"No, *you're* supposed to laugh," Ash said.

"Ooops, sorry," said David.

Ash un-muted the call.

"That's pretty funny, David. I never would have thought that," said Ash.

There was no laughter from The Commies.

"Hey, Ash, we have a pretty tight schedule, can we pick this up a little bit?" Lasi requested.

David actually looked relieved. It was Ash who felt more stung by the comment. He felt powerless. What was wrong with sparing a few minutes to try to develop talent?

"Sure," said Ash, although he thought to himself that if David had not looked so unhappy, he would have insisted he continue.

They proceeded through a series of trivial questions that were easily explainable – why did expenses go up last year? That was because of the new product they launched, etc.

"I don't think you have accurately captured the risks in this deal," asserted Lasi.

"How so?" asked Ash.

"What happens if currency goes away?"

"I'm not sure I follow," said Ash cautiously.

"What if there is no more currency? What if only electronic payments exist?"

"Well," said Ash, attempting to pause for a few seconds to let the disbelief clear, "for starters, if that is going to happen, it's a damn good thing I insisted we sell our company GeldXpress."

Nobody laughed except for David and Patricia.

"Look, even if that were to happen, the system could still be used to process electronic payments. The company's machines would just accept credit cards instead of cash," explained Ash.

"This company takes a royalty on each car that comes in a garage, correct?"

"Yeah, it's pretty clever to set it up that way," said Ash.

"Oh yeah, what if people don't use cars anymore?" argued Lasi.

What was going on? Where did all of the doomsday scenarios come into play? This "what if" game could go on forever.

"How would that happen?" asked Ash.

"Well, they have those mobile walkers now. What if everyone uses those?" asked Lasi.

"Those things move at like ten miles per hour. It would take forever to go long distances," refuted Ash. He was rolling his eyes towards David and Patricia.

"But if everyone who lived nearby were to use them, then the number of people using the parking garage would decline," Lasi countered.

"Yeah, but people who would be so inclined are likely either already walking to work or they are cycling. Perhaps they are even using a moped or Vespa or something," argued Ash, getting increasingly more exasperated.

"No, I think the number would increase."

"I don't think it would increase that much to make it material," suggested Ash.

"What if it did?"

"Okay, Lasi, let's say we run a downside scenario. Let's say the mobile walking thing – whatever the hell it is – takes the planet by storm. Let's make it severe and let's say we lose five percent of the number of cars coming in."

"I think that number should be ten percent," said Lasi.

"You would, wouldn't you? Fine, make it ten percent."

"Excuse me?" asked Lasi.

Ash ignored him, "we still end up with a return of thirty-eight percent on the deal, down from forty-two."

"Hmmm….," indicated Lasi.

There was silence as Ash tried to recover from this ordeal.

"Okay," said Lasi.

Ash threw his hands up in the air toward Patricia and David. They all chuckled.

"Now, hold on," said Lasi.

"What is it now?" demanded Ash.

Patricia put the phone on mute, "Ash, I think you should just take a breather.   Yeah, he's being more of a pain, but it's not worth it."

Ash smiled at her, "You're right."   He took a deep breath, "I'll be okay."

"You have us doing all of the debt in this deal," said Lasi.

"Yeah, it's structured like every other one that we have done," said Ash.   Perhaps he should have taken more deep breaths.

"No.   This deal is too risky for us to do all of the debt. We'd better get some banks in here to take some of these loans."

"Risky because of the ridiculous mobile-walking-thing threat?"

"Yes."

Ash opened his mouth and then stopped and closed it. He opened his mouth again and then stopped and closed it again.   He looked to Patricia and David.

"If you don't want to do this deal, just tell us now and we can stop wasting our time," insisted Ash.

"I just told you how we would do the deal.   And don't speak to me that way," contested Lasi.

Ash remained silent for a while.   He observed the hole in the wall.   He observed the clock.   He looked to Patricia and David.

"Okay," he paused a second, "other than that, we have your approval to do the deal?" asked Ash.

"Yes."

"Just come back to us when you have the banks lined up," said Henry.

Ash cringed again.   He didn't want Lasi to have so much time to dream up other doomsday scenarios.

"Okay," conceded Ash.

• • •

Eddie came into Ash's office.

"I got an e-mail from Lasi," he said.

"Thanks for sharing that with me, Eddie," mentioned Ash, "next time I get one, I'll let you know."

"He wants us to take one of these new Operating Partners to Tennessee for Project Flow," said Eddie, ignoring Ash's snide remarks.

"Interesting," Ash commented.

It wasn't actually, but he was hard pressed for anything else to say.

"I guess it's the in vogue thing to do these days?" said Ash.

"What is?"

"Well, it seems like every private equity group is hiring these Operating Partners to try and fix the problem children," Ash pointed out, "and I guess also to look at healthy companies."

"Yeah."

Hey, Eddie, whenever you have an original thought or your own opinion to express, just feel free. Don't hold back on account of me. Even if I am speaking, feel free to interrupt me. I may take out a full-page ad in the Wall Street Journal or Financial Times. I may invite the President, the Prime Minister and/or the Queen.

"So who's the guy and when do they want this to happen?"

"A guy named Joe Nagle. He's done a bunch of distribution work in the past. They think he'd be good at Project Flow."

"And what do you think he'll do there?"

"Oh, probably give us an assessment first."

"And then what, try to improve things?"

"Yeah, I guess."

"This is going to be interesting," said Ash.

"What? Why?"

"You'll see."

• • •

Ash was becoming increasingly concerned about Project Elba. There was all of this surreptitious behavior and his name was being associated with it as if he had involvement. Ash thought he better obtain some help in trying to learn more about the situation.

"Max, I need your help," requested Ash.

"Anything."

"Something is going on with a Popular portfolio company referred to as Project Elba. The name of the company is Jet Manufacturing, Inc. Apparently there is some info that has been leaked publicly. I may be implicated in something, so it is hard for me to go digging. Can you see what you can find out?"

"Sounds serious. You gonna be okay?"

"I'm not sure yet," responded Ash.

"I'm on it. Don't worry," Max assured him.

CHAPTER 19

Ash accompanied Joe to the initial meeting with Ricky and Johnny. For some reason, Eddie was busy. They started out in the conference room at the Company.

"Why don't you tell them a little bit about your background?" Ash suggested.

"Okay. I have worked in a senior management capacity at three Fortune 500 companies, all with market capitalizations greater than five billion US dollars," said Joe.

Ash could just see the reaction in Ricky's eyes. He had the "who the hell do you think you are" look.

Strap in, thought Ash. This is going to be a fun ride.

"Shall I go on?" asked Joe, looking at Ash.

"No," said Ash, "I think that's good for now."

Ash looked at Ricky and Johnny. He probably could have used their cheeks for hammering a nail in the wall. They had yet to smile at Joe.

"Why don't you show Joe around?" asked Ash.

"C'mon, Joe, lemme show you da place," said Ricky, finally moving from the still position with his arms crossed that he had been in since Joe entered the building.

"I guess I'll follow y'all," said Johnny.

As they proceeded to tour the building, Johnny fell back a few feet and approached Ash.

"How much time's he gonna be spendin' down here?" asked Johnny.

"I really don't know," answered Ash.

He regretted saying that after seeing the look on Johnny's face. He looked like someone had just pulled a gun on him.

"Well, I 'ope he ain't plannin' on bein' here lots," said Johnny. "I think's we's is doin' jus' fine withou' any help."

"Absolutely. You guys are doing what you do best; you are running your company like you built it and it's performing really well."

Johnny still had a sullen look on his face.

"Look, he is just here to see if he can apply his successful paradigms from large multi-national corporations to this scale. You know, Six Sigma, and stuff like that," said Ash.

"Do what now?" asked Johnny.

Ash tried to keep from laughing. That's why I love these guys, he thought. Is there any comment more genuine than that?

"Look here, I dunno too much 'bout dhose dhings. What I do know is howta run dhis here bizness," said Johnny.

"And you do it really well," Ash praised him.

"I ain't so comfo'ble widh all dhem changes," he said.

"Don't worry, Johnny. You've made millions doing what you do best. It's my job to ensure that you have what you need to keep doing that."

Johnny still looked worried.

"Even if that means keeping people out of your way who are going to impede progress," Ash concluded.

Finally, he managed to get a smile out of Johnny.

During their discourse, they had fallen so far behind, that Ash didn't notice the fight going on in front of them. Luckily no punches had been thrown – yet. Both Ash and Johnny looked up at the same time.

"We's bes' be gettin' up dhere," Johnny said.

As they approached, Ash saw how aggravated Ricky

was.

"Boy, I oughta smack you right outta here," Ricky threatened.

"Look, I'm sorry you don't like the suggestion, but your process flow here is all primitive."

"Dhere you goes again. Don't be callin' me primitive," Ricky warned.

"Okay, I think we are done here," Ash interrupted.

Ash had to insert himself in between Ricky and Joe.

"Joe, can I see you?" Ash requested.

"Ash, I'm sorry, he just asked me about what kind of help I was thinking of providing, so I tried to show him some of the efficiency boosts we can give to this place," Joe offered.

"I know, it's okay," Ash assuaged, "Sometimes the audience isn't ready to hear what you have to say."

Ash handed Joe the rental car keys.

"Here. Drive yourself back to the airport. I'm going to stick around for a few hours and hang out with these guys to get them to calm down."

"What do I tell Lasi?" Joe worried.

"I'll handle him."

"I don't know why these guys are so stubborn," complained Joe.

"Well, I think there are places in our portfolio where you are going to be able to provide value and others where you won't. This is just an example of the latter. I might even have some companies I'd like you to take a look at."

He didn't actually, but it sure did sound better.

Ash walked to Ricky's office.

"How come's every'ne ya bring here is such a dud?" asked Ricky.

"I suppose I attract them," confessed Ash.

Maybe there was more truth in that statement than Ash would have liked there to be.

"Foller me," Ricky instructed.

Ricky took Ash through a door that connected his office to Johnny's. Inside was a cabinet. Ricky withdrew a key from his pocket and opened the cabinet. There were probably sixty different bottles of alcohol in there.

"Let's 'ave 'rselves a drink," he said.

"Let's," Ash agreed.

Ash looked at his watch. Not quite 10:30 am yet.

● ● ●

The receptionist at the office walked in a fax. The subject read "Letter of Resignation." Ash turned the page and looked at who signed it. It was signed by Glenn Eagle.

Ash called him on his mobile right away.

"Ash, I'm sorry. But I'm not going down with Capricorn. It just won't happen," Glenn expressed with resolve.

"Glenn, the last monthly report showed that you were ahead of budget and things were going really well. We've got the new product launches in two months. What are you talking about?" Ash beseeched him.

"Your guy Phil has been periodically wiring money from our accounts! We have lost fifty million dollars that way!" Glenn roared.

Ash wasn't sure how to react. He was a mixture of shocked and confused.

"How did he do that? Under what authority? Don't you, as President, need to authorize those?" asked Ash.

"Yeah well, our bank has a bunch of Board resolutions from a law firm called McCarthy that granted Phil signature authority on the accounts," explained Glenn.

"Glenn, give me some time, I can sort this out," Ash insisted.

"Ash, I'm not doing it. I have a family. I have worked in business for decades and have always maintained the utmost integrity. I can't be affiliated with people who do this. If you end up at a decent place, call me. I'd love to work with you again," Glenn professed.

"Glenn, please don't make any rash decisions..." Ash was speaking to a dial-tone.

• • •

Ash called Albrecht immediately.

"I have a transaction that has been approved," he told Albrecht, "It is subject to getting a bank to give us some of the loans, but that is the only contingency."

"I thought your company always did the loans as well."

Ash felt conflicted. He felt like he had been caught lying. It's true, thought Ash, but how do I embarrass myself and my firm by telling him the truth about why a bank's loan would be needed.

"Well, it's just that, the size is a bit large..." Ash started.

He paused to see the reaction from Albrecht.

"I see."

Ash felt a sigh of relief. He hated being untruthful to him, but he was glad Albrecht believed what he just told him.

When Ash hung up the phone, he stood up and looked out of his office window. His arms were folded and he was stroking his neck.

• • •

That evening, as he passed the time with Sophie and a rare Pauillac from Chateau Latour, he recalled a promise he made to her earlier.

"So, I told you I was going to give you a better description of what I do for a living."

Sophie turned to Ash. "Tell me."

"Well, in actuality, we as private equity professionals are a lot like movie producers."

Sophie laughed. "Ash, just because we are in LA..."

"No, I'm quite serious."

Sophie carried an expression that showed she was not convinced.

"You see, we are responsible for putting the money in to a deal, as producers do with movies, if there is any other money to go in, like from banks, we as well as producers are the ones responsible for finding that money and bringing it into the company or the film project."

He raised an eyebrow upwards while looking at Sophie. Her smile indicated she was with him thus far.

"Now a company is like a movie. Private equity guys are responsible for assembling the management team, including hiring and firing the President, which is the same thing a producer does with the Director, who is like the President, and the actors and actresses."

"If anything goes wrong in a movie, who suffers? It's the producer. If anything goes wrong in a private equity investment, who bears the losses? It's the private equity Partners. Producers and private equity professionals are the ones who are constantly trying to keep a project or deal on schedule, adhering to a timeline and they are also the ones always concerned about budgets. If there are any changes, those have to get approved by the producers or private equity guys. So you see, doing deals is just like making movies."

"Okay, I'll give it to you, my little *financier*."

She placed her arms around his neck. Ash looked at her. She tugged at his shirt, pulling it from his pants.

"You see, I know how to get you agitated," she commented.

● ● ●

Given Patricia's experience, Ash knew there were whole projects on a deal he could have her spearhead. On Project Triumph, Ash decided to have her run the search for the bank loan financing.

"So contact the various banks out there that are doing these types of deals and see what their level of interest is in providing financing for us," Ash instructed her.

"No problem," Patricia said.

There was an enthusiasm in her voice that Ash loved to hear. At times, she would remind him how he had felt doing deals earlier. The thrill of identifying a target and working towards completing the deal, jumping over hurdles, overcoming obstacles. There was an excitement to it, and the thrill of reaching the finish line and closing a deal had the attributes of taking drugs – there was a natural high in accomplishing it. Those days seemed to be long gone for Ash.

After a few days, she came into Ash's office.

"I spoke with twenty lenders," Patricia recapped.

"What? Did you say *twenty*?"

"Yeah."

"I don't think I could even name twenty banks, let alone know whom to call at each one," said Ash.

They both laughed together.

"Hey, that reminds me. Before you get into the results of your scavenging, I have a friend at a hedge fund, Pedro Fritz. Give him a call. Hedge funds are beginning to do these kinds of deals these days. Let's see if he has an interest. Okay, go ahead."

"Well, six of them said no, fourteen said they want to see some information and five said they definitely want to meet the Company," she continued.

"Great. I'll call Albrecht and set up a time for him to fly here and do a presentation to a group of lenders," said Ash. He rubbed his chin. "On second thought, why don't you call Albrecht?"

"Me?"

"Yeah, introduce yourself and tell him what's going on."

"Oh, just say I work for you?"

"No."

Patricia had a concerned look on her face.

"Tell him you work WITH me."

They both smiled.

Patricia got up to leave. She turned around at Ash's doorway.

"Thanks."

"You're welcome."

• • •

On the day of the senior lender meeting, Ash strolled into the conference room. In a room meant to hold twenty people at the table and maybe thirty inhabitants in total had been crammed forty-five people. There was standing room only.

"Patricia, what happened?" Ash asked.

"Four groups that said they weren't coming, just showed up!"

"Hmmm. I suppose it is an elegant problem to have."

Ash stood in front of the crowd.

"Thank you all for coming out. I am thrilled to see so much interest in this transaction. Perhaps we should have sold tickets."

Laughter erupted from the crowd.

"First, let me thank Albrecht for coming all this way from Germany to present to you today."

A round of applause ensued.

"And second, to Patricia, for doing such a great job in coordinating today."

There was a second round of applause.

"Let's do this. Let's have some of you occupy the lobby just outside the conference room. We'll keep the door open and set up a speaker phone inside and outside so that you can hear Albrecht. Good thing we have a glass wall here. And David, you stand in the doorway, if people have questions, you can alert Albrecht."

The rest of the presentation proceeded without a hitch. Ash noticed one of the bankers try to hold Patricia's hand at the end of the presentation. She quickly yanked her hand back and tried to maintain her decorum.

Afterwards, Ash approached Patricia.

"Someone you know?"

"Oh, I'm sorry about that. He's someone I knew in college. He tried to pursue me then."

"And I guess he hasn't given up?"

Patricia blushed.

"Let me know if that becomes a problem," he offered. "By the way," Ash prided, "Really nice job today."

"Thanks so much."

"Also, I think you have been spreading yourself too thin."

"No, it's been okay."

"I'm going to have Steven join the deal team to help you out."

Patricia's face lit up. "Wow, that will help out a lot."

"Great."

"Thanks so much, again."

After two days, Ash approached Patricia.

"How did we do?" he asked.

"Well, we have three proposals."

"Great. Do you have the letters?"

"They will fax them today, but verbally they all agreed to the structure we laid out," affirmed Patricia.

"Great, well done!" exclaimed Ash.

Ash convened a call with The Commies. He really hated speaking with them these days. That damn musty smell of the conference room was getting more pungent. And then there was that stupid clock on the wall. Seven thirty-three pm.

"We have the financing in place. Three proposals have been made," Ash declared.

Ash was eager to get off the phone.

"Okay, good.   Work it to a close," directed Lasi.

What a relief thought Ash.   If I was going to have to tolerate listening to them go on and on, it would have driven me crazy, he thought.

Ash thought about confronting Lasi about what was going on with Capricorn, but he decided not to.

Ash called Albrecht.

"We are all set.   Let's march towards closing."

● ● ●

"Ash, this is bad."

Max had just phoned him.   He seemed extremely agitated.

"Go ahead, Max," pleaded Ash.   Ash couldn't remember a time when he was more scared.   Max was always very calm and collected.   He thought back to the time he had a knife in his throat as a kid.

"The information sources I found indicated that Jet Manufacturing was supposed to do engine parts for aircraft, selling to Boeing and Airbus," Max indicated.   He stopped to catch his breath.   Ash detected a lot of wind in the background.   He was calling him from his cell phone while outside.

"Sources indicated over a billion in sales," Max stated.

Wow thought Ash.   That would be significantly larger than anything else Popular Capital has done.

"So when I saw the address, I thought there would be an enormous facility," Max continued.

"I drove up here.   It's a one room office that is locked," declared Max.

"Max, where are you?"

"Nevada."

"You drove all the way to Nevada for me?" Ash was eager to clarify.

"Yeah. You know how much I hate those short flights. With security and renting a car it takes about the same time..." Max was relaying.

"Max, I am so touched by what you have done."

"I'm worried for you," confessed Max.

"I'm pretty much scared to death," admitted Ash.

CHAPTER 20

Patricia ran into Ash's office in a panic.

"We have a problem," she said. "We made a mistake in the deal information we sent the banks. We...I, accidentally doubled the amount of equity we were doing."

"So, if this was a mortgage application, instead of the twenty percent down payment we are making, people think we are putting a forty percent down payment."

"I'm sorry.   I screwed up," said Patricia dismayed.

"Have you spoken with the banks?"

"Yes, two of the three said they couldn't do it at that level, and the third wants to have a meeting," she said.

"When?"

"Tomorrow afternoon."

"I can't make it.   Why don't you go alone?" Ash suggested.

"Okay."

Patricia seemed slightly nervous.

"Are you okay with doing that?"

"Yeah, no problem," she maintained.

Ash suddenly had a hunch.

"Who is it that wants the meeting?"

"The bank the guy I know is with."

"Damn.   Are you sure you are okay with going without me?   Perhaps we should wait."

"No.   It's okay," Patricia insisted.

"Are you sure?   It could be a sick ploy."

"Yes, I'm sure."

"Okay…but, make sure you meet in a public place. Lots of people. Grab coffee with him at Starbucks or some place. I don't even want you going to his office alone. Have him come to this area. Let's see what can happen."

Patricia got up to leave.

"And call me when your meeting is over," instructed Ash.

"Okay," Patricia agreed.

• • •

"Hello?"

"Ash, it's Patricia."

"How'd it go?"

"It was a dead end."

"What happened?"

"He made the obnoxious comment of committing to do it if I were to go home with him," Patricia spat.

"I was worried about that. Let's see how we can make this work with another bank."

"Ash?"

"Yeah?"

"I'm really, really sorry. I know how badly you want this deal," Patricia said in a distraught tone.

"Let's not dwell on that. Let's try to find a solution," directed Ash.

• • •

Ash decided that as much as he hated the idea, they had to go back to The Commies.

"How did this happen?" demanded Lasi.

"We sent the wrong information," said Ash.

"Why weren't you more careful?" persisted Lasi.

"Because I wasn't," said Ash.

"What else have you messed up?"

"Guess what, Lasi. If I knew the answer to that, I'd fix it before you found out," Ash proclaimed.

"I don't like the attitude you've adopted lately," said Lasi, clearly incensed.

There was a lull in the conversation. Patricia got up from her chair and put the phone on mute.

"Ash, Lasi is pretty upset and it's because of me. Let me tell them it was my fault. I don't want him doing anything to you because of me," she offered.

"Not a chance, Patricia. Sit down," Ash informed her.

To Ash's surprise, Patricia walked out of the room.

"We aren't putting any more money in," declared Lasi after a few seconds.

"So that's it, you're killing the deal," questioned Ash.

"You're sacrificing what could be substantial returns to your shareholders because you are not pleased with my attitude," challenged Ash.

"No," countered Lasi, "You can still do the deal. Tell Albrecht he needs to leave more money in the company."

Patricia walked back into the room. She put the phone on mute.

"I just talked to one of the banks. They agree to do it if we put thirty percent down."

Ash smiled. "Way to go!" said Ash, high-fiving her. Ash un-muted the phone. He took a deep breath and started talking in a softer tone compared to the last few minutes.

"Guys, I think if Albrecht leaves more money in, it will give him too much ownership. We ought to stick to the current balance of power where we control two-thirds of the company. Look, why don't we increase our 'down payment' to thirty percent? One of the banks will come forward on this, and we will stay have a return in the high twenty percent-range," suggested Ash.

"No," maintained Lasi.

Ash was frustrated by the reluctance. He barely had a chance to recover when Eddie walked into the conference room. Ash's fury rose in him like a pit bull whose marked off territory was being violated. He was tempted to demand what Eddie was doing there. Ash suddenly felt schizophrenic. He had to get back to the task at hand.

"Lasi, can I remind you how upset you were when the buyers of GeldXpress tried to change the terms at the last minute?"

"That was different."

"How so?"

There was silence on the other side. Ash wondered if it might be more prudent to back down at this point. He had tested the limits with Lasi. Ash knew how he could get with shareholders. Maybe he should give it a rest. There was a path to get this deal done.

"Look, I don't think he wants to have close to forty-nine percent ownership, which is the impact of your suggestion, and I don't think it's advisable for us to have a simple majority. I think that we ought to stick with the current percentages," said Ash in a calm tone.

"No."

Ash took another deep breath. "Look, if we do future acquisitions, which is a possibility here, I don't want to have to put more equity into the company," Ash reasoned.

What Ash was really saying was that he didn't want to have to come back to The Commies again.

"No, either you do it this way or there is no deal," concluded Lasi.

Eddie walked out of the room. He used his left hand to open the door. His right hand didn't budge from its customary position. Ash thought he detected a smile on his face.

● ● ●

Eddie came by to Ash's office. It was after seven pm.

"So, you couldn't get the deal through?" Eddie mocked.

Eddie stood, refusing the gesture Ash made to sit. His arm was in its traditional place, stiffly situated in his imaginary sling.

Ash knew he was there to gloat. He usually just moved about with a swollen head. Ash thought he could smell alcohol. He quickly dismissed it though. Eddie never drank much. He wasn't likely to be hitting the bottle at work.

"We just have to pursue some modifications," said Ash, feeling a little tired from being so confrontational with his colleagues today. Being combative didn't feel natural to him, so he opted for a lighter approach.

"Well, from what I understand, you don't have a financing problem," hinted Eddie.

"I don't follow you."

"Well, you've got someone willing to provide the financing," Eddie intimated.

"No, we don't."

"Sure you do. Patricia's old friend."

Ash stared at Eddie. How the hell did he find that out? Ash was really drained. Let me just try to be rid of Eddie, thought Ash.

"That guy is a clown. There's no real deal there. He's just after Patricia," Ash affirmed.

"No, he's senior enough to make it happen," refuted Eddie.

This is so ridiculous thought Ash. He reminded himself to remain calm.

"That's not a condition we are going to accept," said Ash standing.

"We are running short on fees this year," Eddie revealed.

"What are you talking about? I have booked over twelve million in fees."

"Yeah, but two of the other offices have bombed. We need to cover for them."

"What?"

"Yeah," said Eddie, "If you want a bonus, we've got to bring in a bunch more fees."

"I don't know what to do."

"This deal, Project Triumph, is worth fifteen million in fees," Eddie pointed out.

"Eddie, are you nuts? You can't ask her to do that!"

"I'm not going to be the one asking her."

"Are you threatening me?" demanded Ash.

"Anyway, look at her. Someone who looks like her has been around," Eddie persisted.

Ash stopped moving.

"I'm going to pretend for your sake that you never said that."

"Make it happen," said Eddie.

This was now just silly, thought Ash. This can't be really happening.

"Eddie, it's late. I think you have been under some strain. The answer is no. I suggest you get home and get some rest."

"Throw some money her way. Make it worth her while."

"Do you have any clue what you are suggesting to me?" Ash demanded.

Eddie was silent. He began shifting his weight back and forth. Ash thought that it might be best to change the subject.

"Let me guess, you haven't done anything about Bob's sexual harassment?"

"Well, such matters can be handled many ways."

"There's the right way, Eddie. All other ways are wrong!"

"Look, Ash, I'm tired of your little punk ass prancing

around here like you know everything!"

Whoa, thought Ash. Eddie suddenly seemed flummoxed. Was it the force of the words or was it the possibility that he drank? This wasn't him. Where was the pressure coming from?

"Uh…uh," Eddie began.

It had been a while since Ash had felt pity for Eddie.

"Why don't you sit?" asked Ash.

"Get…" Eddie took a deep breath. "Get the deal done. Get the fees."

In a disoriented state, Eddie stumbled out.

● ● ●

As Eddie exited, Steven walked in.

"Ash?"

"Yeah."

"I need to talk to you."

Now what? Ash wondered.

"The mistake on the Triumph deal?"

"Yeah?"

That damn mistake is making me miserable, Ash concluded.

"That wasn't Patricia's fault."

Ash looked at Steven.

"No?"

"No, it was mine. She's been trying to cover for me."

"What a great leader she is," Ash mumbled inaudibly, "And these guys want to destroy her."

"I'm sorry?"

"Nothing, Steven. Thanks for bringing that to my attention. You did the right thing."

"Only because you are so cool about things like that."

"Okay, enough with treating me like a FROG. Get out," Ash said in a jovial tone.

"It's true, you never get mad," Steven pleaded.

"I'm getting mad right now," Ash quipped, "Get out."
They both laughed.

• • •

Ash called Albrecht.

"I don't mind doing it," said Albrecht.

"Are you sure?" asked Ash.

"No. It's okay. I don't mind."

Ash was relieved. He wasn't sure how he was going to explain to Albrecht the full background of what had happened and why.

The deal closed within a few weeks of that. Ash wanted to reward Patricia, David and Steven for their hard work. He threw a party for them one evening.

"Are you sure Eddie's okay with this?"

"He doesn't know about it, because I am not going to expense it to the Company," Ash explained.

Albrecht had flown in for the event. He brought his wife with him. Ash brought Sophie to the event.

When Ash and Sophie arrived, Ash was stunned to see Pedro there.

"Are you crashing this party?"

"No," he said.

He gave Ash a hug. He then walked over to Patricia and kissed her on the cheek.

"Thanks for sending her to me," said Pedro appreciatively.

"You sly little fox," teased Ash.

"I sent her to you to look for financing. And you started dating her?"

They both smiled as they held hands.

"Are you okay with this?" asked Patricia.

"Oh, I am only kidding. I couldn't think of a nicer pairing."

"It is so good that I finally get to meet you," Sophie said to Patricia and David.

"I hear so much about you."

"David, where's your girlfriend?"

"Well, we are kind of in a trans....she broke up with me," David revealed.

Ash felt really badly for David after hearing the news.

"Is it because of work? Have I been working you too hard?" asked Ash.

"Yeah, well, it's okay. This is important. I want to do a nice job for you. I'd hate to let you down," David confessed.

"Well, I feel like I have let *you* down," said Ash.

"Don't worry," said Sophie, "We'll find a very nice girl for you."

David blushed.

They had a wonderful dinner, several bottles of expensive wine and superb dinner conversation.

"When do we start the next deal?" asked Patricia at the end of the evening.

CHAPTER 21

Albrecht called Ash. It had been less than a month since the deal closed.

"MagnaTech, our biggest competitor, has a rumor in the marketplace they are looking to merge with someone," Albrecht shared.

Ash began rubbing his chin. "Do you think I should call?"

"Yes."

Ash made the call and arranged to have dinner with the President. MagnaTech was publicly traded, so they had to be as secretive as possible.

"Yes, I'm interested in a deal with SLK," the President of MagnaTech confirmed.

Ash went back to the office that night. He knew he'd find David there. He asked him to run the numbers.

"It all works, except for one thing. Our resultant ownership is less than fifty percent."

"Hmmmm….," reacted Ash.

"What's wrong?"

"I think The Commies will make an issue out of it," said Ash.

"I won't do it," said Lasi.

"I'd like to point out that because you insisted that Albrecht keep more money, which kept our ownership lower, this deal doesn't work. We end up with forty-five percent.

Had you done the deal *I* suggested, then we wouldn't be having this problem. We'd have fifty-one percent ownership," Ash stipulated.

There was silence on the other end.

"Guys, our stock could be worth $500 million with this deal. That's quadrupling our investment!"

There was continued silence.

"Do you guys have a response for us?" queried Ash.

The silence persisted.

"We're leaving," declared Ash and he hung up the phone. Patricia, David and Steven looked at him in disbelief.

• • •

Ash was away from the office for a few days. He went with Boas to visit a potential add-on acquisition. Ash suggested to Boas that he feel free to bring additional members of his team to review targets. While Ash was away, he would come to learn, Eddie decided to conduct the employee reviews.

"Why did you put in my review that 'I have a tendency to lie'?" asked Patricia.

Her tone was not hostile, but he could tell she was upset. She was doing her best to restrain her unease, trying to professionally have it come across as a bid for improving herself.

"I didn't," said Ash.

Patricia presented a paper to him. There it was written.

"Oh no," Ash complained, "I completed these and sent them to Eddie. He changed them."

"Now this is a part of my permanent HR file," Patricia said, her valiant effort at fighting back her emotions being tested to the extreme.

"I too want to be Partner some day," she said. Her voice cracked. She said "some day" so softly that it was barely audible.

"And WHEN you do get it, you will deserve it," Ash championed.

Ash offered her some Kleenex.

"You can't imagine how hard it is here," Patricia began.

"No," Ash said, "I can't ever empathize, but I see enough that I have a sense of how difficult it is."

"Nobody laughs or jokes with me," said Patricia, "They all behave so stiffly when I am around."

Ash motioned for her to sit.

"Unless they are drunk and are trying to grab at me," she concluded humorlessly.

"How is that going by the way?" asked Ash.

"It's the same as it was before," said Patricia.

"Nothing has changed?" asked Ash, shocked over what he was hearing.

"No," she said.

"Why didn't you say anything to me?" asked Ash.

"Well, the head of HR and Eddie told me the three of you discussed this, and that if I had any other concerns I should just mention them to Eddie – that I shouldn't mention them to you."

Ash listened intently.

"I was never a part of any such decision," he revealed to her.

It was Patricia's turn to look stunned.

"So have you told Eddie?" Ash asked.

"Yes," admitted Patricia.

"What did he say?"

"He keeps telling me 'I'm on top of it.'" Patricia said.

"But nothing changes?"

"No."

"I'll look into it," promised Ash.

Ash was troubled. The series of events that were occurring around him were creating a great deal of anxiety for him. He then realized that if Patricia's review had been changed, there was a strong likelihood that Jason's had been altered as well. Ash recalled putting in Jason's review that 'he was a bit too keen in finding faults with others without properly validating his assertions'. But to whom could he turn? Where could he go to seek relief for what was happening?

● ● ●

Albrecht called Ash.

"I am faxing something to you."

Ash went to the fax machine. There was a press release coming through.

"MagnaTech buys BC Systems."

BC Systems was another competitor to SLK. A combination with them meant a merger with SLK was not necessary.

Ash called Albrecht back.

"I'm sorry we missed our window, Albrecht," Ash apologized.

"Not as sorry as I am, Ash. Not as sorry as I am."

Ash's guilt reached a new high.

"My company is left out in the cold. If you guys were not in the way, I would have combined with MagnaTech. That combination needed to happen. We have a limited chance to survive now."

Damn those stupid mobile walking things, thought Ash. No, he realized. Damn Lasi.

● ● ●

Ash went to visit Samuel again. He had not yet even updated him about the fund he wanted to launch with Max and Benson.

"I'm afraid it is off," said Ash.

"What is off?" asked Samuel.

"The fund. We're not going to be able to get it off the ground," said Ash.

"Oh, I see," said Samuel.

Ash was quiet for a while. Sometimes, he just liked to be in that garden. The world seemed less confused.

"Ash, these things take time. You'll find your way," Samuel encouraged.

"I am staying at Popular because they gave me a significant raise, but I am as miserable there as I was before. I just feel badly for you," Ash began to admit as he looked up at Samuel.

"Why would you say that?"

"Most of the people that you affiliate with are highly successful."

Ash paused briefly and looked down.

"I feel like I have been a constant failure. After all of the coaching and mentoring you have done, I feel as if I have let you down," Ash said.

Ash didn't look Samuel in the eye. They both sat in the garden for awhile. Ash could hear the birds chirping, watch the tree leaves responding to the wind and observe shadows lengthening as the day matured. He took note of the row of flowers close to the house. He noticed as a butterfly fluttered away. He became hypnotized by the path of its flight. Samuel's voice brought him back to the conversation.

"I don't think it is me you have disappointed," Samuel said to Ash.

CHAPTER 22

Another quarter had passed and another shareholder call was hosted. The press release this time caused quite a bit of a stir. Over a dozen transactions had been valued downward. Shareholders were diligently scrutinizing the numbers.

The operator came on the phone, "We have a question from Mr. Bruce Katz of Killiney Capital."

"How do you value your investments?"

"Well," said Lasi, "this is a part of our business where we take a great deal of care to provide the best information to our shareholders..."

"I'm not interested in your being a toady! What's the process?" demanded Bruce.

"Well," began Lasi, ferocity creeping in on his voice, "EVERY quarter we review EACH portfolio company and determine the value of our securities in them based on the traditional valuation methods...THIS IS THE RIGHT WAY TO DO IT"

"You seem to be loosing your cool," Bruce shot back, "Are you trying to hide something?"

There was silence from Lasi. It was a very crisp silence. Someone in the room with him must have had the good senses to put the phone on mute.

"So you do this all in-house?" asked Bruce after several seconds had passed.

"Yes, but it is reviewed and validated by an outside valuation firm."

It was Jake's voice.

"That doesn't matter. You guys are doing the work, not them."

"Right, but they issue an endorsement of…"

"You know how easy it is to manipulate numbers and convince somebody else that they are fine? You do it to me every quarter with your financials!"

"MAYBE IT'S TIME FOR ANOTHER QUESTION," suggested Lasi, returning to the call.

The operator came back on the line, "We now have a question from Mr. Ron Biddeford of Biddeford Funds."

"Is it true if you write down all your investments that have been performing badly, you will have negative net income?"

"NO, we don't anticipate that to be the outcome."

"I've been trying to reconcile some of the valuations you have with news available on those specific portfolio company websites and the websites of their competitors. In two instances, I found news releases on a competitor's website that a large section of the company's management team, starting with the President, have left to join competitors. In a third instance, there was a news releases of a competitor coming out with new products in areas your portfolio company is silent on. It seems like more than merely a coincidence."

"THAT'S ALL IT IS," Lasi insisted with a stern tone.

"Right," said Ron, "Nonetheless, don't you think that when a company loses its senior management team, not just one person mind you, but an entire team, that its value goes down?"

"NO, we are actively seeking replacements," Lasi assured.

"So, by that logic, if you and the four senior most guys were to walk out of Popular Capital, the stock price shouldn't change?"

"THAT'S RIGHT!" Lasi's tone indicated a lack of conviction, coming from a man who knew what he had to say while simultaneously knowing that there wasn't a bit of truth to it.

"No, it's not! Of course the stock price would decline! The stock price always declines when there is volatility and uncertainty in the management ranks. Everybody knows that. Everybody but you!"

Either Lasi had no response or someone had forethought once again and precluded his response from being heard.

That day, the stock price took a dive. It tumbled by thirty percent.

● ● ●

Ash had been putting off a visit to one of the portfolio companies that he had inherited shortly after becoming partner. He decided that it would be a useful excuse to be away from the office. The Company was VirtuTech, an inventor of a new water filtration technology. Popular Capital had acquired the business two years ago. Ash made a trip to San Jose to meet with the President.

"I'm your new point person from Popular Capital. If you need anything, I am now the one to call," said Ash as he introduced himself to the President, Roger Erdmore.

"Right. Right. Okay," he said with a chuckle.

Ash extended his arm. Roger was holding a coffee cup with his right hand that he turned around and walked five feet to place on a receptionist's desk before he shook Ash's hand. He could have just moved it to his left hand, thought Ash. Roger kept moving his head up and down, even after the two were done shaking hands. Ash felt like he was talking to an ostrich. At one point, Ash almost felt like he had to move in unison, as if he was out-of-step in some dance routine.

Roger had bushy, brownish-red hair and a thick mustache. It looked like he hadn't had a chance to cut his hair in a while. He had round eyeglasses that looked in need of a cleaning to reduce the smudges. He wore khaki pants, a blue shirt and a bowtie. Ash wondered if the bowtie had been worn just for him.

"Why don't you show me around?" suggested Ash.

"Right. Okay. But first, I want to show you my latest prototype. Would that be okay? Is that all right?" he asked, an eagerness bubbling over in his voice. He spoke at a rapid clip. Ash wanted to suggest to him that he try to limit his daily intake of coffee to say, ten cups.

"Sure," Ash agreed.

They walked down the corridor to his office. Ash noticed many of the offices were empty.

"Are people out sick?" asked Ash casually.

"No. No. People here are healthy. Very healthy. No sickness. No problem," Roger assured.

They went into Roger's office. There was a buzzing sound coming from one of the light fixtures. After five seconds, it gave Ash a severe headache.

"I guess you haven't had a chance to fix that bulb?" asked Ash.

"Fix? Fix? Oh the bulb? Is something wrong with it? It's still giving off light. Is everything okay with it?" asked Roger.

He had walked underneath the bulb and was staring at it.

Ash surveyed the room. Behind his chair, he saw three degrees, all from CalTech. A Bachelor's, a Master's and a Ph.D.

"Never mind," said Ash, "Why don't you show me the product?"

"Yes. Yes. Okay. Okay. So here it is."

He pulled out a contraption from under several design

drawings on his desk.

"This is the MX325-X," Roger stated proudly, holding the device up at Ash.

I guess he thinks that is supposed to mean something to me, thought Ash. Ash didn't want to break his heart.

"Wow, that's the new MX325-X?" asked Ash.

"Yes. Yes. Isn't it great? Isn't it great?"

Ash was staring at a white, honeycomb scaffolding that had a plastic grey covering and a lot of electronic circuitry protruding from the top. There was a panel displaying numbers.

"So how is it different from the...."

"... the MX325-P?."

"Yeah, I guess," said Ash, nodding his head in agreement.

"Okay. Okay. It has all these new measuring capabilities. With these buttons, I can display pH, calcium and magnesium hardness, potassium, nitrates...."

Between the buzzing of the light bulb and the jerking cadence of Roger's voice, Ash stopped listening after pH.

"So how many of the original one..."

"...the MX325—P..."

"Yeah, have been sold?"

"Okay. Okay. None."

"None?"

"Yeah. Yeah. None."

"Oh, is that why you made all of these modifications? Because the customers weren't buying it? They wanted to see these changes?"

"No. No. Well, actually, I don't know."

"So why did you make these changes?" Ash queried.

"Oh. Oh. The MX325-X is so much better than the MX325-P. Just look at all of these new capabilities."

"Does it filter the water any better?"

"No. No. It's the same."

"I see."

Ash couldn't handle the buzzing anymore. Parts of his brain were beginning to go numb from the sensation.

"Why don't you show me around?"

They walked through the office door into the factory part of the building.

"How many people do you have in the back?"

"Okay. Okay. Twenty. Twenty people back here. Twenty outside of the office."

Roger took Ash to a portion of the building that was an enclosed space with floor to ceiling glass. Inside it was carpeted. There were spacious lab benches, wooden desks, tons of computer equipment, cushions on the floor and several whiteboards with writing on them.

"Okay. Okay. This is our engineering department."

"Let me guess," said Ash, "They handle all of your new product development."

"Yes. Yes. Okay. Okay."

I wonder who winds up this toy every morning? Ash mused.

"Roger, are you married?"

"Yes. Yes. My wife is a professor of chemistry. Yes."

"Any kids?"

"No. No."

That's a relief, thought Ash. Poor kids would suffer immeasurably. Ash suddenly felt guilty for feeling that way. Maybe it would skip a generation, he hoped.

Ash counted fourteen people in that cordoned off area.

The rest of the building looked really empty. Ash met the Production Manager, the General Manager, the Shop Manager, the Shop Foreman, the Shipping Manager and the Warehouse Manager.

"A lot of chiefs."

"What? What? A lot of what?"

"Never mind."

"Now, Roger, you said that the predecessor to the prototype you just developed, the...."

"Yes. Yes. MX325-P."

"Right. That one. You said it didn't have any sales. However, I have seen your financials, you are having *some* sales."

"Yes. Yes. Some sales. Some sales. It's from the CX100 and CX150."

"What are those?"

"Okay. Okay. Those are the basic filters."

"Can I see some?"

The two rounded a corner and there in front of Ash were four large industrial racks full of boxes. There must have been over a thousand boxes.

"How long has this been here?"

"Okay. Okay. It keeps changing. We sell some. Build some more. Okay. Okay."

"Right," Ash thought to change the subject.

"You must have had your headcount figure off," said Ash, "I already counted twenty people."

"Yes. Yes. That's everybody. Yes."

"What about your salespeople?"

"Okay. Okay. The salesman quit."

"You haven't re-hired anyone?"

"No. No. No time."

"I see."

Ash was quiet for awhile as he looked around.

"Roger, I think I'm all set."

"Okay. Okay. You wanted to have lunch together. Shall we go? Shall we go?"

"Yeah, you know it is pretty early for lunch. I think I'll try to catch an earlier flight back to LA."

"Okay. Okay. See you then. Bye. Bye. Bye."

Ash felt his blood pressure decrease as he drove away from the facility.

• • •

"That's the last time I visit a company on my own," said Ash to David after coming back from his VirtuTech visit.

"Well, at your level, you shouldn't be visiting companies on your own at all," David countered.

Ash looked at David askance.

"Do you really think I am a FROG?" said Ash.

David was startled, "I... I'm s-sorry. I didn't mean to."

"It's all good," said Ash smiling.

They had assembled in the conference room to discuss next steps with the CCCP on VirtuTech.

"Is everyone there?" Ash asked.

"Yeah, except for Lasi."

"Shouldn't we wait for him?"

"No, go ahead and get started."

"Okay," said Ash "in order to fix this company, you need to hire a President to run it who knows how to operate a business. The guy there now is a technical guru, but he should only be responsible for new product development. We need to replace the sales team, re-allocate people from their engineering department into other areas like quality control and purchasing, and we have to bring their inventory down. There is just way too much product in there. We will need to fund another seven million dollars. The current President put too much cash into new product development, and we are going to hit a wall soon. If we just use all of the cash to pay our debt, there won't be any to make the adjustments on the sales side which will be the key to saving this business," Ash commented.

Ash and David stayed quiet. They waited. Several minutes passed.

"You guys still there?" asked Ash.

He repeated himself.   Ash and David heard a beep.

"Yeah, hey, we're here," said Henry.

"Did you guys hear what I said or shall I repeat it?" Ash queried, his tone calm and very matter-of-fact.

There was another minute of silence.

"So, what's the problem here?" asked Ted.

Ash looked at David, who shrugged his shoulders.

"The guy running the place should only be in charge of new product development. He isn't suited for any other role," Ash reiterated, speaking in a slow tone and enunciating the key words.

"Why don't we just hire a President who can run the thing?" suggested Jake.

Ash looked at David in disbelief.   He shook his head in disgust.

With clenched teeth, Ash responded, "Brilliant idea."

"Okay," said Jake, "Go make it happen."

"Wait, did you guys also approve the funding request?"

"What funding request?" asked Henry.

"We sent you a detailed analysis of why the business needs another seven million dollars of cash to save it," Ash reminded the group.

"You sent that to us?" asked Ted.

Ash looked at David who was punching at his laptop. He looked up at Ash and nodded his head yes.

"Yes, we did," said Ash.

"You need seven million?" asked Henry. "Seems like a lot."

"We've laid out the use of the funds," said Ash.

"Okay.   It's fine.   Seven million," concluded Henry, "Just pile it onto the existing debt.   See you, guys."

"Whoa, hey," Ash interjected, "Hang on a second.   We can't put that on as debt.   It needs to be equity!"

"Equity?   No way," Jake denied.

"Guys, they don't have a way to pay the interest and principal on the debt and have the cash to get the business back on track," argued Ash.

"No can do," said Jake.

"Why not?" asked Ash.

"It has to do with our funding and the limits we have on how we can deploy capital," explained Jake.

That explanation makes no sense to me whatsoever. Thanks for the brush-off response, thought Ash.

"Guys, it's like buying an investment second home, where you need the monthly rent to pay the mortgage, but you take the mortgage out before the house is even built. How are you going to pay that mortgage?"

"These guys need a mortgage? Are they buying a building?" asked Ted.

"No, they are not buying a building," said Ash with exasperation.

"Yeah, we get it, but you can't do it as debt," said Jake.

"So this business will fail because of how we are structured?" asked Ash.

"You'll think of something," Jake assured.

"See ya, guys," said Henry.

"Guys, we'll never be able to hire a credible President with this amount of debt."

As Ash spoke, the line went dead.

● ● ●

"Ash, Magnatech and BC Systems have launched a bundled service," Albrecht pointed out, "they have slashed their offering price to thirty percent below ours."

"Oh no," bemoaned Ash.

"Ash, I told you before, I don't know how we are going to make it," divulged Albrecht.

"What can be done?"

"If Popular Capital can fund some additional capital, we can try to jump start development efforts on the next generation technology. But I can't do that without engineering talent," suggested Albrecht.

"Let me see what I can do," Ash offered.

• • •

Ash approached The Commies again with the request.

"No, no more money," indicated Lasi.

Ash had not thought of how yet to respond. He just thought about Albrecht and stressed about what would happen to the Company that he built.

"How much cash do they have?" Lasi asked.

"Twenty-three million dollars," indicated Ash after David put a piece of paper in front of him with the number on it.

"Oh!" said Lasi.

There was a long silence. It seemed like Ash, Patricia, David and Steven had been placed on hold.

Lasi came back, "did their performance slip last month?"

"That's a rather specific question, isn't it?" Ash asked.

"What's the answer," asked Lasi adamantly.

"Yes," informed Patricia, "they were off eighteen percent."

There was another long silence.

"Ash I want you to listen to me carefully," Lasi began.

"Tomorrow, you must fire Albrecht, have the twenty-three million wired to us, and then get rid of the rest of the employees," Lasi instructed.

"Let me guess, by 'get rid of' you mean killing them, right?" Ash asked sardonically.

"Ash, you need to fall into line," ordered Lasi.

Ash rolled his eyes. "On what grounds are you dictating me to fire Albrecht?"

"He missed his budget."

"Are you kidding me? Let me tell you something, you yourselves can never meet a budget that you articulate. And you want me to fire Albrecht, who has only missed one month? If you hold to that logic, you ought to be firing yourselves!" elucidated Ash.

The line went silent again.

• • •

Patricia came into Ash's office.

"Are you busy?"

"No."

"How's Pedro?"

"He's doing great. He wants to do something as a foursome soon."

"That sounds like a good idea."

"I found out more about Project Elba."

"Tell me," encouraged Ash.

"Well, it had been an actual company at one point, but now it is just a shell," she began, "an Operations Partner, with some link to Lasi, had gone into the portfolio company and started firing people. He started with the Vice President of Sales, and by the end of the month, eight heads rolled, including that of the President. They replaced them all with a lot of high-powered talent from multi-billion dollar companies."

"I hate when they just don't leave things alone," lamented Ash.

"Well, it gets worse. All of the customers bailed. They went down to ten percent of the sales that they had before in just three months," she exclaimed.

"You know," said Ash, "it always amazes me. Sometimes with these smaller companies there is an art to the way they work and function well. Maybe it's a certain process or procedure that the President or the VP of Sales follows that a customer really likes that makes them keep coming back. When you change that, customers get agitated and contemplate going elsewhere."

"So, are they going to put it into bankruptcy?" Ash asked after a momentary silence.

"That's the thing. Lasi knows he can't. They put close to a billion dollars into it," Patricia pointed out.

"Writing that down to zero would do us in," indicated Ash.

Ash was beginning to piece it together. They needed to keep inserting cash into the business but couldn't do it directly. They were using him to move money from legitimate businesses. That's why they destroyed Capricorn. That's why they want to destroy SLK Technologies.

• • •

"Ash, we have a problem. I took a team, and we went to visit this lab supply company. They are experiencing some financial difficulties, and I thought they might be a good acquisition target. Actually, it was one of the deals that your friend Charles recommended. They sell chemical reagents, including acids. Unfortunately, there was an accident in their hydrosulphuric acid tank. It exploded while we were there," Boas reported.

"Oh my god, were there any injuries?"

"Yes, several, but only three major ones," Boas indicated.

"A large pipe fell on Peter Dawson's leg. He is in critical condition. We were in a remote area, so they had to use a helicopter to get him out."

"Tyler Jones had some acid spill on his arm. He was behind Peter when the pipe fell. The acid missed Peter but hit Tyler. He is suffering from multiple degree burns."

Boas was silent for a while. Ash was busy trying to digest all of this information.

"What about the third one?"

"It's me."

"What happened to you?" demanded Ash.

"The pipe that landed on Peter's leg."

"Yeah?"

"It hit me on the head on the way down," revealed Boas.

"Are you okay?"

"I had some pretty intense bleeding, but I am okay now."

"Is everything okay internally?"

"Yeah, should be. I just had some stitches on my scalp."

"When you say should be, what do you mean?"

"I didn't have time to run a scan. I wanted to see how Peter and Tyler were doing."

"I think you oughta have the scan done."

"Yeah, Wendy is saying the same thing."

"Please listen to us."

CHAPTER 23

"Ash, we have a problem. I called to get pre-qualified on the CT Scan and MRI. They said that our monthly premiums were in arrears. We have no medical insurance."

Ash was stunned and suddenly became very nervous. His heart sank.

"Let me find out what is going on," said Ash. Ash considered the situation for a moment. "Don't worry," he said to Boas, as a knee jerk reaction.

"I am worried," Boas admitted.

• • •

Ash's cell phone rang. He thought it might be an update from Boas so he picked it up without checking whom it was.

"Ash, I trusted you, Ash," Albrecht lamented.

Oh no thought Ash.

"Albrecht, how did I betray your trust?" Ash implored.

"My company is gone now. It has been destroyed by your firm."

He felt like a man who no longer had any control or say at his firm. Some Partner title this turned out to be.

"Somebody named Henry was here today. He took over control of the business. He fired everybody."

"Albrecht, I don't know what to say," offered Ash.

"What could you possibly say? What could you comfort me with? I needed to take it easier on myself, not destroy my business. Do you have any idea what it feels like to see decades of hard work disappear in one day?"

Ash had no way of commiserating. He wished he had heeded his compunctions earlier.

• • •

Ash tried to recall the name of the person at headquarters who dealt with insurance matters.

"Is Barbara there, please?"

Ash had to wait for what seemed like an eternity.

"Barbara, this is Ash from the LA office. I understand you were inquiring about the healthcare coverage at High Performance Systems. There seems to be a problem now. What exactly did you do?" asked Ash.

"I did my job," she retorted.

Oh brother, thought Ash.

"I'm sure you did, Barbara. What exactly was it?" asked Ash.

Ash's voice was urgent. He was becoming more and more agitated with the situation.

"Look, don't you get snippy with me," snapped Barbara.

I can't believe this is happening, thought Ash.

"I did what I was s'posed to do," she insisted.

"Give me the insurance company's contact info," asked Ash.

"I'm busy at the moment, I'll e-mail it to you when I can," she said.

"Barbara, you and I are on the same team," Ash reminded her, "Let's try and work together."

"Listen, before I do anything and stick my neck on the line, I need to get permission from my supervisor, so I don't get myself into trouble," said Barbara forcefully.

"Get yourself into trouble? What are you talking about? I want some information on one of my companies."

"It ain't your company," Barbara declared.

"Yeah, I meant that figuratively and not literally," said Ash.

He rolled his eyes. Why do I even bother?

"Your name ain't even on here. That's the problem," said Barbara.

"Whose name is there? Who is listed as the Partner?"

"Eddie."

Ash's head was swimming. He hung up the phone. He called Boas's assistant.

"Can you get me the name and contact of your health insurance provider?" Ash asked.

"Sure, Mr. Gyan. Just one second."

Ash called the insurance company. To his horror, he learned that only half of the premium amount was being paid, and the policy had been canceled.

He called Boas.

"Boas, I am still sorting out the situation here. Why don't you go ahead and have the scan? We'll get it resolved."

"They had to amputate Peter's leg."

"What??"

"The pipe that fell on him was really rusty. An infection started and spread quickly. He hadn't had a tetanus shot in decades. It was a regional hospital. They didn't give him a vaccine."

"Is he still at risk for tetanus?"

"The doctors say he should be fine. They believe they stopped the spread. But, I have bad news about Tyler as well."

"What happened?"

"The burns damaged a lot of nerve tissue," Boas said. His voice was quivering. It was the first time Ash had really heard Boas get emotional. "He can't move his right arm," he choked out.

Ash was himself becoming a bit teary-eyed. There was a long silence on the phone. Ash could tell that Boas was feeling responsible.

"It's not your fault, Boas," soothed Ash.

"It'll cost several thousands for me to get the scans if we don't have insurance," was his reply.

"Don't worry about that now, just get checked out."

"I'll speak to you in a little while."

"Make sure you...."

The line had gone dead.

Ash couldn't tell what bothered him more, the sense of letting Boas down or the fear of finding out what actually happened.

Ash tried contacting Eddie.

● ● ●

Ash couldn't sleep that night. He had tried Eddie numerous times. When he woke up in the morning, he called Boas. He had to leave him a message.

"Look, Boas, I feel like I should make my way out there, but I'd like to discuss it with you first. Call me when you can."

Ash was frustrated with waiting. He called Lasi.

"Yeah?"

"What happened on High Performance Systems?"

"What do you mean?"

"Did you alter the deal after we had finalized it and closed the transaction?"

Lasi was silent.

"You cut their health insurance contribution, didn't you?"

Further silence.

"Look, we were standardizing our procedures across the entire portfolio."

"Each company is different, Lasi. Why didn't you tell me so they could have done something about it to have some kind of insurance?"

"These are tough times. We need to sharpen our pencil on each investment, create the most value."

"These are tough times? The stock you own is worth over one hundred million dollars and you need to wring another fifty thousand a year in savings from a tiny company?"

"Don't get that way with me," Lasi warned. Ash was quiet for a while.

"We agreed to it before, and we changed our minds," Lasi stated.

"Why didn't you tell me?" questioned Ash. More dead air.

"Isn't it a policy to inform the Partner about what is going on with their deals?" challenged Ash.

"There you go with your policy crap," said Lasi condescendingly.

"Policies protect people."

"We managed to find Eddie, and we told him," Lasi defended.

"And you intentionally told him not to tell me." Lasi was quiet. Ash was thinking.

"We have to make this right. There has been a major accident," he finally stated. Lasi was quiet.

"We have to make this right," Ash repeated.

"Look, I have to go. But just remember the money, Ash. There's a lot of money here for you."

Before Ash could say anything, the line went dead.

He called Boas again, "Listen, buddy, I need to chat with you. Why don't you give me a call when you get a chance? I think I'll definitely come out there. Maybe I can do it next week."

● ● ●

He and Sophie were planning a trip to Napa Valley that weekend.

"Do you still want to go?" asked Sophie.

He held her in his arms.

"Yeah, hopefully it will help clear my head," said Ash.

She kissed him.

"Sometimes I wish you were cold like the others," she said.

"What?"

"Then I wouldn't see you suffering the way you do."

"But then I would likely be cold with you too," said Ash.

"Better not change then," she reconsidered.

The two kissed.

The following day, Ash tried to get an emergency meeting of the CCCP. They wouldn't give him a definitive until very late in the day. He still hadn't heard back from Eddie and Boas was, unfortunately, still ignoring him.

I wish he'd call me, thought Ash.

When The Commies convened, there was a tension in the air.

"Ash, this is Henry speaking…uh, go ahead, you have some concerns you wanted to raise," said Henry.

That was odd, thought Ash, why did Henry announce himself?

"There has been an accident with the management team of High Performance Systems. Unfortunately, it has been severe for at least two of them. One has lost his leg, and the other has lost the mobility in his arm."

Ash could overhear whispering from the CCCP. That is odd, he thought, usually they just throw it on mute or they chatter amongst themselves.

"There was a lapse in their insurance coverage. It seems as if that decision was made by the CCCP, but I had no knowledge of it. Rather than waste time on figuring that out though, I'd like to get some funding into the company to cover the medical expenses for the employees in case we hit a brick wall with insurance," said Ash.

There was a several second pause. Ash looked at David. David shrugged.

"Ash, this is Lasi…"

What the hell? I know your voice. I've been listening to it for years.

"…we have here the minutes from the April 12th CCCP meeting. It was approved by the CCCP to alter the health care insurance reimbursement to conform with the practice of a majority of our other portfolio companies."

"I wasn't informed of that meeting," defended Ash.

"We have noted here that, as per policy, there was a member of the deal team present on the call," indicated Lasi.

Ash again looked at David.

"Who was it?"

"It was Eddie Cache."

"Did you tell Eddie to inform me?" asked Ash.

"I can't recall at this time. There is no indication of that in the minutes, and our policy doesn't actually require it," explained Lasi.

Now Ash got it. This conversation was being recorded. They probably even had their lawyers on the phone.

"Well, I can't get a hold of Eddie, so I can't ask him why he didn't tell me."

"I'm here," said Eddie.

His voice appeared on the conference call. Ash could just envision the short wiry punk, cowered in a corner somewhere, his arm brazenly held in place with his imaginary sling.

"This is Eddie. By my recollection, I do remember informing you, Ash."

Ash looked at David in disbelief. For both of them, their jaws dropped. It was a marvel. Eddie would show integrity through customs when re-entering the country and on his personal income tax returns, but never integrity towards people. Being honest was not a priority for him.

Ash felt like he was at the center of a tornado. His head was spinning. Why didn't I see this coming? How *could* I have seen this coming? Why didn't I trust my instincts? Maybe I did, but not enough? Forget about the brick wall with insurance, I'm hitting a brick wall here. What was that Russell Crowe movie? Ah yes, *The Gladiator*. Knowing that history had played this trick on many a man gave him some comfort, albeit twisted. He had a one-man army, Ash felt, as he looked over at David, okay, maybe a two-man army. Suddenly, David's spiked hair and braces came into focus. Maybe one and a half.

"Ash, do you have any further comment?"

Ash was tempted to hang up again.

"For the sake of your lawyers present," Ash said, "there never was such a conversation between me and Eddie."

"Ash, this is Jake, did you have knowledge of the management team's whereabouts on the day of the accident?"

"We all knew they were pursuing acquisitions. Don't you remember the commitment he asked us to provide?" queried Ash.

"It's a yes or no question," insisted Jake.

"I do not recall."

Ash recalled. Boas hadn't told him. Boas rarely told him unless it was something worthwhile. Ash had that trust with Boas. Ash never demanded that Boas tell him his whereabouts.

"You don't recall whether you knew or not," Jake asked him again.

"That is what I said."

"We have the minutes from the last several Board meetings at the company where you presided as Chairman."

Oh man, thought Ash, shaking his head in disgust.

"There is no approval of pursuing an acquisition of that company or a motion granting them the right to investigate a link-up with them."

"That's not how we typically worked," Ash pointed out.

"Acquisitions always require the approval of the Board of a company," informed Lasi.

Ash looked up at David again. He mouthed to Ash, "I'm so sorry."

Ash hung up the phone.

"David?"

"Yes, Ash?"

"CCCP doesn't stand for Capital Commitment Committee of Popular. It actually stands for Clueless Condescending Chameleons of Popular."

Ash got up, he walked to the wall where the clock was hanging. He lifted the clock off the wall. He let go of his grip and simultaneously walked away. He was about five feet away when it crashed to the floor and broke into several pieces.

● ● ●

Ash went into his office and closed the door. His phone was ringing and there were knocks at his door. He ignored all of them. Sitting at his desk, at first, he stroked his neck. Then he began rubbing his chin. After about two hours he stood up.

"We have to cover their medical bills," he said to David after calling him into his office.

"I know," said David.

"What about worker's compensation insurance?" Ash considered aloud, "Won't that cover it?"

David looked into it and came back to his office.

"They weren't on site at their company when it happened. They can't get covered under the Company's policy."

"What about the company they were visiting?"

As Ash started to ask the question, David was already shaking his head.

"Because of their financial distress, they actually stopped funding their worker's compensation insurance," said David.

"Isn't that illegal?" asked Ash.

"Yeah, but what can we do about it? Reporting them to Health and Human Services isn't going to pay for Peter, Tyler and Boas anytime soon."

Ash stood up from his desk.

"David, find out what the cost of their hospital bills is."

• • •

Despite Sophie's persistent, and at times gallant, effort to cheer Ash up, he was inconsolable during their time in Napa. Benson had bought a property there and had loaned it for the weekend to Ash. It rained all weekend long. The atmosphere matched Ash's mood. There was a somber clarity being immersed in that setting. Ash mostly brooded that first morning and afternoon, leaning against walls or door frames, sitting in arm chairs or deck chairs looking out into empty space.

"If you rub any longer, the skin on your chin will come off," Sophie chided.

Ash looked down at her. She sat on the floor, set one glass on the floor beside her and raised the second one to Ash's lips. Ash held the glass and she placed her head in his lap. He could feel her breasts pressing against his shin. She had taken her bra off.

"You're clever," said Ash, as he set the glass down and lifted her up.

He carried her in his arms to the bedroom.

It was late afternoon when they emerged.

"I feel thirsty," said Ash.

They set out on their visits to the various vineyards.

"This one is a Bosch – aka Ash's head – there is way too much going on," Ash quipped.

They headed to another vineyard. They were getting more and more wet with each visit. The rain was a drizzle but at times it became severe.

"This is a Goya; it is screaming of desperation."

He continued to drink it, the buzz effect of the alcohol welcome.

By the time they got to the last vineyard, they were soaked through, and the sky was becoming ever darker shades of gray.

"This one is a Fragonard."

Sophie looked at him.

"It arouses me..."

He grabbed Sophie's hand and escorted her to behind the building.

"Not here!" she protested.

He lifted her up and headed for the vines.

"Oh no," she said.

There was a gleeful abandon in the sound of her voice. She wasn't dismayed. She was looking forward to it.

There, among the vines, they rolled about in the mud, their progress occasionally impeded by stakes in the ground.

When they emerged, they were covered in mud, and it was completely dark. It started to rain again. They removed their outer layers of clothing and sat in the car. Laughing together, they drove back to the house where they were staying. They had been prescient enough to purchase several bottles of the Fragonard before leaving the last vineyard. The rest of the evening was lost for Ash in a haze of alcohol, soft skin, acrobatics involving furniture and eventually, succumbing to a sweet slumber.

His eyes opened with a start. He looked at the clock. It was 3:28 am. The last visual of the clock that he had was 2:29 am. He lifted Sophie's arm and head off of his chest.

He was wide awake. He put on a robe and wandered to the deck. There was a chill in the air which Ash found welcoming. He sat on a deck chair. As the air around him intensified in illumination, he could see that he was ensconced in a thick cloud of fog.

He liked the feeling of anonymity it gave him. It was okay for his thoughts to be muddled here. It was a chance for him to leave the confusion, the uncertainty. Perhaps when these storm clouds disappear, the world will be clear again, he thought to himself.

Sophie came outside. "Are you going to be lost in your thoughts again today?"

Ash didn't respond.

"I haven't had enough of you lately," she bemoaned, "You are always so preoccupied."

He couldn't deny that she was right. He had been there, but he hadn't been there. He wasn't living in the moment. His thoughts were elsewhere.

"I have been waiting to share so much with you, but I haven't because you have been so lost in your head," said Sophie.

"I know, I'm sorry," Ash pleaded.

"Well, you should be."

Ash was taken aback by her more aggressive posturing.

"I want to go to France. I have been wanting to go for months now," she said.

"Then why don't you go, visit your family?" said Ash.

Sure, he'd miss her, but if that's what she wanted.

"I want you to come with me."

"Oh, it's just that it is so busy at work right now," Ash tried to beg off.

"You are always saying that, always saying that," said Sophie.

Her voice showed additional strain.

"Look, now is a particularly bad time," he said.

"It's always that way," she said.

Ash absorbed what she was saying.

"Why don't you just leave your job, if you hate it so much?" she implored.

"I tried, remember?" he defended himself.

Sophie stood up and walked inside. The two were quiet with each other the rest of the day. There were no more vineyards visited. They drove to the airport in the early afternoon and flew home. The aircraft was delayed in landing, circling LAX because the rain had followed them south.

They were silent in the car ride from the airport home.

CHAPTER 24

Ash's cell phone was beginning to beep and ring on the drive to his house from the airport. He let it go.

When they arrived, Sophie was startled to see someone at the front door. It was still raining. Ash ran to the front after hearing Sophie scream. He recognized the person. It was Wendy Cole.

"Wendy? How long have you been out there? You know I've been trying to reach Boas, and I haven't been able to get through."

Wendy moved with the speed of a snail. She shifted her weight from one foot to the next. Perhaps she was slowed down by the weight of her rain-drenched clothes or perhaps it was heaviness in her heart.

The sight of her made Ash panic. He suddenly worried.

"He's gone."

It was barely audible when she said it. Sophie immediately embraced her.

"Let's get you inside."

Wendy lifelessly followed Sophie inside. She was without strength, without a will, without thoughts, raw. Her legs moved like she was wearing concrete cinderblocks on her feet and not shoes. There was a zombie-like periodicity to her gait. It was as though she had suddenly aged sixty years and her muscles had lost their ability to function. As if each of her joints had been administered anesthesia, and the effect had yet to wear off. She was lost.

Ash stood there. He was teeming with questions, but the sudden impact of the news needed to make its way through him. It was like an echo he was suddenly hearing. The words penetrated him. Rippled through him. Made him scared, confused, sad, angry and created his own sense of loss. His desire to console was profound. All manners that presented themselves seemed shallow. What could he say now? What could he do? Boas was gone. There was no way for Ash to replace him. Nothing could bring him back. Nothing.

Was it his fault? Was it Popular Capital's fault? Was it Lasi's fault? Was it Eddie's fault? Whose fault was it? No one was to blame, yet everyone was to blame. What was true was they *all* had a hand in it.

● ● ●

"Wendy, I don't know what to say," Ash admitted.

Wendy was quiet. Ash was searching for things to say.

"The important thing is to survive now," Ash thought to say. He felt like he was balancing an expensive crystal vase on the edge of a precipice.

"You have to think of your children," he added.

"Look, this is probably the last thing on your mind, but maybe it can provide you comfort. There is a life insurance policy for Boas."

As soon as he said it he experienced regret on numerous levels. Firstly, perhaps she wasn't ready to hear a discussion of practical matters, Secondly, he hadn't had a chance to confirm that it was still in place and hadn't been tampered with.

Wendy found her voice. "What about the others who don't have life insurance, Peter or Tyler who make forty or fifty thousand a year? What will their families do?"

Wendy amazed Ash. She really was a lover of man. Not just an anthropologist, but an anthrophile. After all that she was going through, she could be so concerned for others. Suddenly Ash felt a sense of guilt. All those times he complained about his salary which was a multiple of what these people had. All the comparisons he made. How angry he got for not having more, for not being paid the millions that he had convinced himself that he deserved.

Greed is not good. You are wrong, man with the last name intentionally sounding like the slimy lizard that you are.

Ash felt tiny, petty, inconsequential, for being allured by the pull of money. He was smarter than that. He knew better. He had disappointed himself. Oh, how upset Samuel would be with me now.

And then he remembered what he had said, "It's not me that you are disappointing."

It's true, thought Ash. He didn't like himself very much at the moment.

• • •

Sophie came over to Ash. He was seated on the sofa, staring into space. Sophie sat next to him. She took his hands into hers.

"Ash, I love you," she said.

Sophie didn't give Ash a chance to respond.

"But I am going to leave you if you don't leave Popular Capital."

"Sophie…." there was a pleading in his voice.

"No," she stopped him, "I don't want to become a Wendy Cole."

Within one hour, she had packed her bags and headed for the airport. She kissed Ash on the lips. They stayed intertwined for a long period of time. Ash didn't want to let her go, but somehow he knew she needed some space from the trauma.

She left, and they didn't say a word to each other.

• • •

Ash called David.

"David, I need you to look into something although I already know the answer."

Within fifteen minutes, David called him back.

"It's true," he said, "They did cancel the life insurance policy."

"David, by the morning, can you determine the amount of the total damage?"

"Sure."

"About two million two hundred thousand. Two million dollars for the lost life insurance proceeds and close to two hundred thousand for all of the medical bills," indicated David as soon as Ash walked in.

"I see," said Ash.

He turned to David.

"I think you ought to go to Business School. Get an MBA," said Ash.

"Will you help me?" asked David.

"I'll do more than that. I'll make sure you get in. I have a friend on an admissions committee. She'll make sure you check all of the right boxes."

"How did Boas die?" asked David.

"Severe brain hemorrhage due to internal bleeding," said Ash.

"Had he gotten the MRI or CT Scan on time, could it have been prevented?" asked David.

"They certainly would have seen it. Whether it could have been prevented or not is a question I – I mean we – will have to live with not knowing the answer," said Ash.

• • •

Ash walked into the office.

He saw Eddie in his office. He was about to storm into his office to tell him what happened. To expose the evils of what he had done, the damage he had caused, the pain and suffering he had been a party to. He then stopped. Eddie would never get it.

He saw a bunch of stacks of papers in his office.

"Hey, Ash?"

"Yeah?"

Ash turned around. Is that the first time he called out to me?

"I need you to do something," he said.

When Ash walked in, he noticed that Eddie's hand – the one that was typically stiff and in suspended animation was shaking, at times violently.

"You don't look okay," Ash observed.

"Um, there are some problems in the portfolio."

He shifted papers from one stack to another. Ash thought he smelled alcohol.

"We need to hit our numbers for the quarter."

"We closed SLK; that's another fifteen million in fees."

"It's not enough."

"We need to modify…. We need to modify the…." Eddie took a deep breath.

"We need to modify the valuations that we did."

"Those have all been completed, Eddie." Ash spoke tentatively and with caution.

"They need to be modified."

Eddie turned around and grabbed a stack of papers.

"Here are yours."

At this point, Eddie's hands were shaking violently. He couldn't hold the papers up. He had to bring his other hand to hold it even moderately steady.

Ash took the papers. He thumbed through them. All of the numbers had been adjusted upwards for his companies.

"These values are overstated," Ash noticed.

"Just sign them, okay?" Eddie said exasperated.

And that's when Ash felt pity. Here was a broken man. At his wit's end. He was threadbare. He had a skeleton of an existence to hang on to.

"Eddie."

Eddie kept moving papers about.

"Eddie?"

Ash walked around to the other side of the desk.

"Eddie!"

Ash had to grab him by the arms.

"People like me and you go to jail for things like this. Don't do it."

"Just sign the papers, damn it!"

"I'm not going to."

Ash walked to his office.

CHAPTER 25

"We have a Mr. A. Yan Rand from Fountainhead Capital who'd like to ask a question," announced the operator.

"Actually this is Ash Gyan."

"Ash, what are you doing, buddy?" asked Lasi, slightly panicked.

"I'm tendering my resignation."

"This is HARDLY the time or the..." Lasi shouted.

Ash cut him off.

"But as my last official duty, I wanted to keep you from making a material mis-statement. The debt on High Performance Systems should be $2.2 million higher. As my last act, I just approved a cash infusion for that amount in order to cover the health care and forfeited life insurance liabilities of the injured and deceased employees," declared Ash.

There was silence on the line.

"You know, I'd hate for you to do something wrong and have to suffer the consequences," said Ash to Lasi. "Oh and lest I forget," added Ash, "I never signed the letter covering up the Enron-esque mis-statement of your financials."

"YOU LITTLE..." began bellowing Lasi.

"You know, to cover-up the fiasco at Project Elba that you and Eddie were trying to pin on me."

"HANG UP!"

"And another thing…this is for the shareholders…,"

"SHUT UP!" demanded Lasi.

"…you all are trying to argue with a man who spent a significant portion of his life…"

"SHUT HIM UP!" demanded Lasi.

"…fighting for the flawed construct of communism…"

"GET HIM OFF THE PHONE!" screamed Lasi.

"… why would he back down with you because you're pointing out the flaws in his construct of private equity?"

"OPERATOR!" protested Lasi.

"Lastly, shareholders should get out before interest rates go up, Popular's going to loose a bunch of money!"

"OPERATOR!"

Ash slammed down the phone.

CHAPTER 26

A sh went in search of Sophie. He found her where his heart had always been. In Bordeaux.

"I did it! I left my job."

"I know. Both Patricia and David called me," mentioned Sophie.

"I never want to be separated from you again."

Ash went down on one knee.

● ● ●

He woke up every hour wondering if it was time. The Bordeaux seller was going to be there in Los Angeles today. He found that at five am, he just couldn't stay down any longer. He showered, placed his copy of the purchase agreement, the registration statement for the SEC for the IPO and the new mock-up of the catalog into his briefcase and went to his car. He carefully placed his briefcase on the back seat, propping it against the back of the seat so that it would move about minimally. He drove to the store. There would be three hours before the seller showed up. Ash couldn't have been more elated.

As he approached the store, a man exited a black sedan. He wore a suit and a trench coat.

"Ashwin?"

"Yes?"

"Ashwin *Guy-an*?"

"Yes?"

This guy doesn't look like a seller of Bordeaux wines,

Ash assessed.

He handed Ash a stack of papers.

"You have just been served," the man declared.

"What the hell took you so long? Do you know how many months I have been waiting for this?" Ash yelled out at the guy.

The man gave him a quizzical look.

Ash knew it was coming. The civil lawsuit. He opened it up. Ah yes, Plaintiff, Popular Capital, Defendant, Ashwin Gyan. He looked for the amount. There it is, two million two hundred thousand. The lawsuit didn't bother him. Sure, it was a nuisance, but this is how people like Lasi and Eddie cope with phenomena they don't understand or can't appreciate. There are many ways for them to attempt to assert their control. He thought about Boas and Wendy. He mostly thought about karma.

• • •

Ash opened the newspaper. He saw Mayfair had just been sold after only nine months of ownership. The investment group, TTW, bought the business from their London office, led by Partner Benson Wong for $175mm and sold it for $325mm, making a tidy profit in less than a year.

Ash smiled to himself. Popular had paid $140mm for the business and held it for five years before Ash was able to sell it to Benson's firm.

• • •

Ash was back at the wine store. George came in with a walker and a nurse following closely behind.

"Ash, my guhd vriend," said George.

"Shouldn't you be resting?" asked Ash.

George's head was tilted and his smile was broad. He looked around.

"I luff vhat you have done vith da place," George beamed.

He made a sweeping motion with his arm. His voice

had gotten increasingly more heavy.

"Well, George," said Ash, "it's okay for a vine to have multiple caretakers. I hope I do right by you in making it grow."

While he was there, Warren came into the shop. A man walked in with him.

"Hey, Ash," said Warren, "sorry to bother you, but I have those IPO documents for you to review."

"Warren, come here, I want to show you the man who started this place and the other shop on Santa Monica Boulevard," said Ash.

Warren shook George's hand.

"Oh and this is Lewis, my partner," Warren introduced.

"We are going to be a public company," said Ash to George.

"Vhat?" asked George.

"Your store is going to be on the stock market, George," said Ash, deliberately emphasizing "your store" and "stock market."

"Vhat? Dhis liddle store?"

"No," said Ash, "we have a chain of thirty-five now."

George shook his head in delight.

"It iz like dream come true," George gushed.

Ash turned to Warren.

"We got those contracts signed with the help of Sophie's father," said Ash.

"Whoa. So, now you are the exclusive distributor for all five first growth Bordeaux vineyards in Southern California?"

Ash was nodding his head yes.

"Your valuation is going to go through the roof," exclaimed Warren.

"Oh, don't listen to him when he talks that way," said Lewis, faking a slap on Warren's face.

Ash wasn't expecting that. Now he understood what

kind of partner Lewis was.

"Come on, sweetie," said Lewis, "I want to get something for tonight."

They grabbed a bottle and brought it to the counter. Ash couldn't help but smile.

"Didn't you suggest going to a strip club that one time?" enquired Ash.

"Sometimes you have to keep up appearances and sometimes it's okay to let your guard down," said Warren as he smiled back at Ash.

Warren and Lewis left the store. Holding hands.

• • •

Lothar arrived at the event. Ash and Sophie were throwing a large party to launch the opening of a wine mega-store. It would be the largest in California. Ash asked all of his financial backers to attend the event.

Ash was pleased to see Lothar again. Ash became shocked when he saw that following closely behind him was Albrecht.

"Lothar, it's great to see you," said Ash as he embraced Lothar.

Ash stood in front of Albrecht. Ash offered his hand tentatively. Albrecht moved forward and gave him a hug.

"Lothar had told me what happened to you," Albrecht indicated.

"Does those mean you forgive me?" inquired Ash.

"Not only do I forgive you, I thank you," proclaimed Albrecht, "you provided me with a lot of money. And after SLK fell apart, I joined Lothar's business. We are creating a whole new division of his company that will make some of the equipment that SLK once did. I am even hiring my best people back."

Ash thought about karma.

• • •

Ash's phone rang. It was Benson.

"I just wanted to say congratulations!"

"Thanks, buddy. It's great to hear from you. How are you doing? How was the move?"

"Oh, I'm shattered," said Benson.

"And of course you mean that in the strict British sense of being 'extremely exhausted' and not like us Americans for whom it means 'emotionally distraught,' right? I suppose I have to stop giving you grief. Now that you have *moved* to London."

Both laughed together.

"How's Max?"

"He's good. He's here with his father. I'll put him on."

"Yeah," said Max, "it's a shame you couldn't come out. Yeah, they're working out great. Patricia and Steven are a nice addition to my team."

Patricia approached with Pedro.

"Ash, you left me in great hands. Max is a great boss."

"I'm thrilled to hear that," said Ash.

"Also David sends his regards from Stanford. He apologizes he couldn't come down but he had some MBA project due," added Patricia.

Patricia kept smiling.

"What is it?" inquired Ash.

"Have you been reading the Wall Street Journal?"

"No, I really haven't had a chance."

Patricia pulled a copy out of her bag. The main headline read, "POPULAR CAPITAL FILES FOR BANKRUPTCY: Shareholders File Class Action Lawsuit Over Questionable Valuations, Fraudulent Companies."

"No wonder they sued me," exclaimed Ash, "they need all the money they can get their hands on!"

● ● ●

Ricky and Johnny were able to attend the opening.

"Sure was nice o' ya to invite us here," said Ricky.

"Well, I'm glad you were able to make it," said Ash, "It's an honor for me. I'm so glad you guys were keen on backing me on this."

"Ricky, I'd like you to meet two good friends, Lothar and Albrecht," said Ash.

"Lo, Al, how the heck are ya?"

"We are fine, thank you," they responded, almost in unison.

Ash ducked out of the scene, laughing to himself

"Dhis here '03 Petrus is mighty nice," said Johnny, "But I think I like da 2000 I gots sittin' at home better."

"The 2000 is a bit bolder, isn't it?"

"It's got mo' body to it," Johnny reported.

"Kind of like a huge Botero," said Ash, smiling.

"Do what now?" asked Johnny.

Johnny leaned in intently, straining to hear what Ash was about to repeat.

Ash put his arm around his friend. No imposter here, thought Ash to himself.

"I said – 'Could I get you another bottle?'"

● ● ●

Max turned to Sophie. "So what have you decided to name the place?"

"Butterfly Wines of Bordeaux," she said with a smile, "because even the best wines need time to achieve their top form."